Jokes
and
Their Relations

Jokes
and
Their Relations

ELLIOTT ORING

THE UNIVERSITY PRESS OF KENTUCKY

Copyright © 1992 by The University Press of Kentucky

Scholarly publisher for the Commonwealth,
serving Bellarmine College, Berea College, Centre
College of Kentucky, Eastern Kentucky University,
The Filson Club, Georgetown College, Kentucky
Historical Society, Kentucky State University,
Morehead State University, Murray State University,
Northern Kentucky University, Transylvania University,
University of Kentucky, University of Louisville,
and Western Kentucky University.

Editorial and Sales Offices: Lexington, Kentucky 40508-4008

Library of Congress Cataloging-in-Publication Data
Oring, Elliott, 1945-
   Jokes and their relations / Elliott Oring.
     p.   cm.
   Includes index.
   ISBN 0-8131-1774-7
   1. Wit and humor—History and criticism. 2. Jewish wit and humor-
-History and criticism. 3. Freud, Sigmund, 1856-1939—Views on
humor. 4. Jokes—Psychological aspects. 5. Cognitive styles.
I. Title.
PN6147.075   1992
809.7—dc20   91-35254

This book is printed on recycled acid-free paper meeting
the requirements of the American National Standard
for Permanence of Paper for Printed Library Materials. ∞

For Benjamin Fass, M.D.,

whose humor is the most potent of his healing arts

Contents

Preface   ix

1. Appropriate Incongruity   1
2. To Skin an Elephant: On the Presumption of Aggression in Humor   16
3. Jokes and the Discourse on Disaster   29
4. On the Structure of a Humorous Repertoire   41
5. Redundancy in Repertoire   53
6. *Rechnitzer Rejects*: An Unorthodox Humor of Modern Orthodoxy   67
7. Between Jokes and Tales   81
8. Freud and Humor: Analytic Reflections   94
9. The People of the Joke   112
10. Self-Degrading Jokes and Tales   122
11. Dyadic Traditions   135

Notes   145

Index   168

Preface

In this book I bring together a number of my essays on humor. While most of these essays have been published before, they have been more or less rewritten for this volume. New materials have been appended, redundancies have been eliminated, some essays have been completely refocused, and two essays are new. One reason for bringing these essays together was to make them more accessible. Another was to illustrate an approach to the analysis and interpretation of humor that others may find both stimulating and productive.

My approach has several strands. First and foremost, I do not accept the notion that the motivations, techniques, and functions of humor are fully known and understood. I reject the idea that the analysis of jokes and other humorous expressions is merely some kind of mopping up operation in which old established paradigms may be mechanically applied to yield reliable results. Most particularly, I challenge the assumption that humor is simply a species of aggression. I view the reduction of humor to a form of symbolic attack—often racist or sexist—on an individual or group as unnecessarily parochial. While humor can serve the aims of aggressive impulses, it may serve other aims as well. I view it as a mistake to certify humorous expressions—even those with explicit sexual or violent contents—as aggressive without considering other possible interpretations. Humor is crafted ambiguity, and ambiguities do not easily yield certainties.

The ambiguity of humor is rooted in its structure. Humor depends upon the perception of what I call an "appropriate incongruity." Incongruity was first characterized as a property of humor more than two hundred years ago and has since been incorporated in a number of humor theories. Nevertheless, these theories have generally been restricted to demonstrating that a particular expression is or is not funny. Once an appropriate incongruity has been shown to reside within some joke, the source of its humor is regarded as explained and analysis ceases. No attempt is made to push through such analysis to interpretation. Incongruity theory is thus employed only in the discrimination of humorous from nonhumorous forms. It has not been marshaled to explore the range of messages that are articulated within a particular humorous structure, or to explain why one particular joke might be employed in preference to another, or to characterize the ways in which a set of humorous expressions could be said to constitute a socially and psychologically coherent repertoire. Analysts of humor have generally ignored aspects of structure in favor of elements of character and action thereby restricting their interpretive possibilities. If humor is everywhere based in appropriate incongruities, it seems necessary to explore the bearing this structure has upon meaning.

To date, the overwhelming emphasis in humor analysis and interpretation has been upon the favorite and familiar. Certainly, if there is anything worthwhile to be said about the meaning of humor, it must illuminate those examples we ourselves employ and admire. However, there is a danger in focusing analysis exclusively upon such familiar material. We may see too little because we presume too much. We can learn from the humor of an exotic or unfamiliar group because it challenges our comfortable notions and plays havoc with our facile generalizations. The essays in this volume engage both the familiar and the exotic. The essays confront the kinds of jokes that we have all heard—and perhaps told—as well as those we may scarcely recognize or understand.

The interpretation of humor also demands an attention to the contexts of its expression. Humor does not exist in a vacuum. It succeeds or fails in particular social situations and specific interactions. It is dependent upon the social and cultural conventions and understandings that a group shares. It may be part of a repertoire of expression subsumed within some larger system of meaning. Humor may also serve as a form of personal expression reflecting aspects of individual disposition, circumstance, or life experience. Humor is not a puzzle that can be solved solely within the matrix of a mathematical imagination. It must be confronted in the social, cultural, and psychological spaces of the real world.

All these strands of my approach emerge in the essays that follow. Chapter 1, "Appropriate Incongruity," introduces the concept of appropriate incongruity and its application to various forms of humorous expression. Chapter 2, "To Skin an Elephant: On the Presumption of Aggression in Humor," critiques aggression theory in relation to a reanalysis and reinterpretation of the elephant joke cycle of the 1960s.

Chapter 3, "Jokes and the Discourse on Disaster," treats the jokes that emerged following the explosion of the space shuttle Challenger in 1986 and offers an alternative explanation of their motivation and popularity. Both chapter 4, "On the Structure of a Humorous Repertoire," and chapter 5, "Redundancy in Repertoire," decode an abstruse form of Israeli humor known as the *chizbat* to reveal its role in the creation and transfiguration of identity and self-image. Chapter 6, "*Rechnitzer Rejects:* An Unorthodox Humor of Modern Orthodoxy," links a series of humorous songs to changing conditions in the New York Jewish community during the 1980s. Chapter 7, "Between Jokes and Tales," focuses upon the punchline as a device that serves to distinguish jokes from other forms of humorous narrative. Chapter 8, "Freud and Humor: Analytic Reflections," presents a psychobiographical investigation and interpretation of a portion of Sigmund Freud's own joke repertoire. The question of why Jews have been perceived as a humorous people is raised in chapter 9, "The People of the Joke," and a potential solution is offered. Chapter 10, "Self-Degrading Jokes and Tales," scrutinizes the hypothesis that certain forms of humor can be characterized as self-deprecating and degrading and reviews the alternatives to such a proposition. Finally, chapter 11, "Dyadic Traditions," describes a type of personal, private communication that raises serious questions about the impulses that inform humorous expression.

Although I have tried to arrange the essays of this volume in a felicitous sequence, the order is not obligatory. Only chapter 1 needs to be read first since it introduces the structural perspective basic to the analysis in the other essays. It is also recommended that chapter 4 be read before chapter 5 since the two chapters deal with the same esoteric materials and much is explained in the former that is merely assumed in the latter. Otherwise, readers are free to pick up and leave off as they choose.

Many have contributed to the essays in this volume. Richard Bauman, Jan Brunvand, Frank de Caro, Larry Danielson, Alan Dundes, Robert Georges, Henry Glassie, Arthur Hofmann, Barbara Kirshenblatt-Gimblett, Jay Mechling, Victor Raskin, Barre Toelken, and Bert Wilson have all said things that I remember that they probably do not. Mahadev Apte, Dan Ben-Amos, Michael Owen Jones, and Tom Peterson read one or more of these essays and offered helpful suggestions. Don Ward was particularly generous in reading and commenting on manuscript versions of these essays as well as sharing his deep knowledge of German humor, folklore, and literature.

Although this is not a funny book, my appreciation for and interest in humor stems from times spent among friends and relatives with lively senses of humor: Foley Benson, Bruce and Inta Carpenter, Lillian and Jerry Cirker, Patsy Colvin, Kerstin Danielson, Norine and Harold Dresser, Jim Durham, Robert Ewald, Mary Georges, Max Gimblett, Bruce and Gen Giuliano, Jess and Naomi Hordes, William Ivey, Jane Jones, Judit Katona-Apte, Norman Klein, Michaela Lang, Irving Levinson, Lawrence and Dorothy Levinson, Jon and Natalie Olson, Mark Oring, Renee Oring, Marge Power, Judyann and Neil Rabitoy, Fred and Gloria Reinman, Dianne Smith, Anthony and Kathleen Stocks, Judith Terzi, Mirna Velcic, Jon and Hilda Yoder, and Taffe Semenza. Without them, the world would be a far less interesting and amusing place.

Elements of chapter 1 can be found in my book *Israeli Humor: The Content and Structure of the Chizbat of the Palmah* (Albany: State Univ. of New York Press, 1981), pp. 39-45; chapter 2 is derived from the essay "Everything Is a Shade of Elephant: An Alternative to a Psychoanalysis of Humor," *New York Folklore* 1:3-4 (Winter 1975): 149-59; chapter 3 from "Jokes and the Discourse on Disaster," *Journal of American Folklore* 100:397 (July-Sept. 1987): 276-86; chapter 4 from "Hey, You've Got No Character: Chizbat Humor and the Boundaries of Israeli Identity," *Journal of American Folklore* 86:342 (Oct.-Dec. 1973): 358-66; chapter 5 from "Arab Images and Jewish Identities in an Israeli Folk Humor," *Shofar: An Interdisciplinary Journal of Jewish Studies* 8:1 (1989): 61-70, and *Israeli Humor: The Content and Structure of the Chizbat of the Palmah*, pp. 126-30; chapter 6 from "Rechnitzer Rejects: A Humor of Modern Orthodoxy," in *Between Two Worlds: Ethnographic Essays on American Jewry*, Jack Kugelmass, ed., (Ithaca: Cornell Univ. Press, 1988), pp. 148-61; chapter 7 from "Between Jokes and Tales: On the Nature of Punch Lines," *Humor: International Journal of Humor Research* 4:2 (1989): 349-64 by permission of Mouton de Gruyter, a division of Walter de Gruyter and Co.; chapter 8 from *The Jokes of Sigmund Freud: A Study in Humor and Jewish Identity* (Philadelphia): Univ. of Pennsylvania Press, 1984), pp. 1-26; chapter 9 from "The People of the Joke: On the Conceptualization of a Jewish Humor," *Western Folklore* 42:4 (Oct. 1983): 261-71; and chapter 11 from "Dyadic Traditions," *Journal of Folklore Research* 21:1 (Apr. 1984): 19-28. Permission to reprint is gratefully acknowledged.

1
Appropriate Incongruity

Two major theories have held sway in the conceptualization and analysis of humor. The better known is psychoanalytic theory that was first formulated by Sigmund Freud in his 1905 classic, *Jokes and Their Relation to the Unconscious*.[1] Psychoanalysis, and consequently the psychoanalytic theory of jokes, is basically a theory of motives. As such it articulates the motives that lie behind expressive forms. In the case of jokes, these motives are invariably aggressive or sexual, although aggression is the more pervasive of the two; for even sexual motives are transformed into aggressive ones as they are inhibited by particular social conditions and circumstances.[2] Freud's emphasis on the aggressiveness of jokes conveniently corralled earlier notions that laughter depends upon a sense of superiority or the expression of malice.[3] Thomas Hobbes, for example, held that laughter resulted from the sudden perception of a superiority of the self relative to the inferiority of someone else.[4] The views merge as humor does not merely register the awareness of some eminency of the self, but actually spawns such eminency through the regular and deliberate diminution of others. Henri Bergson also saw laughter as an unconscious form of ridicule designed to humiliate and correct others.[5] While Freud's analysis of jokes is deeper and richer than either Hobbes's casual observation or Bergson's treatise, popular belief in the aggressive aims of humor probably owes much to these other theorists, although validated and justified through reference to Freud's seminal work.

The only perspective to rival psychoanalytic theory in its global applicability to the analysis of humor of all types and provenience is incongruity theory. Incongruity theory was already fully formulated in the early eighteenth century by poet and essayist James Beattie: "Laughter arises from the view of two or more inconsistent, unsuitable, or incongruous parts or circumstances, considered as united in one complex object or assemblage."[6] To rephrase Beattie in my own terminology: the perception of humor depends upon the perception of an *appropriate incongruity*[7]—that is, the perception of an appropriate interrelationship of elements from domains that are generally regarded as incongruous.[8]

An example should serve to resolve any of the difficulties of the abstract terminology:

Q: When is a door not a door?

A: When it's ajar.

The basic incongruity is formulated in the riddle question; there is something that is both a door and not-a-door at the same time. The answer suggests a means by which such an incongruity can be made appropriate. A door that is "a jar" is clearly not a door, but at the same time is virtually indistinguishable phonologically from "ajar," a state in which a door most certainly can be. The logical contradiction of the riddle question is resolved by recontextualizing the problem in terms of the homophonies of the English language.

Riddles, in our culture, are widely recognized as humorous expressions, although generally more appreciated by children than adults. Their humor depends upon the perception of an appropriate incongruity. The appropriate incongruity is often transparent in riddles because it is generally the function of a riddle question to propose an incongruity that the riddle answer must in some way appropriately resolve. What may serve as an "appropriate" relation between incongruous categories is rather open. In the riddle, the mere coincidence of sounds bearing different meaning is sufficient to establish appropriateness even though it is recognized by all that this coincidence is fortuitous and artificial. Appropriateness need not be rooted in any kind of logical validity, however; it requires only a psychological validity—the recognition of a connection even if that connection is logically or empirically questionable. In the riddle, we allow the coincidence of sounds between "ajar" and "a jar" to serve as the basis for the transfer of meaning thus making the incongruity appropriate. Humorous expressions often, although not always, establish appropriateness through means that would be regarded as spurious in expository forms of discourse.

Riddles do not always depend upon soundplay to establish the appropriateness of the incongruity.[9] More often they simply invoke the secondary sense of a word or phrase:

Q: What has a head but can't think?
A: A match.

The incongruity of having something with a head that is unable to think is appropriately resolved by the answer "a match" because we can understand the word "head" in both its literal and its figurative senses.[10] Thus "head" not only refers to the part of the human anatomy that contains a thinking brain but to many other objects whose parts can be conceptualized as analogous to a head in a head-to-body relationship and are so named. There are, in fact, as many solutions to this riddle as there are objects that can be characterized in this way: a pin, a hammer, a beer, etc.[11] Riddles such as this one thus rely upon a double meaning; one primary and one secondary. Which meaning is primary and which is secondary is not absolute, however, but is contextually conditioned. The riddle question proposes some "head that can't think." Because "head" is embedded in a proposition concerning thinking, the kind of head that contains a brain is established as the primary meaning. The riddle solution then resorts to a usage in some secondary but nonetheless appropriate sense.

Jokes also depend upon the recognition of appropriate incongruities. Some jokes, in fact, resort to the very same strategy as the riddle above: they establish a primary meaning that is disestablished by some secondary, yet appropriate, interpretation.

> A1: A doctor, as he left a woman's bedside, said to her husband with a shake of his head, "I don't like her looks."
> "I've not liked her looks for a long time," the husband agreed.

When the doctor comments on the "looks" of a woman, we assume he is referring to the state of health of his patient. The husband's echo of the doctor's evaluation would at first suggest he is commenting on her medical condition as well. But "not liking a woman's looks" generally has a different significance for a husband than for a physician. When a husband comments on the "looks" of his wife, we may assume that he is referring to her physical attractiveness. In the joke, the husband's claim that he has been concerned about his wife's looks for "a long time" implies that his evaluation predates the onset of her illness, thus diminishing the likelihood that he intends the same meaning as the physician.

While the incongruity of the riddle is explicit, the incongruity in this joke is implicit. A reader or listener must register the potential discrepancy between the doctor's and husband's assessments, despite their seeming agreement. Yet the incongruity is appropriate because the phrase "I don't like her looks" bears pulchritudinous as well as medical connotations.

If any incongruity or the appropriate connections between incongruous words, behaviors, or ideas are not perceived, there is no humor. This failure may result from an inability to register or organize the relevant information. Thus joke A1 about the doctor and husband could not succeed if the listener only knew "looks" to refer to one of the two forms of evaluation—health *or* attractiveness. It also could not succeed if the listener either overlooked the secondary meaning and assumed the husband's remark, like the doctor's, related to his wife's medical condition, or assumed that the doctor himself was commenting on the woman's attractiveness rather than on her medical condition. The likelihood of such misunderstandings depends in part on the openness of a hearer to multiplicities of meanings in general, as well as familiarity with particular English idioms and usages. Successful jokes generally give clues to reduce the possibility of misinterpretation. Thus the husband's comment that he has not liked his wife's looks for "a long time" would seem an unnecessary elaboration to simply register agreement with the physician about the health of his wife. This elaboration consequently becomes a sign that the husband is not necessarily in agreement with the doctor at all.[12]

There are a number of ways that a text might destroy or severely reduce the possibility that an appropriate incongruity might be perceived. Text A2 offers one extreme:

> A2: A doctor, as he left a woman's bedside, said to her husband with a shake of his head, "She seems very sick."
> "I've thought her ugly for a long time," the husband agreed.

Although the sense of the doctor's and husband's comments have been retained, their reformulation without the phraseology of "looks" destroys the possibility of establishing an appropriate connection between the unrelated assessments of the two principals. There is simply no appropriate incongruity to apprehend. Consequently, no humor is perceived.[13]

At the other extreme is a performance that retains the full sense of incongruity and appropriateness but fails to accentuate them sufficiently.

> A3: A doctor, as he left a woman's bedside, said to her husband with a shake of his head, "I don't like her looks."
> "I don't either," said the husband.

In the above formulation, the possibility of regarding the husband's agreement as referring to attractiveness rather than health exists, but it is so economically expressed that it would be possible to overlook it entirely. His agreement with the doctor might be taken at face value and the prospect for perceiving the joke thus destroyed. If instead of "I don't either," the husband in A3 responded, "I never have," the likelihood for perceiving the joke would be greatly increased.

Riddles, jokes, indeed all forms of humor, are rooted in appropriate incongruities. The boundaries between such forms are not always hard and fast. What seems to distinguish the riddle from the joke is the question-answer format in which the riddle is framed; the fact that the presentation of an incongruity in the riddle is often the function of the riddle question and precedes the revelation of its appropriateness[14]; the greater amount of time permissible in the riddle between the presentation of an incongruity and the demonstration of its appropriateness; and the fairly limited conventions for establishing appropriateness within the riddle genre.[15]

The question-answer format is not, in itself, sufficient to define the riddle. Jokes may also employ a question-answer format. Relative to the appropriate incongruities that underlie them, this format is merely one report strategy.[16]

> Q: How late does the beadle sleep on Sunday mornings?
> A: It depends upon the length of the sermon.[17]

In the above question-and-answer sequence we perceive a structure of appropriate incongruity. At first we suppose that how late a church functionary may sleep depends upon the time church services begin and how much time might be necessary for any preparatory activities that might be required. The answer to the question reveals our assumption to be totally mistaken. Incongruously, how late the beadle will sleep depends not on when church services begin but when the sermon, which is a part of that service, ends. The incongruity is made appropriate once we access our knowledge concerning the monotony of sermons and the tendency of parishioners to sleep through them. We would probably regard the above question-answer set as a joke rather than a riddle because no incongruity is presented or implied in the question, and the conditions posed by the question do not establish a framework for a solution. Perhaps the basic requirement for a riddle is that it is solvable. It poses an explicit *problem* and not merely a *question*.[18] Consequently, joking questions, unlike riddle questions, do not admit solution. They are open-ended and relatively unpredictable. Almost anything may follow. Riddle questions, however, tend to pose a problem with a restricted range of potential answers.

In jokes there can be only a short delay between the presentation of the question and the answer. If the time between question and answer is unduly extended, the puzzle function of the expression is emphasized. Although jokes are kinds of puzzles,[19] they are puzzles that demand instantaneous solutions on the part of the listener—that is, an instantaneous recognition of the underlying appropriate incongruity. Delay between the presentation of the joke and the perception of the appropriate incongruity drains the joke of its humor. It will be less funny. A joke, consequently, that has to be explained is rarely very funny.

A joke will be successful only if the listener can identify and access the background knowledge relevant to the conceptualization of an appropriate incongruity. At root is the basic linguistic knowledge without which verbal humor cannot proceed.[20] To understand the riddle concerning the door that is not-a-door, it is necessary to recognize the morphemes "a," "jar," and "ajar," to know that the first two of these may be combined into a noun phrase, and to understand the different meanings of the wholes "the door is a jar" and "the door is ajar" while registering their phonological similarity. Jokes often demand linguistic knowledge beyond phonological, morphological, and syntactic levels, however.

> A kangaroo walked into a drinking establishment, walked up to the bar and asked for a scotch and soda. The bartender looked at him a bit curiously and then fixed the drink. "That'll be four seventy-five," said the bartender.

The kangaroo pulled a purse from his pouch, took out the money and paid. The bartender went on about his business, glancing from time to time at the kangaroo, who stood sipping his drink. After about five minutes the bartender went over to the kangaroo and said, "You know, we don't get many kangaroos around here."

The kangaroo replied, "At four seventy-five a drink, it's no wonder."

In the fictional world of jokes, virtually anything is possible. Talking animals and machines, Martians, and even God may serve in a joke's cast of characters. In a joke, a kangaroo entering a bar and ordering a drink is not necessarily anomalous, no matter how strange it might seem in real life. In this joke, the situation is characterized as anomalous, however. The behavior of the bartender, who looks at the kangaroo "curiously," glancing at him "from time to time," marks the presence of the kangaroo in the bar as deserving of some explanation. When the bartender finally asks the kangaroo outright about his presence in the bar, the kangaroo incongruously comments on the price of drinks.

The incongruity is appropriate, however, because of the way the bartender framed his question. In fact, it was not a question at all but a statement: "You know, we don't get many kangaroos around here." In colloquial English discourse, statements are often employed to elicit information. If I tell my stockbroker, "You know, the stock you sold me dropped twenty points last week," I am less likely to be informing him of the fact than requesting an explanation for the collapse of the stock he recommended. Consequently, we intuitively hear the bartender's statement as a question about the presence of a scotch-drinking, English-speaking kangaroo in a bar. But the particular phraseology of the bartender's query, "We don't get many kangaroos around here," implies the existence of a class of scotch-drinking, English-speaking kangaroos of which only a very few ever come around. Thus the kangaroo is free to respond to the literal observation of why so few come around, rather than the implied question about the existence of a class of articulate, liquor-drinking kangaroos. The kangaroo thus seizes the opportunity to propose that it is the price of drinks that keeps his fellow kangaroos from frequenting the bartender's establishment. His response, while incongruous at one level, is entirely appropriate at another.

Two particular kinds of knowledge must be swiftly accessed by a hearer of this joke. The first demands a knowledge of colloquial English discourse: a statement can serve as a question. The second is a piece of cultural information: four dollars and seventy-five cents is a lot to pay for a well drink in a bar.[21] If the bartender's intended query were recast in an explicit interrogative format, "How is it that a kangaroo comes to walk in off the street and order a drink in a bar?" or the price of the drink were changed to fifty cents, the appropriate incongruity, and the joke, would evaporate.

The range and depth of the cultural knowledge that may be required for understanding humor can be considerable. The sharing of jokes presumes a community of knowledge that can be readily accessed through mere hints and allusions.

> A Frenchman and an American are arguing about the number of [sexual] positions they are familiar with. "I have read the *Kama Sutra*," insists the American, "and I have tried them all. There are exactly sixty-four positions." "No monsieur," says the Frenchman. "You must be mistaken. I know of only sixty-three, and if I know only sixty-three, that means there are no more." "All right," says the American. "Let's enumerate them. First, she's lying on her back, and he is lying on top of her. . . ." "Oh, monsieur, I am devastated," says the Frenchman. "You're right. You win!"[22]

To understand the above joke, it is necessary to recognize the existence of an idea that Frenchmen are experienced and sophisticated lovers. It is also necessary to recognize the first sexual position described by the American—often called the "missionary position"—as the most common and least venturesome. In this joke the incongruity resides in the fact that the Frenchman, despite his knowledge of dozens of sexual positions, does not know the most basic one of all. Yet the incongruity is appropriate because it implies that the Frenchman really is so sophisticated that he could never be acquainted with so commonplace a position. Despite the fact that the Frenchman knows fewer positions than the American, the Frenchman emerges as the true sexual sophisticate.[23]

To understand this joke, it is not necessary to believe that Frenchmen are experienced and sophisticated lovers. It is only necessary to know that such a typification exists. Similarly, jokes whose appropriate incongruities depend upon the recognition of Jews as clever, Poles as stupid, Scots as stingy, or blacks as hypersexed, do not demand the acceptance of these predications as sociological facts. They only demand an awareness of them as ideas. It may be that certain typifications are only invoked in jokes and are totally irrelevant to other forms of discourse or interaction. The introduction of the term *script* into humor analysis is particularly helpful in this regard. A script has been defined as a "large chunk of semantic information surrounding a word or evoked by it. The script is a cognitive structure internalized by the native speaker and it represents the native speaker's knowledge of a small part of the world."[24] The word is useful because it designates a semantic category rather than a sociological one. Scripts enable us to speak of the knowledge one needs or possesses to decode humor without implying that that knowledge constitutes a basis for social evaluation or interaction. A script is not a stereotype. A script is knowledge about a category; a stereotype is a belief that rationalizes conduct in relation to that category.[25] The attributes of Frenchmen, Jews, Poles, Scots, or blacks regularly accessed in jokes are first and foremost scripts. These are fictional figures inhabiting fictional worlds. Whether there is a relationship between a script and stereotype, and the nature, degree, and direction of that relationship, is a matter for independent psychological and sociological investigation. It should not be presumed that the two are identical.[26]

The Frenchman as sophisticated lover is a conventional script employed in many jokes. Often humor demands an access to knowledge that is not so conventional. Consider for example the famous witticism by the satirist G.C. von Lichtenberg:

> Not only did he disbelieve in ghosts;
> He wasn't even frightened of them.[27]

The incongruity resides in the logical and linguistic formulation of the statement. If a man does not believe in ghosts, it goes without saying that he won't be frightened by them. However, the expression "He wasn't even frightened of them" conveys the impression that his lack of fear is, in fact, something additional; something independent of his lack of belief. This incongruity is appropriate, however, because the intellectual position of not believing in ghosts can be reconciled with an emotional disposition to be afraid of them. Many a person who would claim not to believe in ghosts would be loath to spend a night alone in a cemetery. The witticism does not depend upon any conventional joke script nor does it invoke some artificial connection between incongruous categories. It depends upon the ability to access a particular piece of implicit knowledge—in this case, a psychological truth concerning the relative independence of intellect and emotion.

While appropriate incongruity is the fundamental structure of humor, appropriate incongruities are only engendered through the use of specific techniques. For example, we might characterize the riddles and joke A1 (about the doctor and husband) above as depending upon a "double meaning" in which appropriateness is established through a word or phrase that bears more than one meaning. Even the joke about the kangaroo in the bar depends upon an apprehension of the bartender's utterance in both its declarative and its interrogative senses. Little serious attention has been devoted to the analysis of joke techniques. Freud provides perhaps the most extended and useful discussion.[28] He tends to view most linguistic techniques as specimens of "condensation."[29] Others have conceptualized them as forms of reversal.[30] I would view the underlying unity of humorous techniques as proceeding from the fact that all of these techniques must ultimately produce appropriate incongruities. But the particular techniques by which incongruities are generated and made appropriate need elaboration and discussion.[31]

For example, one technique—which might be termed "vacuous reversal"—depends upon the reversal of a sequence that unexpectedly results in no change in the sense or significance of the whole.[32] Vacuous reversal is clearly characteristic of the palindrome, a sentence that is identical whether read backward or forward. The one linked with Napoleon is: "Able was I ere I saw Elba."[33] The startling and amusing characteristic of the palindrome is not that it bears multiple meanings, but that its alphabetical reversal unexpectedly leads to an identical meaning rather than to meaninglessness. Vacuous reversal is also characteristic of certain jokes.

Q: Explain to me the difference between communism and capitalism.
A: Capitalism is man's exploitation of his fellow man.
Q: And what is communism?
A: Just the opposite!

Actually the vacuous reversal here depends upon two senses of the phrase "Just the opposite," for there are two ways in which the characterization of capitalism can be reversed. The initial and final words of the phrase "man's exploitation of man" may be reversed with no change in meaning whatsoever. But the word "exploitation" can also be reversed—man's "nurturance" (nonexploitation) of his fellow man. The incongruity resides in the fact that the "opposite" can result in the exact same. The incongruity is appropriate, however, because there are two ways that "man's exploitation of his fellow man" can be reversed, only one of which is vacuous.

If a reversal or opposition may be manipulated to produce identities, identities may lead to the perception of difference. We might term this technique "contrastive iteration," where repetition of the same or a similar expression signals difference, even reversal.

> She is a rarely beautiful girl—very rarely.[34]

> A man tells his friend that his wife has the biggest vagina that he has ever seen. His friend is skeptical so he invites him to see it. He asks his wife to undress and tells his friend to get real close and take a look at it. His friend gets up real close and says, "Oh, that's not so big. . . . Oh, that's not so big."[35]

> Mr. and Mrs. Jones live rather well. Some people think that Mr. Jones has earned a lot so that Mrs. Jones has been able to lay back a bit. Others think that Mr. Jones has been able to earn a lot because Mrs. Jones has lain back a bit.[36]

In each of the above examples the iteration of a word or phrase changes or even reverses its sense. The rarely beautiful girl is beautiful only rarely. The denial of the enormity of the wife's vagina is belied by an echo that only a vagina of superhuman proportions could produce. The significance of Mrs. Jones "laying back a bit" is dependent upon whether it is viewed as the cause or the effect of Mr. Jones's accumulated wealth.

With the elucidation of humorous techniques we may be in a position to ask some new questions about humor: What kinds of techniques predominate in a particular society or social group? Are some groups more limited than others with respect to the range of techniques employed? Do dominant techniques correlate with any other aspects of thinking style or world view? Are some jokes technically more complex than others? Is there some developmental scheme in the acquisition of humorous techniques?[37] It is not my intention to attempt a listing, or even an outline, of techniques here. The task is complicated and demanding. Even with the few examples I have provided, there is a basis for disagreement and debate. For example, the reversal signaled by the repetition of "Oh, that's not so big" is dependent upon the mediation of a concept—the echo—to create the sense of reversal. The iteration does not suggest the phrase holds some secondary linguistic meaning as does the phrase "She has lain back a bit" in the joke about Mr. and Mrs. Jones. Should these two jokes really be conceptualized as employing similar techniques? Is the technique of the joke about the differences between communism and capitalism really comparable to the palindrome? The incongruity of the former is dependent upon vacuous reversal while its appropriateness depends upon the two senses of the word "opposite." How should the technique be characterized? And how might we describe the technique of the von Lichtenberg witticism about the belief in ghosts, where appropriateness is rooted in a particular understanding of human nature and the world? Such questions remain, as yet, to be resolved.

Techniques create appropriate incongruities. However, the perception of appropriate incongruities is not coincidental with the appreciation of humor. While humor cannot be appreciated without the perception of an underlying appropriate incongruity, an appropriate incongruity may be perceived without being appreciated. A number of factors may inhibit this appreciation. The technique may be regarded as contrived, hackneyed, or transparent. Ideally, the perception of an appropriate incongruity should occur apart from the understanding of how it has occurred. A technique that is too transparent, while leading to the perception of humor, is likely to produce a diminished appreciation of that humor. Transparent technique is, in part, what leads to a groan rather than a laughter response to humor. For example, puns, which are particularly transparent, are often met with groans. Groans register the recognition of humor while devaluing it socially and intellectually.[38] If a technique is too transparent, it leads to a sense of intellectual superiority on the part of the hearer that is incommensurate with a sense of full appreciation.

Emotion may also inhibit the appreciation of a perceived appropriate incongruity. An emotional tie to a particular topic may produce the feeling that the subject should not be joked about at all, or at the very least that the joke must avoid the use of certain categories, images, and linguistic expressions. A joke that fails to live up to these standards may not be regarded as funny. The emotional attachment to the topic overpowers the appreciation of the intellectual structure of the joke. "That's not funny!" is a reaction that recognizes but discounts the joke structure and categorizes the expression as some form of serious statement—an insult or obscenity. This is not to imply that individuals cannot joke about people or events that are important to them—they can. To do so, however, they must be able to suspend their involvement with them. For the purposes of the joke, they must detach themselves sufficiently from these personages and events to recognize them as ideas that can be manipulated for some particular semantic value.

The fact that people may respond seriously, even angrily, to certain jokes, suggests that they feel jokes contain some serious message—that they are something more than laughter-provoking stimuli. Freud believed that every joke could be reduced to a serious thought.[39] As humor structures ideas in appropriately incongruous ways, ideas are often conjoined in ways that can be expressed as propositions. Thus in the joke about the differences between capitalism and communism we are surprised to discover that there is none; that both can be thought of as systems of exploitation. The joke introduces the thought that communism and capitalism (and perhaps every other form of political-economic organization) often benefit the few at the expense of the many and are, in this basic sense, similar. For a brief moment, listeners are asked to *entertain* this notion. This thought can be characterized as "serious" because outside the frame of the joke, such a thought might be seriously engaged and debated. But the joke does not and cannot make a serious claim for the thought. For example, no one would seriously accept the joke as an *argument* for not caring which of the two systems they lived under.[40] Furthermore, the identity of the two systems is only established in the joke through the dual sense of the word "opposite"; a mechanism that would be rejected as spurious if employed in serious discussion. The thought of the joke can only be made serious if it is negotiated into seriousness; that is, if it is translated into some form of nonhumorous discourse.[41]

Furthermore, jokes that establish thoughts with a claim to seriousness must be examined against the background of the multitude of jokes whose thoughts evince no such claims.

> There's a parallel between a martini and a woman's breasts: One is not enough, and three is too many.[42]

Given the extraordinary differences between martinis and breasts, we may be surprised to discover identities in the numbers of each that are deemed insufficient, excessive, and felicitous. This correspondence, however, in no way establishes a serious relation between martinis and breasts as such a thought cannot be seriously engaged outside the frame of the joke. Why should we assume that the correspondence established between capitalism and communism is intended more seriously than the one between martinis and breasts? The fact that we may engage the correspondence between capitalism and communism seriously while rejecting the correspondence between martinis and breasts rests solely upon our appraisal of the world and the kinds of relations that we recognize as legitimate within it. Jokes may establish all manner of relations. Those we are seriously willing to engage owe nothing to their formulation as jokes and everything to our prior understandings of the world.

In any event, it would be difficult to reduce all jokes to propositional format let alone to serious propositions. While the joke on communism and capitalism lends itself to such formulation (both capitalism and communism are systems of exploitation) as does the witticism by von Lichtenberg (it is easier to say you are not afraid than to free yourself from fear), many jokes do not. How might we reduce the joke about the kangaroo in the bar to its underlying thought? Is it merely that four dollars and seventy-five cents is too much to pay for a drink or that kangaroos can be motivated by the same economic forces as people? Certainly in order to understand the joke listeners must be able to access such thoughts. But they must also access the idea that statements can serve as questions and that kangaroos can't speak English and don't drink whisky. Are these to be considered underlying thoughts of the joke as well?

It is exactly such complications that make humor such a singular form of communication. It is not that jokes and other forms of humorous expression convey no messages, but that it is often not clear what these messages might be and to what, if any, degree they might be seriously intended. Humor is fundamentally ambiguous. First, it is grounded in an ambiguous system of relations—relations that are simultaneously incongruous and appropriate. To recognize the joke, weight must be given to both. Second, if humor contains a message, that message may be far from self-evident. It may not be easily grasped let alone formulized in some compact proposition. Or there may be several equally viable formulations. Third, jokes often establish connections by spurious means that carry no legitimacy in rational discourse. Fourth, even when some primary message might be formulated (as in the capitalism-communism joke), it is unclear how seriously the message is intended, for there are simply too many analogous expressions whose messages could never be meant or taken seriously at all (e.g., the martini-breast joke). Finally, humor is recognized as a species of play which—by definition—is something other than seriousness.

The interpretation of humor requires a reduction of these dimensions of ambiguity. Discerning the messages of humor demands close analysis of the categories that are brought into incongruous opposition[43] as well as of the means by which they are made appropriate. To neglect these structural elements in conceptualizing the messages of humorous expressions is to risk reading into them messages that may not be there, thus increasing rather than reducing levels of ambiguity. Ambiguity may also be reduced through attention to context: the context of rules, conventions, and understandings of the culture in which humor is communicated; the context of the humorous repertoire of which a joke is but a single element; the context of the situation and interaction in which it is expressed; the context of the life of the individual who performs and enjoys it. Each of these contexts can serve to reduce the ambiguity that permeates a humorous expression. In the following chapters, I shall try to show that an attention to both the structures and the contexts of humorous expression can yield understandings of humor that are both novel and rich.

2
To Skin an Elephant
On the Presumption of Aggression in Humor

In 1905, humor was decidedly removed from the domain of the trivial when Sigmund Freud set forth his theory of jokes: "There are only two purposes that it [a joke] may serve. . . . It is either a *hostile joke* (serving the purposes of aggressiveness, satire or defense) or an *obscene joke* (serving the purpose of exposure)."[1] Freud's pronouncements on joking have received surprisingly widespread acceptance, even in quarters that typically suspect or discount psychoanalytic insights. Indeed, the presumption of aggression has become something of an interpretive axiom: "Under the mask of humor, our society allows infinite aggressions, by everyone against everyone. In the culminating laugh, by the listener or observer . . . the teller of the joke betrays his hidden hostility and signals his victory."[2] Jokes, then, are assaults against real individuals and groups in the social world. They serve the emotions by allowing the expression of aggression safely "masked" as play. The aggressions are successful because they are not recognized, or if they are, they are not taken seriously.

However, in the wholesale adoption and application of this approach to the analysis of jokes, some fundamental problems have been overlooked:

1. Aggression theory has been adopted with little regard for the unique properties of humor. Humor is viewed merely as a mask for the expression of aggression. But from a psychoanalytic perspective, *all* expressive forms—myths, fairytales, songs, rituals—serve to disguise forbidden impulses so that they can be expressed in a socially acceptable fashion. Consequently, aggression theory does not adequately distinguish humorous communication from other forms of expression.[3]

2. Many jokes that have been analyzed as socially aggressive (ethnic

humor perhaps being the most notable example) are told by various groups about themselves. If aggression theory is not to be abandoned altogether in such instances, one is forced to posit masochistic tendencies in all these groups and to regard such humor as a vehicle of self-aggression.[4] This masochism is never independently established, however, because the jokes are not conceptualized as *correlates* of aggressive impulses, but rather as *signs* of such impulses. When the sign is present, the referent is merely assumed. Thus the relationship between joking and aggression is really not a scientific hypothesis but an identity that is not subject to empirical challenge.

3. How does one reconcile the fact that the aggression purportedly *disguised* or otherwise made acceptable in humor is often consciously expressed in nonhumorous ways? What contribution does humor make to a thought that can be and is articulated as a serious proposition? For example, blacks who tell jokes about whites seem quite capable of articulating their hostilities without the aid of joking forms.[5] What purposes do these jokes then serve?

The emphasis that has been placed on aggression has stifled humor interpretation and analysis. The data are merely manipulated to evidence an *a priori* perspective. The open and interesting question, "What does this joke communicate?" is collapsed into the less open and less interesting, "Against whom is the aggression directed?"

For example, in their analysis of the elephant-joke cycle, Roger Abrahams and Alan Dundes do not begin with questions of structure or function but rather ask: "What is the nature of the reality for which elephant jokes are a sanctioned means of combat and escape? What early anxieties have been triggered which necessitate the reactivation of such childish forms of defense and release?"[6] Rather than acknowledge the possibility that elephant jokes may be socially nonaggressive, Abrahams and Dundes set out to identify that element in the social environment that lurks behind the symbol of the elephant.

Abrahams and Dundes conclude that the elephant is an ambivalent father figure, alternately admired and hated. In the 1960s, the trigger for such Oedipal concerns was the Civil Rights movement and the entry of blacks into white society. With the traditional social barriers between white and black under attack, with the increasing demands for equality and integration at all levels of the society, the joke gave expression to white fears and fantasies. In reality, it is the black man (perceived as a sexual threat) that stands hidden behind the image of the elephant. That is why the jokes concern the *color* of the elephant (Q: Do you know why elephants are gray? A: So you can tell them from blueberries); his *intrusion* into the most intimate areas of the home (Q: How do you know if an elephant is in the bathtub with you? A: By the faint smell of peanuts on his breath); and his prodigious *sexuality* (Q: What's big and gray and comes in quarts? A: An elephant). Elephant jokes, in Abrahams and Dundes's view, masked the aggressive impulses of white, liberal, middle-class society, while providing a means by which blacks could be symbolically subjugated, controlled, and feminized (Q: How do you keep an elephant from stampeding? A: Cut his 'tam peter off).[7]

I am less bothered by the conclusions of Abrahams and Dundes's ingenious essay than by the assumptions upon which they are based: that jokes are attacks against groups of people; that interpretation consists in identifying the target groups and the motives for the attack; that these targets of aggression are hidden from consciousness and identified through symbolic interpretation. While one or more of these assumptions might hold true in a particular situation, they are unacceptable as a *program* for interpretation. Furthermore, their interpretation itself depends upon overlooking some contrary evidence.

Abrahams and Dundes consider elephant jokes to be riddle-jokes that concern elephants. But many riddle-jokes that were told in "elephant-joking sessions" in no way involved the figure of an elephant. Canaries, rabbits, mice, whales, grapes, as well as other flora and fauna were also featured. Nor did tellers conceptualize or perform these jokes differently from those of the elephant variety. Thus, the corpus of jokes considered by Abrahams and Dundes for interpretation has been, to some extent, artificially restricted.

More important, in the effort to establish the plausability of the elephant-equals-black equation, Abrahams and Dundes point to other riddle-jokes—"color riddles"—told in the era of the elephant jokes that *explicitly* invoke racial images and epithets:

Q: What do they call a Negro with a Ph.D.?

A: Nigger.

Q: What's black and has a red cape?

A: Super Nigger.

Q: What's black and white and rolls in the grass?

A: Integrated sex.[8]

These jokes, however, do not support but challenge Abrahams and Dundes's thesis. Why resort to the disguised aggression of the elephant joke when explicit joking aggressions were available and acceptable? Unless Abrahams and Dundes are able to demonstrate complementary distribution for the telling of the elephant jokes and the "color riddles" above (that is, that the people who told elephant jokes did not tell color riddles and vice-versa), we must assume that these expressions could be and were being explicitly expressed in joke form by middle class whites during the 1960s. Thus the disguise supposedly afforded by the figure of the elephant for aggressive impulses against blacks should have been entirely superfluous.

The problems raised by aggression theory demand a fresh approach. In addition, the oft-repeated assertions of informants who state that their jokes are without hostile intent should be seriously entertained. There is probably more to be gained by initially accepting such statements at face value than by assuming that the reverse is necessarily the case. That jokes are meant to be funny is relatively certain. That they are also intended as assaults is far less certain.

The communication of a joke requires the perception of an appropriate incongruity; that is, the perception of conceptually distant ideas that are "appropriately" linked. An interpretation of humor should begin with the delineation of such incongruities. Only after such analyses have been performed can hypotheses about the relationship between humor and its psychological and cultural milieus be proposed.

Q: Why are elephants gray?
A: To distinguish them from blueberries.[9]

The key to the humor in this riddle-joke does not lie in the figures of the elephant or blueberry or the quality of grayness per se. Rather, the humor lies in the incongruous proposition that the grayness of the elephant is intended to distinguish it from a blueberry. The proposition is incongruous because the color difference is but one of a myriad of substantial differences between elephants and blueberries, *and* because this color difference can in no way be presumed to be telic. But the incongruity has a measure of appropriateness because elephants and blueberries do differ in color. Thus the joke is able to "appropriately," though absurdly, imply that were it not for their color difference, elephants and blueberries would be virtually indistinguishable. Thus the sources of the elephant joke's humor lies not in the particular characteristics or antics of the elephant but in the perversion of logic and the violation of an established conceptual order.

When we examine the elephant-joke repertoire as a whole, we can more precisely delineate the kinds of order that elephant jokes seek to abrogate. They are, most particularly, the rules and conventions associated with riddling.

1. Traditional riddles often pose contradictions that are resolved in the recognition of the multiple attributes, both figurative and literal, of some familiar, local, or even homey object or event.[10] For example, "What has teeth but cannot eat?" The apparent incongruity of having teeth but being unable to eat is resolved in the riddle solution—a comb—which has teeth in a figurative sense but which literally cannot eat. Many riddles depend upon the presentation of incongruities that are resolved with the recognition that they can be unified if they are viewed at figurative and literal levels simultaneously. Moreover, the objects and events that serve to resolve the incongruities are familiar and encountered in everyday life: a comb, an egg, a spinning wheel, snow, an icicle, a newspaper, the wind.

Elephant jokes trade upon the riddle genre by deliberately ignoring these riddle conventions and violating traditional expectations:

Q: What's gray and comes in a bottle?
A: Liquid elephant.

Q: What's gray and comes in a red and white can?
A: Campbell's cream of elephant soup.

Q: What's gray, black, and white?
A: Sister Mary Elephant.

Q: What's purple and conquered the world?
A: Alexander the Grape.

Q: What's long, yellow, and goes "click-click"?
A: A ball-point banana.

Q: What's black, dangerous, and lives in a tree?
A: A crow with a machine gun.

Q: What's green, weighs one thousand tons, and lives on the bottom of the sea?

A: Moby pickle.

Q: What's red and dingle-dangles?

A: A red dingle-dangle.

Rather than unifying the incongruous attributes of the riddle question in some *familiar* object or event, the incongruous attributes remain essentially incongrous in the improbable or impossible objects characterized in the answers. Thus the traditional expectation of the familiarity and unity of the riddle answer is violated because the elephant-joke answer lies beyond probability. Liquid elephant, for example, is outside our experience. It is incongruous. But because of the existence of a number of solids and gases that have been transformed through the wonders of modern chemistry (liquid waxes, liquid soaps, liquid oxygen, liquid vitamins), we can entertain the idea of the liquification of anything. Consequently, the notion of liquid elephant, though incongruous, merely extends the idea of liquification; hence the incongruity is appropriate and consequently humorous. Campbell's Cream of Elephant Soup involves a similar extension. Given the ever increasing variety of soups, an elephant soup, though improbable, becomes conceivable (in a purely semiotic realm; it is unlikely that an actual elephant soup or any other form of liquified elephant would naturally be gray). When the answers to these elephant jokes are compared with the solutions to traditional riddles, the differences are striking. Riddle solutions highlight an ordinary and familiar world. In themselves they are only funny in relation to the incongruities of the riddle question. The elephant-joke answers, however, construct an absurd image. Each answer is often humorous in its own right.

2. Traditional riddles condition audiences to the expectation that incongruous questions are resolvable. Audiences expect appropriate and acceptable resolutions to the irreconcilable contradictions of the question. Thus riddle questions can be entertained seriously even though their solutions may depend upon a playful use of metaphor. Elephant-joke answers, however, resolve nothing. The appropriateness of these answers is contingent upon the acceptance of the situation posed in the question, and these situations exceed the boundaries of mere incongruity.

Q: How do you know an elephant has been in your refrigerator?
A: Footprints in the cream cheese.

Q: How do you know if an elephant is in the bathtub with you?
A: By the smell of peanuts on his breath.

Q: Why do elephants wear green tennis shoes?
A: To hide in the tall grass.

Q: Why do elephants paint their toenails red?
A: To hide in cherry trees.

These elephant-joke questions do not demand the resolution of an incongruity but the entertainment of an absurdity. If such questions are not rejected outright, these absurd images are, in a sense, legitimated. By awaiting an answer, the listener accepts the idea that elephants do paint their toenails or rummage through our refrigerators. Since the listener has suspended critical judgement in entertaining such questions, the patent absurdity of the answers becomes appropriate. While it is certainly ridiculous to think that painted toenails would hide an elephant in a cherry tree, it is not much more ridiculous than accepting the notion that an elephant might paint its toenails in the first place. (Note that even absurdity is rule-governed if it is to be humorous; it would not do to answer that elephants paint their toenails red to hide in lime trees—the absurdity must still be "appropriate.") While traditional riddles present seemingly impossible contradictions that evaporate with the recognition of the literal and figurative dimensions of language, elephant jokes conspire to implicate the listener in one absurdity in order to legitimate another.

3. Riddles that are based on categories of color and animal behavior are traditionally regarded as innocuous and childlike. Again the elephant joke violates these staid expectations.

Q: Why did the elephant marry the ant?
A: Had to.

Q: How did the male elephant find the female elephant in the grass?
A: Refreshing.

Q: What is gray and comes in quarts?
A: Elephants.

Q: How do you get an elephant in the back of a Volkswagen?
A: You don't! You can't even get a little pussy in one.

4. Another convention consistently violated is the principle of the discreteness and integrity of text. Riddles are traditionally self-contained entities, with independent structures, content, logic and aesthetic unity. Yet in the elephant joke, the boundaries of text becomes vague.

Q: Why are elephants gray?
A: To distinguish them from grapes.

Q: What did the colorblind man say when he saw the elephants coming?
A: Here comes the grapes.

Q: How does a colorblind man tell the difference between an elephant and a grape?
A: He jumps on it. If it doesn't turn to wine it's an elephant.

Q: Why do ducks have webbed feet?
A: To stamp out forest fires.

Q: Why do elephants have flat feet?
A: To stamp out flaming ducks.

Q: Why do elephants wear springs on their feet?
A: So they can rape flying monkeys.

Q: What is the most fearsome sound to a flying monkey?
A: *Boing! Boing!*

In these jokes, the information that appears in one text becomes the premise of subsequent texts. The jokes must be told in a prescribed order. In riddling, although one may extrapolate from the techniques of one text in the solution of another (e.g., the concrete descriptor should to be thought of figuratively rather than literally), specific content does not carry over. The texts are discrete entities. Elephant jokes regularly violate this convention of discreteness.

In violating old conventions, however, the elephant joke establishes new ones. Even absurdities are in danger of becoming routinized. As the nature of the rules by which elephant jokes operate begin to become familiar to listeners, elephant jokes must change. Any single line of absurdity can be pursued for too long. Elephant jokes are always told in sets or exchanges, rather than individually. Their raison d'etre is to establish patterns of expectation that then can be creatively violated.[11]

One way the elephant joke can unsettle newly formed expectations is to retreat from absurdity. The elephant is defined solely by his context, and his "elephantness" is simply ignored. This, of course, creates its own absurdity because an elephant in any context is difficult to ignore.

Q: What do you call elephants who ride on trains?
A: Passengers.

Q: What did the elephants say when they saw Tarzan leaving the jungle?
A: Goodbye!

Q: How does an elephant get out of an elevator?
A: The same way he got in.

Q: How do you get six elephants in a Volkswagen?
A: Three in front and three in back.

Q: What do you do when an elephant sneezes?
A: Say "Gesundheit!"

Another way that such expectations are violated is by recognizing the absurdity of the question and denying its legitimacy.

Q: What did the banana say to the elephant?
A: Nothing. Bananas can't talk.

Q: What did the elephants say to General de Gaulle?
A: Nothing. Elephants don't speak French.

Because the elephant joke is predicated upon violating conventions through absurdity, it can even return to more traditional forms and revitalize their powers to surprise and amuse:

Q: What is larger than an elephant but weighs less than an ounce?
A: His shadow.

Q: What do elephants have that no one else has?
A: Baby elephants.

Q: What has four legs, a trunk, and is gray?
A: A mouse going on vacation.

Q: What has two trunks, four eyes, eight legs, and two tails?
A: Two elephants.

These riddle-jokes are identical to the riddles and conundrums that constitute children's entertainment in our culture. If these jokes are capable of amusing adults, it is because the context of gross absurdity has made the old rules and techniques surprising and pleasurable once again.

One final way the elephant jokes avoid routinization is by declaring all rules null and void and asserting that they are beyond predicability. (Bracketed statements indicate responses, expected and/or actual, to the joking question.)

Q: How do you kill a blue elephant?
A: With a blue elephant gun.
Q: How do you kill a red elephant?
   [With a red elephant gun?]
A: No, you hold his nose until he turns blue and shoot him with the blue elephant gun.

Q: What's red and dingle dangles?
A: A red dingle-dangle
Q: What's blue and dingle dangles?
   [A blue-dingle dangle?]
A: Sorry, they only come in red.

26   Jokes and Their Relations

The rules of the game are in constant flux. In conditioning the listener to certain expectations that are abruptly and deliberately disappointed, the elephant joke emphasizes that rules are irrelevant; the situation is evolving, and the past is of no consequence in anticipating the future. The only constant would seem to be rule-breaking itself.

Q: What is blue, hangs on the wall and whistles *Dixie*?
[I don't know]

A: A herring.
[But a herring isn't blue.]

A: You can paint it blue.
[But a herring doesn't hang on the wall.]

A: You can hang it on the wall.
[But a herring doesn't whistle *Dixie*.]

A: So I lied a little.

In this last example, the reliability of the information in the question itself is discounted. Nothing can be taken for granted.

Elephant jokes are absurd jokes. It has been maintained that unlike absurd drama, the absurd joke makes no reference beyond itself. It designates or captures no aspect of reality.[12] This may or may not be true. But if we are forced to look for some correlative of elephant joking in the society at the time the jokes were popular, we need not start by trying to decipher the symbol of the elephant. The elephant is only one component of a much larger phenomenon. If the elephant joke is anything, it is a parody. It dismisses conventional questions and answers. It repudiates established wisdom and the authority of traditional knowledge. It is a denial of the reliability of rules and conventions learned and accepted in childhood.

The elephant joke craze exploded in 1963.[13] Coincidental with the emergence of the jokes was the emergence of the counterculture. Spawned mainly on university campuses, teach-ins, strikes, demonstrations, and building seizures overturned the traditional educational order. It was the students who made the demands for faculty and administrators to meet. New, "relevant" courses would be offered and new interdisciplinary programs established. Efforts to recruit black students would be implemented. Universities were pushed to abandon their traditional roles as parent surrogates. Residence, dress, and sexual regulations were abolished or relaxed. The time had come for students to educate their teachers; indeed, for youth to educate and reform the society as a whole.

The jokes both augur and reflect something of the spirit that came to animate this era. The rejection of traditional conventions and the assault upon traditional knowledge and authority were common to both the jokes and the movement. *Disestablishment* was the purpose of both. Perhaps it was no accident that many of the elephant jokes emphasized the intrusion of sex into the most innocuous areas. The sixties brought about a sexual revolution that not only transformed sexual attitudes and behaviors, but thrust these attitudes and behaviors into public view. It also makes sense that the elephant jokes regularly violated the discreteness of text. The counterculture held that knowledge could not be rigidly compartmentalized. All things were related, and knowledge could not be gained through adherence to strict disciplinary boundaries.[14]

The Civil Rights movement, of course, was an integral part of the countercultural revolution. But there is no reason to view it as the single force conditioning the joke cycle. Much more than the relations between the races was being turned on its ear. Reducing elephant jokes to a mere front for racial aggression, it seems to me, not only misses the larger sense of what the jokes are about, but the larger sense of what was going on in the society at the time.

Humorous communication first involves conceptual and cognitive processes. An interpretation of humor must begin with a consideration of humorous structure; otherwise it is likely to miss the locus of the humor in the analysis. Elephant joking is more than a description of the episodic career of an animal with a phallic nose.[15] What engenders the humor in such jokes is the violation of categories of expectation and not images of subjugation, degradation, or feminization of the elephant.

I believe my interpretation is at least as plausible as that offered by Abrahams and Dundes. I regard among its virtues the fact that it does not depend upon the unmasking of the elephant figure (although the image of something large, wild, and powerful abroad in the land is not inconsistent with my interpretation); nor is it wedded to the idea that jokes are invariably socially aggressive expressions. Interestingly, Freud himself offers no symbolic interpretations of jokes or joke elements. Although he regarded symbolism as appropriate to the interpretation of dream and fairytale, he did not employ it in the understanding of jokes. Those who would apply it to jokes miss the important distinctions that Freud recognized between jokes and these other forms of expression.[16]

Furthermore, Freud was not wedded to the idea that jokes were always socially aggressive.[17] He recognized that jokes could be directed at cultural and social institutions or challenge the certainty of knowledge itself. (And indeed, it would appear that the elephant joke strongly inclines toward inclusion in this latter category.) Eventually even he came to believe that jokes could be liberating mechanisms, serving to elevate the ego and assert its invulnerability in the face of the slings and arrows of outrageous fortune.[18]

Humor depends upon the intellect for its creation and appreciation. This is not to deny that humor can serve some emotional end. Experiments with select jokes communicated under particular circumstances indicate that sexual and aggressive impulses may marshall the forces of humor in their behalf.[19] But the use of a joke sexually or aggressively reveals the manipulation of a structure of ideas to serve the aims of a particular participant in a particular social interaction. When joking has sexual or aggressive goals, those goals are often quite conscious to the joker. The joke is employed, however, because it has proven a strategically superior tactic in some analogous aggressive and/or sexual social situation. Jokes may, on occasion, prove to be highly disguised expressions of unconscious libidinous or aggressive wishes. This, however, should not be the hypothesis of first choice. It is a hypothesis to be entertained in the presence of substantial and compelling evidence.

Humor, first and foremost, appears to be a subspecies of play. Like aggression, play must be considered a primary impulse, an impulse sui generis, not reducible to more fundamental impulses. Despite occasional similarities in their surface behaviors, aggression and play are semiotically distinct: "The playful nip denotes the bite, but it does not denote what would be denoted by the bite."[20] Aggressive impulses may, on occasion, utilize forms of intellectual play (i.e., jokes) as weapons, but the impulse of play, mediated by the intellect, can similarly manipulate forms of aggression in the construction of jokes.

3
Jokes and the Discourse on Disaster

One day I received a telephone call from a newspaperwoman who was preparing an article on how men use humor to harass women in the workplace. She needed both joke material and commentary, and she asked for my help. I provided her with the following example:

> A businessman was having economic difficulties and was in the position of having to dismiss some of his employees. He had three secretaries, and he would have to let two of them go, but he didn't know which two to let go and which one to keep. He explained his dilemma to a colleague over lunch one day, and the friend made the following suggestion:
> "Listen, this may cost you a little money up front, but it will be well worth it and will pay for itself in the long run. Next payday, add an extra five hundred dollars to each of their paychecks and see how they respond. That will give you an idea of who to keep."
> The next payday came around and he took his friend's advice. The first secretary looked at her check and said to herself, "The boss overpaid me by five hundred dollars. I'd better get that extra money back to him right away. I know the business is in trouble, and he can't afford such errors."
> The second secretary looked at her check and said to herself: "He overpaid me by five hundred dollars. He will eventually discover the error, but in the meantime, I will bank the money. When he asks me to give it back I'll return it, but I will get to keep whatever interest accumulates."
> The third secretary looked at her check and said to herself: "He overpaid me by five hundred dollars. He'll eventually discover his mistake and ask for the money back, but I won't give it back. I'll just

quit. The business is not doing all that well, and it will probably go under. At least I'll be five hundred dollars ahead."

Which secretary got to keep her job?

The one with the big tits.

I asked the newspaper reporter if this was the kind of material that she had in mind. She said that it was precisely the kind of material she was looking for. I did go on, however, to point out a few interesting properties of this joke.

The narrative portion of the joke is remarkably similar to the "Parable of the Talents" related in both Matthew and Luke.[1] In the parable, a man entrusts three of his servants with various sums of money. Two of the servants invest that money and return it to their master with interest. The third, however, buries it in the ground and returns only what his master entrusted to him. The master is pleased with the two "good and faithful" servants who invested his money, but rejects the third as a good-for-nothing.

Despite the fact that in the joke the secretaries are given equal sums of money and the notion of a test is explicitly stated, the two narratives are remarkably similar. The major difference between the two is that the joke revolves around an appropriate incongruity. The incongruity centers on the establishment of an elaborate strategy seemingly designed to assess honesty, loyalty, and responsibility in the workplace. These traits, however, are totally ignored in reaching the final decision about which secretary to employ. The appropriateness of this incongruity depends upon the recognition of the pervasiveness of sexual motivations and their power to shape even nonsexual behaviors. In its most abstract formulation (its deep structure), this joke seems to hinge on the opposition of reason and instinct. This I would argue is its *base meaning*. Base meanings, it should be noted, cannot be formulated as statements; at best they can be formulated as oppositions. Very different jokes may share a similar base. Thus G.C. von Lichtenberg's witticism, "Not only did he disbelieve in ghosts; he was not even frightened of them"[2] has a base similar to the secretary joke: the opposition between thought and feeling.

A joke also has what may be termed *propositional meanings*. Propositional meanings may be formulated as propositions that proceed from the base but incorporate aspects of "plot" (if the joke is in narrative form) and specific elements of content. Thus in the narrative line of the secretary joke, instinct triumphs over reason. Taking into account the specific elements of the joke's contents, we might elaborate that male sexuality overcomes rational economic calculation. This, we might argue, is the joke's propositional meaning. We would also argue that, like a proverb, a joke has specific *performance* meanings that are only discernible in situations of performance in relation to particular tellers, audiences, settings, and interactions.[3]

While I would suggest that a joke has only one base meaning, a joke may have a number of propositional meanings and innumerable performance meanings. This is not to say that there is no restriction on the range of performance meanings, for they should all be restricted by and be reducible to the base. If there were no restrictions on the meanings of a joke (or any other text, for that matter), any joke would be appropriate for any situation, and this is certainly not the case. Indeed, we should only need one text, which we would then perform on all occasions, as it would be capable of bearing an infinity of meanings.

We are now in a position to speculate about someone who might tell or appreciate the joke about the businessman and his secretaries: that is, we are capable of imagining some plausible performance meanings. Several possibilities immediately come to mind:

1. The joke is meant as a hostile expression that denigrates women by transforming them exclusively into sexual objects through coarse reference to their anatomies.

2. The joke is meant to stimulate and arouse through an allusion to the omnipresence of sexual forces and by the direct reference to specific sexual characteristics.

3. The joke is meant to ridicule males who allow sexual impulses to overpower critical reason and judgment.

4. The joke is meant to celebrate male sexuality and the male dedication to sexual pursuit in all circumstances and climes no matter how unsuitable. As such it is a affirmation of sexuality and the "lust for life."

The point should be clear. We can assign no single performance meaning to the joke. We can only hypothesize plausible alternatives that proceed from the base and propositional meanings.

Shortly after the explosion of the space shuttle Challenger on January 28, 1986, a cycle of riddle-jokes emerged and spread rapidly throughout the United States. What follows is a sample and interpretation of the jokes of that cycle.[4] It proceeds from a close attention to the structure, plot, and content of the joke texts. While this interpretation is only a hypothesis, it offers an alternative perspective on these jokes and their relation to the cultural, social, and psychological environment in which they were told.

Q: What does NASA stand for?
A: Need another seven astronauts. [Alternately: Now accepting seven applications; Not a soul alive; Need another seven assholes.]

Q: Why do they drink Coke at NASA?
A: They can't get 7 Up.

Q: What's the favorite drink at NASA?
A: Seven-up with a splash.

Q: Where are the astronauts spending their next vacation?
A: All over Florida.

Q: Why didn't they put showers aboard the Challenger?
A: Because they knew everyone would wash up on shore.

Q: What's worse than glass in baby food?
A: Astronauts in tuna.

Q: What do sharks eat at Cape Canaveral?
A: Launch meat.

Q: What color were Christa McAuliffe's eyes?
A: Blue. One blew this way and one blew that way.

Q: How did they know that Christa McAuliffe had dandruff?
A: Her head and shoulders washed up on shore.

Q: How do we know that Christa McAuliffe wasn't a good teacher?
A: Good teachers don't blow up in front of their class.
   [Alternately: How do we know she was a good teacher?
      She only blew up once.]

Q: What were Christa McAuliffe's last words to her husband?
A: You feed the kids, I'll feed the fish.

Jokes and the Discourse on Disaster   33

Q: What were Christa McAuliffe's last words?
A: What's this red button for?

Q: What was the last thing to go through Christa McAuliffe's mind?
A: A piece of fuselage [Alternately: her ass].

Q: What was Christa McAuliffe's favorite drink?
A: Ocean Spray.

Q: What was the cause of the Challenger explosion?
A: The crew was freebasing Tang on the mid deck.

Q: What were the last words said on the Challenger?
A: I want a light. . . . No, no a Bud Light.

Within a month of the disaster, the existence of the joke cycle was acknowledged in the press. The opinion of Roger Simon, writing in the *Los Angeles Times,* is quoted at length:

> A friend from New York called me to ask if I heard the latest Christa McAuliffe jokes. . . .
> My friend's call did not shock me because I had already heard the jokes. Some jokes involved just McAuliffe, and others involved the death of all seven astronauts. . . .
> Let me disappoint you right now if you expect me to reprint these jokes. I am not going to do it. If you have never heard these jokes, count yourself lucky.
> A colleague here at the paper has a whole list of the jokes. They had upset him greatly, and newsmen are very hard to upset. Bleak, sardonic humor is common to newsrooms. These jokes, however, went beyond that.
> "How could people joke about a thing like this?" he asked.
> But people will joke about anything. Maybe that's the point. Maybe it is some people's way of saying that nothing is sacred. . . .
> True, almost all jokes are based on someone else's misfortune. That is the basis for humor. . . .
> Take any joke you can think of. Take one of my favorite comic, Henny Youngman: "Doctor gave a guy six months to live. Guy couldn't pay the bill; doctor gave him another six months!"
> Why is that joke funny? Why is it not cruel? Because the object of

the jokes is not real. We can joke about a guy having six months to live, because there is no such guy. It is harmless, anonymous joking. . . .

The McAuliffe jokes are different, however. In them, the targets and the tragedy are only too real. Psychologists I have talked to tell me that is the point. They say we joke about the truly horrible as a way of distancing ourselves from it, as a way of isolating ourselves from tragedy. By joking about it, we make it unreal.

Well, maybe. But maybe we joke about such things for a different reason. Maybe we do it to satisfy some, deep, dark urge within us to speak the unspeakable, to push against the limits of decency. . . .

I am not sure who makes these jokes up. I am not sure why they do it. I am not sure how they get the jokes spread around the country so fast.

I'm only really sure of one thing.

They are not doing it to be funny.[5]

There are undoubtedly many individuals in the United States who, like Simon, would attribute the Challenger jokes to human depravity. However, scholars and physicians are inclined to be more forgiving: "They help people cope with anxieties," stated psychologist Harvey Mindess. Psychiatrist William F. Fry agreed: the jokes are a way "of trying to cope with the horror." "TV and perhaps the newspapers make everyone a witness," opined folklorist Alan Dundes. "We all saw those smiling people getting aboard—including one of *us*, a civilian. . . . We all share and we share immediately. . . . The more horrible things are the more you need these things."[6] "People who were sensitive to the disaster can find some need later to distance themselves from it and to joke about it."[7]

Neither the depraved nor the therapeutic hypothesis depend upon a close reading of the jokes themselves. Both positions are equally based upon the fact that people are laughing at disaster. It is solely a matter of formulating an opinion as to the motives that inform that laughter— cruel and depraved, or therapeutic and liberating? But as with the discussion about the businessman and his secretaries, there are other possibilities.

Simon has characterized the Challenger jokes as tasteless and cruel. It may be worthwhile to examine the *specific* properties of these jokes that excited Simon's commentary. The jokes are not all of one piece. In the first place there are several jokes that conjoin NASA with images of death and failure. In one sense they may be simply recognizing that the privileged place held by the Space Administration in

American consciousness was compromised. NASA had been presented as one of the few American bureaucracies that worked—that got the job done. The jokes suggest that NASA was no longer unique among bureaucratic institutions. Although such jokes may be used as a criticism of NASA, such criticism is not necessarily implied by the jokes.

Many tellers of these jokes were committed to NASA's mission and wanted to see it continue. They were fearful about the effect of lengthy delays on the shuttle program. Perhaps they were also concerned about the nation's resolve to press on despite the setback. The conquest of space had always been regarded as an enterprise that would exact a toll in human life.[8] Yet the very lethal potentials of space flight somehow had become divorced from the public consciousness of NASA's mission. And this, in fact, is precisely what these jokes assert: that death or failure is inevitably conjoined with NASA's space effort. To every seemingly innocuous question about NASA, the response betrays its human cost. Whether these jokes are meant as criticisms of NASA or whether they merely served as some sort of commentary on the inevitability of such disasters depends largely upon individual assessments of the worth of the space program and the extent to which the risks were and are subjectable to human control.[9]

Most of the Challenger jokes do not mention NASA, however, but trade on responding to seemingly innocuous questions with graphic images of death and dismemberment. These incongruous images are made appropriate and hence humorous by several transparent techniques, but usually double meaning (e.g., "head and shoulders," "blue," "blew up," "go through," "I'll feed," "ocean spray"). Certainly these graphic images are a major contributor to the "tastelessness" of the Challenger jokes.

It would seem to me, however, that there are alternative hypotheses beyond cruelty or working through the horror of the tragedy to account for these formulations. Indeed, Simon articulates one hypothesis very well: it centers on the notions of "decency" and "unspeakability."

Jokes are forms, par excellence, that deal with situations of unspeakability because they may conjoin an unspeakable, and hence incongruous, universe of discourse to a speakable one. This is not necessarily the joke's raison d'etre, but it certainly is one of the joke's unique talents.

The shuttle disaster was a "disaster" in the original sense of that word. It was a fiery explosion in the heavens—the undoing of a star [*dis + aster*]. Without imputing any malevolence to newspeople, it should be recognized that such disasters are media triumphs. They are what make the news. Indeed, our awareness of national or international disasters is dependent upon the media—particularly television news broadcasting. Furthermore, the frame for communication of information about a disaster is established by the media. In doing so, they establish canons of speakability and unspeakability (or viewability and unviewability). Graphic images of death and bodily mutilation are generally beyond speakability or viewability. When they do make their appearance, they are usually preceded by explicit warnings and/or apologies.

The shuttle disaster was a photojournalistic coup. It happened "live on TV"[10] and could be replayed countless times to viewing audiences. It could be replayed not only because it had been captured on magnetic tape, but because the view of that human disaster miles above the earth was shielded by flame and the opaque wall of the shuttle cabin. The crew had "vaporized," the gleaming spacecraft "blown into a thousand fragments."[11] These images of the disaster were not only decided to be "speakable" but endlessly repeatable, and viewers were bombarded with images of launch and explosion again and again.[12] But beyond these speakable images of flame and falling debris, beyond the "evaporation" of the seven astronauts, lay the imaginable but unspeakable images of horrific trauma and mutilation. The "abstract" incendiary images of television news belied the "concrete" destruction of human muscle, bone, brain, and being. But this level of destruction was unspeakable and indecent, and hence unacknowledged. The jokes, however, call this unspeakable destruction to our attention and force us to confront what lies behind the speakable media images that are created and manipulated for our consumption.[13]

It is worth pointing out that in jokes these images of destruction often are responses to some innocuous question about details: What was Christa McAuliffe's eye color? What were her last words? What was the last thing said on board the shuttle? Why were there no showers aboard the shuttle? These are precisely the kinds of questions that are regularly entertained by television newscasters and commentators. They do attend to details of description such as eye color (especially when describing a young female in the fullness of life whom a misfortune has befallen). They are passionately concerned with "last words" uttered or last deeds done before death. They have been particularly attentive to the last words preceding air disasters that are preserved on flight recorders. These last words are usually played for their "human interest" value rather than for what they may contribute to an understanding of the accident.[14] (One example was the playing of the flight recorder from the 1986 Aeromexico flight that collided with a small plane over Cerritos, California, on its approach to Los Angeles International Airport. When the pilot's very last words were finally released over the airwaves, they were broadcast with his final expletive deleted. This brings us back once again to the issue of unspeakability as the last words of this doomed man became unspeakable according to some public code of acceptability.) Even the question about "Why didn't they put showers aboard the shuttle?" seems to echo the questions of the news commentators immediately following the disaster as to why no escape hatches were put aboard the craft.

Another of Simon's complaints about the Challenger jokes was their lack of anonymity. Jokes about death and dying are all right so long as they are anonymous. "The targets and the tragedy are only too real," said Simon of the Challenger jokes. Who were these tragic heroes of the ill-fated Challenger mission? To family and friends they were persons intimately woven into the fabric of their lives. The loss to loved ones could have been no less great or wrenching had they been killed in an automobile accident or a plane crash. But in the media, the distinction between a private, personal loss and a public, symbolic one was rarely kept in view. Although many people were genuinely moved by the shuttle disaster, the shuttle crew members had not been woven into the fabric of their lives. Their sense of loss, if any, could not be enduring. For the shuttle crew were not persons; only media personalities.[15] Among those personalities only one stood out—Christa McAuliffe.[16] She too was a star undone in the Challenger disaster. Only she is mentioned by name in the shuttle jokes. The other names quickly faded into the generic "other astronauts." Indeed, at this late date, it would be difficult to ascertain how many of the public even knew there were seven astronauts until after the disaster occurred. While the prominence of Christa McAuliffe might bear several interpretations,[17] the most economical one is that her unique status as a nonastronaut attracted significant media attention. It is no exaggeration to claim that her presence aboard the space shuttle was purely symbolic—that is, she was there solely to give the media something to report. In fact, the joke, "What were Christa McAuliffe's last words? . . . What's this red button for?" clearly articulates the teller's and listener's shared understanding of Christa McAuliffe's superfluousness to the technical and scientific mission of the Challenger.

Again, it was the media that attempted to prescribe the significance of the shuttle disaster for its viewing audience. Their insistent rhetoric of tragedy, grief, and mourning might well have been regarded as an affront and intrusion by a viewing public who felt that they were perfectly capable of determining their own emotional responses to the event.[18] It was perhaps inevitable that a rebellion against such media homiletics might surface. Humor was a tactic in that rebellion. The jokes ruptured the conventions established and maintained in public discourse. They asserted the existence of attitudes not reflected by media or other public expression.

I find it interesting, and perhaps significant, that a number of the shuttle jokes (as well as other disaster jokes) incongruously employ the names of familiar and amiable commercial products from television advertising: Coke, Seven-Up, Tang, Head and Shoulders, Ocean Spray, Bud Light. "What were the last words said on the Challenger? . . . I want a light. . . . No, no a Bud Light." In this joke an incongruous image is created of the Challenger destruction being caused by someone mistaking an order for beer as a request for an explosion. The incongruity is appropriate because incendiaries were indeed part and parcel of Budweiser Light Beer commercials in the mid-1980s. This linking of the Challenger disaster with television commercials does not seem entirely coincidental. Even occasional television viewers were aware of the degree to which Bud Light commercials had saturated the media. Like the Challenger newscasts themselves, they were so omnipresent that it was almost inevitable that they would be employed in parody.

But the juxtaposition of commercial products with images of disaster seems a particularly appropriate commentary on the television medium and images it presents to viewers at home. Television news programs regularly conjoin images and stories of death, disease, and destruction with images of commercial products. Virtually every television report of a news disaster is preceded and followed by a commercial message (or each and every commercial message is preceded and followed by the report of a disaster). Thus the concatenation of brand name products and images of disaster achieved in the jokes is really no more incongruous than that achieved several times each evening by national and local television news programs.[19]

I do not mean to argue that these jokes need be viewed as a conscious and deliberate assault on the press.[20] Rather, the jokes may be viewed as a rebellion against a world defined by the media. Much of the world that we have come to know and about which we worry is a media construction. Were it not for the media, our disasters would be far fewer. In part, Challenger jokes challenge this media definition of the world. They are part of a battle for the control of discourse about death and disaster. Indeed, it is appropriate that Roger Simon should be so puzzled by the Challenger joke phenomenon, for it is against such desires as his to define tragedy and control feelings that the jokes are so militantly and pervasively arrayed. It is even more appropriate that the humor takes such an outrageous form; because this outrageousness guarantees that the media will prove unable to report the humor in any detail. Against an all-consuming and expropriating media, these "tasteless" jokes are a form of discourse that cannot be readily coopted.

This is clearly not the only interpretation that has been or could be proposed. But this interpretation is more than a statement about why people would joke about disaster. Interpretations that intimate deep, dark, and cruel motives or those that regard the jokes as ways of coping with horror, need not—and often do not—attend to the details of the jokes themselves. Furthermore, the depth analysis of human psyches are usually accomplished without any reference to individual human beings, either depraved or grieving. As such, their interpretive efforts seem somewhat a priori. If jokes seem cruel or horrible then the people telling them are either cruel or they are simply coping with a horrifying situation. Both of these propositions are crude reductions of Freud's psychology of joking.

Ironically, my own interpretation, in its effort to avoid any adherence to Freud's psychological propositions, is probably more faithful to Freud's rich and subtle psychology. It was Freud who pointed to the significant similarities and dissimilarities between jokes and dreams. Among the most important dissimilarities is that dreams are unintelligible and the inhibitions that motivate them are unconscious. Jokes, on the other hand, are *communications* and have a requisite condition of intelligibility.[21] The inhibitions that motivate jokes are accessible to consciousness and, indeed, are highlighted by the joke itself. People who tell disaster jokes know that one is not *supposed to* talk about human suffering and disaster graphically or flippantly. Indeed, the joke tellers and their critics share the very same sensitivities, but the joke tellers are willing to ritually suspend these sensitivities when they are elevated by others to the level of moral imperatives. Mine is not a depth analysis of jokes; it proceeds from an understanding of inhibitions and forces that we all recognize and share.

It may be worthwhile to re-examine some of the reported American joke cycles from such a perspective. It may be that Auschwitz jokes, ethnic jokes, dead baby jokes, AIDS jokes, as well as other disaster cycles may also be reactions to the conventionalization of discourse.[22] It would seem that the "What's Grosser than Gross?" joke cycle acknowledges the enlarged boundaries of discourse created by sick jokes themselves.[23] It is certainly not my intention to reduce the discussion of jokes to platitudes about the media or public proprieties, but it certainly seems worthwhile to explore such suggestions as well as the deeper psychological hypotheses.

The newspaperwoman did go on to write her article about the use of jokes as a form of sexual harassment in the workplace. She even included the joke I told her about the "big tits" although as a responsible reporter she felt compelled to call them "big breasts." But something that I said to her about jokes must have shaken her faith in the simplicity of jokes and the transparency of their intentions, because when the article finally did appear it was entitled: "The joke's on you—or is it?"[24]

4
On the Structure of a Humorous Repertoire

Since the eighteenth century, incongruity theory has been reinvented several times under the guise of new and seemingly different terminologies. Thus, the "incongruous assemblages" first proposed by James Beattie[1] have yielded to "bisociation,"[2] "appropriate incongruity,"[3] and "compatibly opposed scripts"[4] in the works of other commentators. But nothing except the terminology had fundamentally changed. Each new terminology has been put to exactly the same use as the previous one. Commentators have been content to demonstrate how the humor of a few familiar—often favorite—jokes stands revealed once their appropriate incongruities or compatibly opposed scripts are made explicit.

Incongruity theory, in all its terminological redactions, has proved important in the conceptualization of humorous communication. But as incongruity theorists have been more concerned with identifying the essence of the joke rather than exploring the messages of jokes, the theory has not advanced appreciably beyond its original eighteenth-century formulation. This failure is, in part, due to the fact that humor analysts have restricted themselves almost entirely to exploring their own humor; that is, to scrutinizing those texts that they themselves find funny. While the understanding of one's own humor can be a scientific and entirely worthwhile enterprise, such an investigation is often insufficiently problematized. As the proof texts are those that have been regarded as unambiguously funny by the analysts, the investigation invariably ceases when the sources of that humor have been identified. There is no impetus to ask why these jokes were considered funny while other equally "appropriately incongruous" texts were not. In other words, while incongruity theory has been basic to the definition of humor,[5] it has contributed little to the interpretation of particular jokes and nothing to the understanding of humorous repertoires.

An encounter with the humor of an alien culture is less forgiving, however. Even after the incongruities have been identified—which may be no small task—another problem remains: why do so many of the jokes fail to amuse *us* while providing such an endless source of amusement for *them*? The following analysis will demonstrate that incongruity theory can be extended to the solution of this problem as well.

The Chizbat of the Palmach

There have always been a large number of terms in Hebrew employed in the classification of Jewish verbal culture. Since biblical times, many literary categories have been distinguished: *mashal* (exemplum, proverb), *agadah* (legend), *midrash* (homiletic interpretation), *sippur* (story), *ma'aseh* (tale), *ḥida* (riddle), *ḥokhma* (wisdom), *bediḥah* (joke). Each of these categories bears a Hebrew name and a venerable genealogy in the Hebrew lexicon. However, with the Jewish resettlement of Palestine, a new category came into being—*chizbat* [tʃizbæt]. It is immediately evident that this category sports a non-Hebrew title as [tʃ] is not a Hebrew phoneme. Indeed, *chizbat* is the sound feminine plural of the Palestinian Arabic *chizba* and means "lies." This term came into Hebrew usage in the 1940s with the formation of the Palmach and came to designate their particular repertoire of humorous jokes and anecdotes.

The Palmach was an underground commando organization formed by the Haganah High Command in 1941 in response to the threat of a Nazi invasion of Palestine. After the German defeat at El Alamein, the Palmach was maintained to provide the *yishuv* [the Jewish community in Palestine] with a trained, fully mobilized strike force. Because the Palmach was an illegal organization in the eyes of the British authorities that governed Palestine, and because the funds to support such a force were lacking in the yishuv, Palmach platoons were stationed on *kibbutzim* [collective farms] throughout the country. Because Palmach recruits were virtually indistinguishable from other farm members, the kibbutz offered a cover for Palmach activities. Recruits worked a half of every month to earn their bed and board and were thus able to engage in military training for the other half.

Until the termination of the British Mandate over Palestine, the Palmach worked, trained, promoted illegal immigration, secured yishuv settlements and transportation, and occasionally engaged British police and army units. With the United Nations partition of Palestine in 1947 and the withdrawal of British forces and the declaration of the State of Israel in 1948, Palmach battalions absorbed the brunt of the Arab attacks while the remainder of the yishuv mobilized for war. During the War of Independence, although its battalions remained intact, the Palmach was officially disbanded and absorbed into *Zeva Haganah le-Israel*, the Israeli Defense Forces.[6]

Militarily, the Palmach was a parody of a modern army. Its underground status required that it conduct acquisitions, recruitment, training, and operations while avoiding detection by a British police and military garrison that exceeded 100,000 men. Its arsenal was obsolete or home-made and always insufficient. Membership in the Palmach was voluntary, and those who volunteered resisted strong temptations to serve in the British Army in the war against Germany or in the more extreme underground organizations in their struggle against the British. They served in order to provide the yishuv with a capable and dependable strike force at the command of its elected leaders. The Palmach consisted of dedicated youth, male and female, who were on a first name basis with their officers, devoted more than half their time to agriculture labor, were immersed in the ideals, values, and lifestyles of the kibbutzim on which they worked, and whose concept of punishment was exclusion from some military operation or exercise. The Palmach represented the coming of age of the first significant generation of *sabra* [native born] youth. Their unique situation was not lost upon them, as they said: "The Jews of Israel are the elite of the Jewish people, and the Palmach is the elite of the yishuv."[7] It was within such a group that the chizbat first crystallized.

The chizbat is a body of jokes, anecdotes, and tall tales. Many concern Palmach figures engaged in characteristic Palmach activities: stealing chickens from the kibbutz, using and misusing the Hebrew language, operating against or avoiding the British, conflict with Arabs, training, illegal immigration, playing practical jokes on members of the general population. Certain select characters that had no special association with the Palmach, such as those concerning Old Elyovich of Kfar Giladi, Avraham Shapira of Petah Tikvah, Suramello of Jerusalem, and Dr. Mahmoud of Beit-Jann, also appear prominently in the chizbat repertoire.

But if the chizbat is an anecdote or joke that concerns characters or situations in the yishuv, it cannot be said to include all anecdotes concerning such characters and situations. The word for "joke" in Hebrew is *bediḥah*, and there were many stories about situations in the yishuv that were regarded by the Palmach as *bediḥot* rather than as chizbat: "There were many attempts to make jokes into chizbat so that they would be more acceptable, and they breathed their last. You felt by the smell that it was essentially a joke. . . . It is possible that occasional jokes sneaked into the corpus of chizbat, that were worked into chizbat, but for us it didn't matter because it acquired a new value."[8] What then made an anecdote about a character, situation, or event a chizbat rather than an ordinary joke? What kind of transformation would be necessary to change a joke into a chizbat?

First we must point to the recondite nature of the chizbat. It is by no means a transparent text and often depends upon personal, local, or other esoteric knowledge.

> On Sabbath afternoons, the mayor of Tiberias goes out, generally in the accompaniment of his wife, and strolls pleasantly in the streets. Once he passed the house of Ofer and saw Mr. and Mrs. Beber sitting on the porch.
> "*Shalom*, Mr. Beber," said the mayor.
> "*Shalom*, honorable mayor," said Ofer's father.
> "Can we come in for a bit?" asked the mayor.
> "Please, please," said Ofer's parents. They brought chairs out onto the porch and put on the table a bowl of fruit: peaches, grapes, melon, watermelon, and also a few apples. The mayor took two grapes and his wife took a peach. They ate slowly, and according to their faces did not appear satisfied. Finally, the mayor could not restrain himself and asked, "Tell me Mr. Beber. Do you have any fruit in the house?"
> "All the fruit is in front of you," said Ofer's father.
> "Isn't there even a small cucumber?" asked the mayor.[9]

This chizbat produces incongruity to the point of puzzlement. Why does the mayor ask if there is any fruit in the house when a whole bowl sits before him? Why would the mayor consider a small cucumber to be a fruit when he fails to acknowledge the apples, grapes, melons, and peaches?

In order to grasp the appropriateness of this incongruity, esoteric knowledge is required. Ofer, a Palmachnik [a Palmach member], comes from a family of European socialist Jews. When the mayor and his wife join the Bebers on their porch, the Bebers offer them a bowl of fruit in accordance with the dictates of European hospitality. But the mayor of Tiberias and his wife are eastern Jews. Whereas the offering of a bowl of fruit is an appropriate gesture of hospitality among Europeans, the offering of a small cucumber or pickle is the customary gesture of hospitality among Jews from Arab lands. Thus the incongruity of the mayor's request is appropriate since the cucumber is the functional equivalent of fruit for the purposes of hospitality in Eastern cultures. Thus, humor replaces puzzlement once the perspective that informs the mayor's behavior is appreciated. Ultimately, we can recognize the existence of a joke, even if it is not one we particularly enjoy.

But the delineation of the appropriate incongruity in the chizbat about Ofer's parents and the mayor of Tiberias does not only show us why the text is a joke. It also shows us what the joke is about. At root, this chizbat is not about mayors and citizens or fruit and vegetables. The joke is about the opposition between European and Levantine world views. While hearing the joke, the listener must assume a European perspective towards its content. The listener—like the Bebers—must regard the placing of a bowl of fruit before the mayor and his wife as an entirely proper gesture of hospitality. The listener must likewise be baffled by the mayor's request for a cucumber. But this bafflement is replaced by humor when the listener suddenly recognizes the Levantine perspective that motivates the mayor's seemingly strange request.

A significant number of other jokes in the chizbat repertoire are also structured around the opposition between European and Levantine.

> After dinner the gang went as usual to the culture shack to listen to some good concert. One night they found Abu Layish by the radio turning the knob this way and that, and finally he stopped on Cairo and listened to the reading of the Koran.
> "Let's hear music," they said to him.
> "There is no music," he said. "I already looked. There's nothing. Only concerts, and they give me a headache."[10]

Abu Layish, although Jewish and a dedicated member of the Palmach, must be marked as Levantine. His thinking and behavior are closer to that of an Arab fellah than to the European Jew. When Abu Layish says that there is no music on the radio he means that there is no Arab music. For him, Western classical music is not a subcategory of music at all; it is merely noise that causes headaches. Abu Layish's musical classification is incongruous given a European or Western perspective, which would hold the symphonic concert to be the highest form of music. The perplexity aroused by Abu Layish's comment, "No music . . . only concerts" is resolved once his Levantine perspective is understood.

In the chizbat, it is not always the Levantine perspective that incongruously emerges to challenge an assumed European one. The movement may also take place in the opposite direction:

> One ideological instructor is hiking. In addition, he is a *Jecke*, the most naive person ever to be with a group, and they are hiking and they go to an Arab village, and they see an Arab beating his wife. A very natural occurrence. It's his wife and he wants to beat her. And then he says, "I don't understand why he hits her. Couldn't he try explaining to her?"[11]

The stereotype of European propriety in Israeli folklore is the *Jecke*, or German Jew. The term derives from the German *die Jacke* ["jacket"], a characteristic item of clothing for the German-Jewish immigrants to Palestine. This stereotype is superimposed on yet another stereotype, the kibbutz ideological instructor: a social revolutionary dedicated to principles and theories of socialism even when they ignore the realities of everyday life. In the above chizbat, the *Jecke* displays a complete lack of understanding of family relationships among Arab peasants. He imposes his European perspective onto Levantine society, and it is this perspective that emerges as appropriately incongruous.

European/Levantine is not the only opposition at work in the chizbat. A number of other oppositions underlie significant portions of the repertoire.

> There was never a doctor or veterinarian in Yavne'el. When a mule would break its leg, they would ride to Mesha and bring a farmer from there who called himself a veterinarian. Once the donkey of the Abramsons got hurt, and Amos rode to Mesha to bring the veterinarian. When they reached the yard, the veterinarian tied his horse and took down his sack. In the sack he always had a rope, a scythe, a whip, disinfectant, and a pocketknife. When he came to examine the donkey, the children of Yavne'el gathered around and one opened the sack to see what was in it.
> "*Kinderlakh*" [Yiddish: "children"], he yelled, "don't touch the *instrumentim*."[12]

Mesha and Yavne'el are two neighboring agricultural villages in the

Lower Galilee. Both were founded in the first decade of the twentieth century. Even in the 1940s, the Galilee was still considered the backwoods, the boondocks. Donkeys, mules, and horses were major sources of power for agriculture work and transportation. Trained veterinarians were not available and his functions were usually fulfilled by some local farmer.

The geographical setting, the two villages, the veterinarian, and especially his implements are meant to be characterized as crude and unrefined. But when the veterinarian tells the children of Yavne'el not to touch his *"instrumentim"*—using a Hebraized Latin word—he is characterizing them as technologically sophisticated, thus suggesting that his medical enterprise falls within the domain of scientific culture. This claim, of course, is incongruous given his background, his training, and the tools he employs. Yet it is also appropriate since, technically speaking, the rope, scythe, and pocketknife are his instruments.

The chizbat above depends upon the fundamental opposition between primitive and civilized. An expectation of primitiveness is established only to be shattered by an incongruous expression of culture and refinement which is, however, in some sense, appropriate. This primitive/civilized opposition informs a number of other chizbat as well. In some texts, such as the one above, it is the claim to civilization that shatters expectations conditioned by an otherwise primitively marked scene. In others, it is the primitive that erupts within the framework of civilization.

> When the war broke out in the country, they assembled all the Haganah officers in Tel Aviv and evaluated new methods of warfare against the Arabs, and they especially dwelt upon psychological warfare. Everyone made suggestions and everyone argued about them. Only Yeruḥam sat on the side and kept quiet. Finally, they turned to him as an expert on Arab questions and asked what suggestions he had.
>
> "First of all," said Yeruḥam, "we must know how many regiments the Arabs have."
>
> "All right," they said. "Let's say that we know."
>
> "Afterwards we have to prepare cages appropriate to the number of regiments."
>
> "What cages?" they asked. "What are the cages for?"
>
> "Regular cages with doors that one can open by pulling a rope. Afterwards you have to prepare smoke bombs."
>
> "*Nu?*" [Yiddish: "Well?"]

> "When an Arab regiment mounts an attack, we build a smoke screen behind which are one or two cages. When the smoke disperses, you open the cage doors and let the *dab* [Arabic: "hyena"] loose that was inside. For every regiment one or two *dabs*, and we will win the war."[13]

During the War of Independence, the yishuv military command gathers to discuss strategy—particularly, abstruse concepts of psychological warfare. Yeruḥam, a Yemenite Jew recognized for his knowledge of Arab personalities, culture, and affairs, is asked for his assessment. He proposes some cockamamie plan to release caged hyenas at charging regiments of Arab soldiers. At one level this plan is completely ludicrous and incongruous. It would seem to have absolutely nothing to do with serious strategy let alone scientific notions of psychological warfare. But the plan is in some measure appropriate because of the position that the *dab* holds in traditional Arab belief.

The *dab* was believed to have powers to bewitch solitary travelers in the night—either through its laugh, by rubbing up against them, or by staring into their eyes. It would then lead bewitched victims to its lair and devour them. The *dab* was greatly feared by Arab Bedouin and fallahin and figured significantly in their folk narrative.[14]

Within the context of a discussion of psychological issues, Yeruḥam proposes a crudely crafted scheme whose rationale is a primitive belief. There is no abstract theory upon which his strategy is based nor are there any psychological subtleties in his approach. His suggestion is nevertheless appropriate since the hyena was, in fact, greatly feared in rural Arab communities. In this chizbat, therefore, it is the crude and the primitive that incongruously disrupts scientific "civilized" discourse.

A corollary of the primitive/civilized opposition is the opposition between dirty and clean. Expectations of normal standards of cleanliness and hygiene are regularly violated in the chizbat by some Palmachnik's behavior or reference.

> Say what you will about Avivi, but one thing you have to admit. In the entire Palmach it was hard to find a better rifle instructor than he. That is, not that he was something special, but he simply knew how to find a suitable example for every lesson. And when the guys heard an example, they immediately knew what Avivi was talking about.
> For example, he would say, "Fellows. A rifle is not an ear. The rifle you have to clean daily."[15]

The expectation is that one's body is cleaned regularly if not daily.

But Avivi, the rifle instructor, incongruously assumes that personal hygiene cannot serve as a suitable model for the care of ordnance. Avivi's assumption in the case of the Palmach is appropriate, however, because the Palmach deliberately cultivated a dirty, unwashed image.

If excessive dirt is incongruous within an assumed sphere of cleanliness, excessive cleanliness becomes incongruous within the sphere of Palmach slovenliness and grubbiness.

> Yonah was the most spoiled person in the entire Palmach. They saw him at eight in the morning by a kiosk in the bus station in Haifa asking for a glass of seltzer. When the proprietor gave him the seltzer, he tasted it and asked him to add a little raspberry syrup. When the proprietor added the raspberry, Yonah took a toothbrush from his pocket, put on paste, brushed his teeth and rinsed with soda.[16]

Yonah's excessive attention to personal hygiene is clearly incongruous by ordinary, let alone Palmach, standards.

The chizbat conditions a set of expectations which are incongruously—though appropriately—violated. These expectations constitute what may be called the *stance* of the chizbat. As we have seen in the three oppositions of European/Levantine, primitive/civilized, and dirty/clean, either of the elements in the oppositional pair may be the basis for the stance *or* for an appropriately incongruous violation of the stance. Thus when a European perspective is assumed, a Levantine perspective may be discovered to be operating, and vice versa. Thus the chizbat, indeed all jokes, depend on a tension between incongruous categories or scripts.

But the significance of the chizbat categories emerge only when the full range of oppositional pairs that inform the repertoire have been identified:

A	B
Levantine	European
primitive	civilized
dirty	clean
secular	sacred
boorish	cultured
unemotional	emotional
self-assured	shy
slovenly, unregimented	disciplined, regimented
practical	theoretical
improvisational	ideological

terse	rhetorical
strong, violent	weak, nonviolent
linguistically competent	linguistically incompetent
slang	poetry
age group	kinship
sabra image	*galut image*

The oppositions in the figure above recur throughout the chizbat repertoire. What is surprising is that they are not arbitrary but systematically related to one another. Each column forms a coherent configuration. Column A represents a complex of values and traits basic to the *sabra image*—to the image of the native born Israeli. Column B, however, represents a complex of values and traits associated with the *galut image*—the image of the Diaspora Jew, the ghettoized European, the exile personality.

The elements of the contrasting images represented by the traits in the two columns have long been recognized by commentators on Israeli national character:

> [The sabra] is a buoyant, extrovert type with a heightened sense of living and purpose, centered around the new nation and the New State, and in complete antithesis to the model of the Ghetto Jew. . . . A Jew transformed into an Israeli is a sturdy, robust, and lusty fellow, non-emotional with rough edges and no complexes. . . . He styles himself on a peasant mentality. . . . He rejects complexity and intellectuality, and he likes to think of himself as a simple straight-forward man without far-fetched ideas and claims. He rejects emotionality, softness, familism, possessiveness and the bourgeois mentality. . . . He hates verbosity and long winded phrases, he has little time for big talk, for juggling with words and abstractions.[17]

> [Being a sabra is] knowing what to say at the right moment. Not showing any weakness. Being in the "in." Acting out the tough guy. Behaving like an Arab so as to appear like a native Israeli. Laughing at aliens (newcomers and those not born in Israel). Disrespecting one's elders ("old" commanders who had passed the age of 30). Doing everything for a friend. Dressing simply and modestly, but according to clear and well-defined rules. Not nominating oneself for an important job.[18]

The chizbat repertoire clearly revolves around two images of central concern to the Palmach: the *sabra* image, which they created and after which they modeled themselves, and the *galut* image, which they abhorred and consciously and actively rejected. But what does the chizbat have to say about these images? Does the chizbat's utilization of the elements of these images contribute in any way to an understanding of the Palmach?

Depending upon the particular chizbat being told, the stance moves between columns A and B. Each time a chizbat conditions the expectation of values belonging to one image (e.g., the expectation that offering guests a bowl of fruit is a legitimate gesture of hospitality from a European perspective), it is disrupted by the awareness that values of the opposing image are in some sense appropriate as well (e.g., offering fruit is not a legitimate gesture of hospitality from a Levantine perspective). The definition of a situation solely in terms of a single set of values is not possible. Neither set is totally relevant or irrelevant. In essence, the chizbat explores the images of *sabra* and *galut* Jew and demonstrates that each must lead to a recognition of the other. The chizbat shows that the Palmach's dissociation from the image of the European Jew and their adherence to new characterological and cultural models is not genuine. The transformation is not complete and cannot be completed. Incongruously, the attempt of the Palmach to divorce themselves from their European and Jewish heritage only emphasizes the strength of their connections to it. It was this message, articulated again and again throughout the repertoire, that made the chizbat a special order of joke; an order of joke that merited a distinct name and a distinct place in the minds and hearts of the Palmach.

Incongruity Theory as an Interpretive Methodology

Approaching a joke repertoire in terms of appropriate incongruities leads to an analysis in some ways similar to the structural analysis proposed for myth and folktales by Claude Levi-Strauss.[19] The syntagmatic (plot) structure of a narrative is ignored in the pursuit of paradigmatic (thematic) structures framed in the form of binary oppositions. Both approaches emphasize the conceptual relations of narrative elements independent of their place or function in the plot. Thus in the story of Oedipus, Levi-Strauss does not regard Oedipus's marriage to his mother as a *consequence* of killing his father but as an *inversion* of it. The marriage conveys the idea of extending blood relationships much too far, whereas the killing suggests that such relationships have not been extended nearly far enough.[20] In the joke about the mayor and the bowl of fruit, we have similarly regarded the fruit as being, in some sense, an inversion of the pickle. While they are both hospitality foods, they operate as such only in inverse cultural realms.

Despite these similarities, differences exist between Levi-Strauss's structural analysis of myth and the incongruity analysis of jokes. The binary structure of humor is intuitively recognized by all but the most unreflective of joketellers and listeners. When tellers try to explain a joke that listeners have failed to apprehend, they regularly resort to highlighting the elements that reflect the underlying oppositions: "The mayor is an Oriental Jew where a pickle is offered in hospitality—get it?" Furthermore, certain details of jokes are absolutely crucial, not only to comprehension of the jokes, but to their very conceptualization as jokes. The change or eradication of such a detail can destroy the possibility of regarding the text as a humorous one. One could not, for example, substitute a raisin for a pickle in the story of the mayor and still reasonably expect that a humorous communication would result.

This is hardly the case with myth. The oppositional structure of myth is a theoretical assertion. It is not clear whether this structure is grasped by myth tellers and their audiences. Nor has it been established that changes in narrative detail can serve to vitiate the mythic structure of a narrative. Consequently, it is impossible to say which elements are central and crucial to the symbolic interpretation of a myth and which are truly superfluous details. The appropriate incongruities of jokes, however, are more than armchair formulations about the underlying structures of humorous texts. Such structures are genuinely verifiable with respect to real groups of tellers and listeners. The same cannot be said of myth. Perhaps the analysis of the paradigmatic structures of myth might have benefited from a grounding in the more explicit and verifiable structuring of humor. Perhaps Levi-Strauss should have begun with jokes.

The central point, however, is that incongruity theory can lead beyond definition—beyond the statement of conditions that are necessary and sufficient for the identification of a humorous text. Incongruity theory can serve as the basis for an interpretive methodology that can enhance the understanding of humorous repertoires. Through a close analysis of the categories or scripts incongruously united in humorous expressions, a potential exists for apprehending a society's deepest conflicts and concerns.

5
Redundancy in Repertoire

The sociocultural analysis of humor demands less focus on individual jokes and more attention to repertoire; that is, attention to bounded corpuses of humorous texts associated with particular social groupings. Only when jokes can be situated within specific groups and associated with distinct settings and conditions of performance are their specific messages likely to be discernible.

However, such messages may lie deep within joke structure. A clever joke mechanism may serve to divert attention and further disguise an underlying message. In the previous chapter, I tried to show how the chizbat explored the images of *galut* (Diaspora) Jew and *sabra* (native born) and found them both incongruous yet appropriate to the identity of the native born Palmachniks. The traditional Jewish image could not be entirely denied, yet the newly constructed sabra image could never be entirely natural. Paradoxically, genuine identity rested upon a comic acceptance of these antithetical images rather than in the serious adherence to or rejection of either one. This message was encoded at the deepest levels of text and repertoire. The values made appropriately incongruous in each of the joke texts related to some element in a more comprehensive *sabra* or *galut* image. But how could the Palmachniks themselves grasp the significance of the whole? With messages buried so deeply, how was their effective communication insured?

Successful communication does not necessarily depend upon the accurate reception and decoding of each and every component signal. Communications systems tend to be redundant.[1] The same information may be repeated or encoded at several levels. For example, in the spoken sentence "The -oys chased the girls up the stairs," a basic piece of information, a phoneme preceding "oys" is missing. How is the meaning of the whole to be determined? Theoretically, the gap might be filled by any number of phonemes. But as the sentence is recognized to be in English, we anticipate that a phoneme of English is likely (e.g., "t" rather than "zh"); that this phoneme is one that can stand in an initial position (e.g., "j" rather than "ts"); and that it will combine with "oys" to form a recognizable word in the English lexicon (e.g., "toys" rather than "foys"). Furthermore, because the missing information is preceded by the definite article, we deduce that only an initial English phoneme that would create a noun, rather than some other part of speech, would suffice. Thus "pl," "t," or "j" are candidates but "cl" is not. We are still confronted with an array of possibilities: "toys," "boys," "joys," "poise," "noise" (in speech the sounds represented in writing by "oys" and "oise" are identical [ɔiz]). But because the assumed noun must have the capacity to chase girls up stairs, we anticipate a noun that is both concrete and animate, rather than abstract or inanimate. Since "boys" is the only concrete animate noun in our selection, "b" becomes the likely candidate for filling in the missing information. The fact that "boys" and "girls" are often paired in English and virtually constitute a conventional phrase, increases the likelihood that our surmise is correct. Of course, utterances in English, or any other language, are rarely spoken in isolation. They are generally a part of more extended discourse that also provides information. If the remainder of the discourse had been about the relations of boys and girls, our suspicions would become a virtual certainty. Indeed, we might not even have noticed the absent phonetic data in the first place. However, if the remainder of the discourse had been about some sort of magical carp ("kois"), we might have to entirely revise our previous assumptions. The point is that although spoken language is fundamentally grounded in sound, spoken communication does not depend upon registering each and every bit of phonetic information. Such information may be recapitulated at morphological, syntactic, semantic, and discourse levels as well.

Something similar seems to take place in joking communication. In the chizbat, there also appears to be a high level of redundancy. The basic messages are reiterated as well as encoded at a number of different levels. If gaps, distortions, or misperceptions occur at one level of communication, they may be eliminated, reduced, or corrected at another. Such overlapping signals could serve, therefore, to increase the likelihood that the basic messages were getting through.

The Chizbat Code

The fact that only a portion of the amusing tales, anecdotes, and jokes known to the Palmach qualified as chizbat served to communicate that these individual jokes and tales were only elements of some larger whole. While each chizbat might prove amusing and enjoyable in its own right, its subsumption in the class "chizbat" would promote a search for relations between one text and another and—inevitably—for the meaning of the whole.

Chizbat were generally told in the ritualized setting of the *kumzits* [Yiddish: literally, "come sit"]. In the evenings after an arduous day of agricultural labor or military training, the members of a Palmach platoon would gather in some peripheral area of the *kibbutz* farmstead. They would build a campfire, make coffee, and cook food. They would also sing, dance, and tell chizbat. The kumzits was the distinctive setting for the chizbat.[2] Consequently, the joke texts themselves were unified not only by their distinctive name but by their performance in the context of a regularly recurring event. The recurrence of performance setting enhances the likelihood that the Palmachniks perceived the chizbat as a unified field of expression and not a haphazard and fragmented assortment of amusing anecdotes. I suspect the powers of inference are greater playing over texts performed within a distinct, traditional, event frame than over texts randomly distributed through time and the course of everyday activities. In other words, both the classification of a corpus of humorous texts under a single label and the confinement of the performance of those texts to a limited sphere would enhance the perception of the chizbat as a *code*, not only by scholarly analysts but by their tellers and their audiences as well.

Within the kumzits, chizbat were not told singly but in batches. Consequently, chizbat were never encountered individually but were situated within fields of linked texts. Although we no longer can discern these specific linkages, encounters with clusters of texts is more likely to lead to an awareness of the relations between them. It is within the structure of the repertoire as a whole that the chizbat's basic message is contained. While no situation of performance could ever include even more than a few of the texts in the repertoire, even small assemblages could collaborate to reveal the thematic similarities and oppositions basic to the articulation of the message of the whole.

Textual and Thematic Iteration

The chizbat was inordinately repetitive. In the first place, chizbat telling did not place a premium on novelty. Unlike modern urban jokes, chizbat could be told by the same tellers to the same audiences over and over again. In fact, audiences would often request the telling of well-known chizbat. Although most chizbat texts have the structure of jokes, chizbat performance was more akin to the telling of tales with narrative technique superseding textual novelty as the basis for aesthetic evaluation.

This simple iteration of texts in chizbat performance increased the likelihood that the underlying values would eventually be grasped by those who were exposed to their telling over time. Furthermore, any particular chizbat was likely to be encountered, not in one but in a variety of assemblages. Any chizbat might be linked with virtually any other, thus increasing the opportunity for registering the similarities and differences in their underlying values and the manner in which they were structured. While this kind of redundancy increased the likelihood of a clear and undistorted communication of the chizbat's underlying message, it has another significance as well. The fact that the Palmach encouraged the re-performance of familiar texts, rather than always demanding the production of novel ones, suggests that what they valued in the chizbat was not the surprise afforded by some clever joke mechanism, but something constant and enduring within the chizbat itself.

Concomitant with the iteration of particular chizbat texts was the iteration of chizbat themes. These themes and their component values, which I schematized in the previous chapter, are the basis for numerous chizbat. In that chapter, I employed three different texts to illustrate the opposition between Levantine and European values. I might have referred to a score of texts expressing this theme. The same may be said for the other themes. While it would not be possible to demonstrate here this iteration for the entire set of themes, a few examples should serve to establish the point. Thus, the three following texts, though on the surface quite different, all iterate a single theme:

> When Zemirli returned to Metullah from his first visit to Haifa he said to the farmers, "The bank is sealed with a big iron door—a needle couldn't get through it."[3]

One of the fellows came, and usually he used to come with a violin with one string. And all his music was, "*Ee-ah-ee-ah-ee-ah.*" Nothing else. And so when people used to visit the Palmach, we used to bring in Abdul, I think it was, I don't remember I think it was Abdul, and he used to play and we used to say, "Now music of the Palmach: *Ee-ah-ee-ah-ee-ah.*"

And usually someone would ask, "What do you mean one string on a violin and only *ee-ah?*"

We said, "The people of the West are very primitive. They have five or six strings and are searching for the right tune. We in the Palmach have found it."[4]

This is a story that happened to me with a *Jecke* [a German Jew]. There was one worker who worked with us. It was customary early in the morning to put the plow on the wagon with a sack for sowing, you take food for the entire day, breakfast, lunch, and you go all day. You would work until nine and at nine you would eat breakfast in the field. And in the afternoon you would let the mules, you'd give them food, and also eat your lunch. About an hour. One day in the afternoon I look, our worker is harnessing the mules and is returning to the house. I thought the plow had broken. I know what happened? He appears:

"What happened Johannes?"

"I forgot a fork!"[5]

All three of these chizbat revolve about a single theme—the opposition between primitive and civilized. In the first chizbat, Zemirli is a native of Metullah, a village in the upper Galilee. The upper Galilee was considered the backwoods, and its society and culture were regarded as stereotypically primitive. Zemirli returns to Metullah to report to his neighbors on his experiences in the modern, urban, port city of Haifa. He exuberantly reports on a bank vault door which has no cracks in it. It seems incongruous that his enthusiasm should be reserved for something so unremarkable, given all the potential wonders of a big city, until we realize that given their extremely rustic conditions, a door without a crack might qualify as a genuine rarity and appropriately worthy of report.

In the second example, the Palmach reduces the violin to a single string on which an unvarying and primitive two-note tune is played. The Palmach claim, however, that it is those who play with a full complement of strings who are the real primitives. A full set of strings is only required, the Palmach maintain, by those who need to play a variety of music because they are still searching for the right tune. The Palmach's claim that Western music is primitive in comparison to their own is incongruous because complexity and variety in artistic expression are traditionally regarded as a mark of civilization. The Palmach assertion is, nevertheless, somewhat appropriate because simplicity and unpretentiousness may, in certain instances, likewise be regarded as indicators of improvement and advancement.

The third text is situated in a primitive agricultural setting outside some insignificant Galilean village.[6] When the Jecke returns to the village at lunchtime, his employer can only imagine some disaster has occurred to interrupt the plowing. The Jecke however, has incongruously returned for a fork. Given his primitive environment, he simply should have eaten with his hands. The absence of a fork does not merit the interruption of important agricultural activities. But from the point of view of the Jecke, the stereotype of European propriety and refinement, his behavior is hardly incongruous at all.

In each of the texts we can discern an iteration of the same underlying theme: the opposition between primitive and civilized.[7] Such iterations undoubtedly increased the likelihood that the underlying themes would eventually be grasped by almost all regular participants in the telling of chizbat. It must be recognized that these themes were undoubtedly much clearer to the Palmachniks than they are to us. We have to work hard even to glimpse a chizbat's humor. We have to be informed of the primitiveness of Metullah or the propriety of Jeckes in order to recognize the joke. However, these associations were part of the background knowledge of the Palmachniks. The chizbat accessed and structured this knowledge to highlight values and articulate themes appropriate to the definition of their identity.

Motif and Plot

Redundancy in the chizbat repertoire is not limited to the mere iteration of texts and themes. The chizbat's message is also articulated at other levels. For example, there is a very strong usage in the chizbat of motifs involving guise and disguise, demeanor and dissimulation. Such motifs seem particularly apropos in a repertoire whose basic message concerns issues of image and identity. The instances are numerous: for example, a gang of Palmachniks pretend to be a chapter of the Society for the Prevention of Cruelty to Animals; a British officer appears in the guise of a dervish; a Palmachnik pretends to be a doctor; a Palmachnik pretends to have just been released from prison; a Palmachnik is mistaken for an Arab; a famous Hebrew author hides his identity from Arab villagers; a thirty-year-old Palmachnik assumes the guise of a teenager; a Palmachnik dresses like a Russian partisan; a Haganah commander gives an emotional speech to cover up his own lack of conviction in his arguments.[8] This list could be easily extended. Undoubtedly disguise and dissimulation related to the realities of Palmach life. As a military underground, Palmachniks were compelled to conceal their identities from British authorities. Nevertheless, the prominence of motifs involving all manner of pretense, deception, and disguise would seem to signal that notions of outward appearance and underlying reality are, in some way, basic to the sense of the whole.

In some chizbat, issues of images and identity are explicitly worked out quite near the surface of the text. Plot can be characterized as the structure of consequential action. In a number of chizbat, one of the dramatis personae does or says something that forces a reconceptualization of image and identity. Each of the following four chizbat enunciate a variation of the message that people are other than whom you think them to be. Behind any particular image may lurk a very different identity, and seemingly firm identities are belied by behaviors and ideas appropriate to entirely different images.

> Beni the Politruk [cultural affairs officer] would eat himself alive if he missed one operation. At one of the night disembarkations in Caesarea, they assigned him to the water detail, whose job it was to transfer the illegal immigrants from the rowboats to the shore. He worked like a donkey. He would load a Jew with all his belongings on his back, and slosh through the water in his rubber boots and set him down on the shore. Bubeleh would greet the immigrants, kiss them, and pass them along. In the last boat stood an awesome, pleading figure. *"Khaver, nemt mikh"* [Yiddish: "Friend, take me"]. Beni loaded this mountain on his back and with shortness of breath reached the shore. The immigrant slid from his back, slapped him on the shoulder, and said *"Salamtak,* Beni" [Arabic: "Be well, Beni"].[9]

This chizbat is the recounting of a practical joke played on Beni during one of the night disembarkations of illegal immigrants. Beni, who is known for his enthusiasm and zeal in the fulfillment of all tasks that contribute to the establishment of the Jewish homeland, undertakes to carry a huge Yiddish-speaking immigrant from the rowboat to the shore. He struggles ashore under the massive weight only to discover that the person he is carrying is one of the *hevrah* [gang], one of his fellow Palmachniks disguised as an immigrant.

The following chizbat would seem to be a precise inversion of the preceding one:

> In '46 they sent Juri to Hungary to instruct youth in warfare and teach them hand-to-hand combat and things like that. When the war broke out, Juri requested to be transferred home. Until the request went through the regular sewer pipelines, half the land had been captured. When he returned to the Land, he immediately went to the newly captured Be'er Sheva. He went down the main street where Arabs used to throw rocks at the Jewish buses and was moved by the victory. The fellows with the majestic beards and mustaches, jeeps with heavy guns, young girls with weapons on their shoulders, etc. Suddenly Juri saw a beautiful tan girl who came out of one of the houses. She was wearing short pants, a khaki shirt, a *kafiyah* [Arab headdress] over her black locks, delicate facial lines, altogether there was something to look at. She started to go down the street and Juri after her. She went right, and he went right, all the time keeping the meter distance from her. He wanted to start talking to her but didn't know how to begin. Finally, when the girl gave him a tender glance, Juri lifted his head to the clouds in the sky and with a suitable sigh said, "Ah, the autumn has toiled but it is not comforted."
>
> "*Vos?*" [Yiddish: "What?"] asked the girl with a Galician accent, "you're a sabra?"[10]

On the basis of her dress, suntan, and robust beauty, Juri the Palmachnik mistakes the recently arrived Galician immigrant for a native. She betrays her immigrant status not only by her language and accent, but by attributing sabra status to someone who would address her in poetic rather than colloquial terms. The chizbat regularly makes fun of Juri's poetic proclivities, because Palmach speech was rooted in direct, terse, and slangy forms of expression.

The next chizbat operates with a different set of identities than the previous two:

> In those days when the *grush* [coin of small denomination] had a hole through it and only a few had contemplated their path in life, there was a unit of Palmach that would frequently scout the other side of the border and search among the bushes for Jews that Yeruham would leave at night with a note "pass on" [a reference to the illegal immigra-

tion from Lebanon and Syria]. It was difficult to cross the border without passing through Metullah, and Metullah in those days was a fortress of Hebrew culture in the northern district. On one day of the *hamsin* [Arabic, Hebrew: sirocco], six lads entered the fruit garden of one farmer who was plowing together with his Arab. So that all conversation would be based from the outset on well-mannered and polite words as is customary in the Galilee, Asherkeh turned to the farmer and asked, "Excuse me please. Is it possible to get a little water?"

The farmer called his Arab and said, "Muhammad. *Vos zogt er?* [Yiddish: "What is he saying?"][11]

The references to the upper Galilee as a fortress of Hebrew culture based upon polite and well-mannered conversations is ironic. The upper Galilee, as I have noted earlier, was the backwoods, the region farthest from the refined cities on the coastal plain or in the Judean hills. Politeness was never the norm. Nevertheless, Asherkeh's attempt at politeness with the farmer is to no avail; the farmer speaks only Yiddish and must call upon his Arab laborer to translate from Hebrew to Yiddish. It is the Arab who is conversant in both Jewish languages, Hebrew and Yiddish; and it is the Arab who serves to link the older immigrant generation of the farmer with the native generation of the Palmachniks.[12]

The final chizbat in this set emphasizes a transformation in the opposite direction:

They said about him [Avraham Shapira] that before he went to get married, then everyone asks about the family and this and that. You know, what the family is like, what the girl is like. Like that. He went to see what the mare was like. According to that he determined.[13]

In this chizbat, the old watchman, Avraham Shapira, European-born and raised, reveals himself to be more of a Bedouin than a European Jew. He is more concerned with the worth of the horse that he is to acquire through marriage than with the qualities of his prospective bride.

Each of the above chizbat contains an explicit message about image and identity. Each chizbat illustrates that a particular image does not necessarily confirm an underlying identity, nor does a particular identity yield the expected image. As a set, we can reduce these chizbat to four propositions:

1. In the chizbat about Beni unloading immigrants: what appears to be a European Jew (image) is in fact a sabra (identity).
2. In the chizbat about Juri and the girl: what appears to be a sabra (image) is in fact a European Jew (identity).
3. In the chizbat about the Palmachniks' encounter with the farmer: what is in fact an Arab (identity) appears to be a European Jew (image).
4. In the chizbat about Avraham Shapira and the mare: what is in fact a European Jew (identity) appears to be an Arab (image).

Simply in terms of what transpires in their course as stories—as accounts of actions—these chizbat reveal the fundamental distance between image and identity, between appearance and reality. In real life, Palmachniks modeled themselves after the image of the Arab and divorced themselves from the image of the European Jew. But in these chizbat, all the images—sabra, Arab, and Jew—are in some sense transformations of one another. The system has no center. There is no firm image upon which identity can rest. Once again, although at a completely different level, the basic message of the chizbat is articulated: image is not identity. The deliberate effort to demonstrate a new identity is inevitably doomed to failure. Identity can never be merely based upon the emulation of admired images, for it is rooted as well in those images that have been repudiated and denied.

Synoptic Texts

Within the chizbat repertoire there exist what may be called "synoptic texts." Whereas the message of the chizbat is distributed throughout the repertoire, as specific values within the *sabra* or *galut* images are made appropriately incongruous, synoptic texts condense the overall message of the repertoire within the framework of a single text. In the context of the chizbat, therefore, a synoptic text is one that explicitly deals with the creation or demonstration of image and the inherent complications in representations of self. While there do not seem to be many such chizbat, some do exist and serve to recapitulate the basic message of the repertoire. The following chizbat concerns the sculptor Avraham Melnikov, who goes to Egypt to look for a lion to serve as a model for his monument to Joseph Trumpeldor and the other martyrs of Tel Ḥai:

> Do you know Melnikov? This story is not about his brother and not about his father but about him himself. When they asked Melnikov to

make the statue of the lion on the grave of Trumpeldor, they said that first of all he would have to see a real lion. They said to him, "Find yourself a lion." And in those days there wasn't one lion in the country.

He went to Dr. Bodenheimer in Jerusalem who was knowledgeable about animals and asked him in German where it was possible to see a living lion. The doctor said to him, "Go to Cairo."

He went to Egypt. He came to Cairo and asked, "Where is the zoo?"

They said to him, "Do you hear the roars of the beasts of the desert? There is the zoo."

He walked and walked until he arrived. He asked to get in. They said to him, "Ticket." He bought a ticket, they let him in.

He just got in and ran to the lion cage. He saw a lion roaring, he took out a piece of paper and started to sketch.

The zoo director came to him and said, "Go!, *yalla!* [Arabic: "Go!"].

He said to the director, "I want to make a statue of a lion on the grave of Trumpeldor."

The director said to him, "*Bala Trunkeldor, bala ishi* [Arabic: "Not Trunkeldor, not anyone." The mispronunciation is deliberate because there is no "p" in Arabic]. "*Yalla, yalla.*" He left.

Melnikov didn't know what to do. He went to the chief rabbi of Cairo and asked advice. The rabbi said to him, "My son, go to the Minister of Fields, Trees, and Animals." He put on a suit, he took an *arabiyeh* [Arabic: cart] and went to the Minister of Agriculture.

He came to him and said, "How much?"

The minister said, "What you give, you give."

Melnikov said, "I'll make a drawing of you so they won't forget you even after you die."

The minister said, "Good!" and sent for the zoo director. The director came and saw Melnikov with the minister and started to sweat.

Melnikov said, "He's really O.K. But law is law. You can't go against the law."

The minister said, "The law is shit and its legislators are under my *surmayah*" [Arabic: shoe]. He gave an order that no one should bother Melnikov during his work.

The director was so happy that Melnikov didn't inform on him that he chased away all the people in front of the lion cage and said, "*Taffadal ya sidi* [Arabic: "Please sir"], the lions and I are your servants. Just say the word."

Melnikov said, "Coffee."

They brought him coffee and he started to work. By the time he started sketching, all the lions had fallen asleep. He told them to roar, they didn't roar. He said to them, "*Tzzzzz.*" They didn't bat an eyelash.

He went "*Zrrr*" and all the donkeys in the area started braying. But the lions—nothing. They were finished. He saw that he had no other choice. He approached the cage and started to stick his hands in. One lion saw a hand, he got up and tore his shirt, with the chest. But he didn't roar. Blood started to flow. Great God! Melnikov left the zoo and ran to a pharmacy.

The pharmacist asked him, "What happened?" and poured an ounce of iodine on his chest.

He didn't want to involve the zoo director so he said, "A cat."

The pharmacist said, "*Walla!* [Arabic: "By God!"] a big cat. A cat like that belongs only to Abu Tintan."

Melnikov said, "Does he roar?"

The pharmacist said, "What do you mean roar? A leopard is a dog compared to him."

Melnikov said, "Bring him to me."

They went to Abu Tintan and found a big cat, like a lion, who roared like a leopard, Melnikov bought the cat and starved him. The cat roared and roared until he finished making a statue of the lion. And anyone who doesn't believe can go to Tel Ḥai and see if the lion there doesn't resemble a cat roaring like a leopard.[14]

Joseph Trumpeldor was a pioneer and soldier who was killed in an Arab attack at Tel Ḥai in the upper Galilee in 1920. It is reputed that his last words before he expired from his wounds were, "It is good to die for our country." Trumpeldor stood for everything the Palmach stood for: self-defense, pioneering, sacrifice. He was a symbol of the new Jew that would rebuild the Jewish homeland.[15] Avraham Melnikov was commissioned to sculpt the monument for the grave of Trumpeldor and the others heroes of Tel Ḥai. Erected in 1934, Melnikov's stylized lion was one of the first pieces of modern sculpture in Palestine.

The chizbat relates a fictional account of how Melnikov came to fashion the image of the lion on the monument. When Melnikov undertakes his commission there are no lions in the country. It is not entirely surprising, therefore, that despite all his efforts, he utterly fails to produce an image of a real lion. There are, after all, no real lions to represent. The implication is clear. Those who would sacrifice and die for the Jewish homeland are not lions; at best they are house cats made to look like lions.[16]

The following chizbat also deals with the problem of image, but focuses upon the inherent impossibility of deliberately and genuinely representing the self.

A friend of ours was riding in a boat at night, fishing, and you need a lamp for that. And another fellow said to him, "Have you got strong character? Are you a strong character?"

He said, "Why?"

He said, "Show me if you're a strong character; take the lamp and throw it in the water."

"What is it? A joke?"

"No, let's see have you got the character or not."

"O.K., I got the character." He took the lamp and threw it in the water.

So the other one said, "Hey, you've got no character. Everybody can influence you."[17]

The attempt to demonstrate identity results in its own negation. When identity becomes a matter of deliberate, organized, and controlled expression, it is no longer identity but image. One who truly has character need not prove it, and one who is compelled to prove it, probably does not have it. This chizbat aptly summarizes the Palmach situation and encapsulates the fundamental message of the repertoire as a whole.

Conclusion

I have tried to show the various encodings of the fundamental message of the chizbat. The most basic encoding was in the structuring of elements of the *sabra* and *galut* images iterated throughout the repertoire. But there were other encodings as well: the plethora of motifs concerning disguise and dissimulation; the actions of characters that reveal the distance between image and identity and that collaborate to deny the reliability of those images in which the Palmach had invested; and the synoptic texts that challenge the genuineness of a calculated identity altogether. This redundancy at all levels of the system reduces the possibility of distortion and enhances the clarity of the communication.

The chizbat was a continual communication. It was told night after night, month after month, and year after year. Its power could not be exhausted in one or even many tellings. But it thrived only as a humorous and ambiguous form of expression. The chizbat could never have survived the translation of its message into expository language—

the kind that characterizes this scholarly discourse, for example—because the chizbat was more than mere communication. At the same time it articulated the problems of identity, it served to resolve them. As it explored and celebrated the paradox of Palmach identity, the chizbat came to serve as the correlative of that identity. Paradoxically, the chizbat came to symbolize the very identity it claimed was beyond representation. Were the message of the chizbat formulated in expository terms, its very explicitness would have undermined its value; for as the chizbat has taught us, deliberate representations of self are never genuine and always doomed to fail.[18]

If the message of the chizbat was never, and could not be, formulated in ordinary language by the Palmach, how can we determine whether it was in fact received and understood? I suggest that we do so in the same way we ensure that many of our ordinary communications have been understood. We ask those who have received them to repeat, or better yet, to *reformulate* them. We ask, in other words, for the production of redundant expressions. Ultimately the Palmach's comprehension of the chizbat's message can only be evidenced in the same way—in the production of redundant expressions. But we have already demonstrated such redundancy. As the members of the Palmach generated numerous jokes and anecdotes that they told as chizbat, that articulated the same messages as other chizbat, and that were accepted as chizbat, we must conclude that the basic message had been received and understood. The redundancy of the repertoire, therefore, not only ensured that a message was clearly communicated; it also registered the very success of that communication.[19]

6
Rechnitzer Rejects
An Unorthodox Humor of Modern Orthodoxy

Several years ago, a friend bought me a Jewish comedy record as a present. At first the record was entertaining, but the more I listened to it, the more I began to wonder about the significance of this comedy and its relation to that larger question of "Jewish humor." American-Jewish humor has been mainly thought of in terms of jokes and anecdotes orally circulated or published in various popular anthologies and compendia. These jokes and anecdotes require, for the most part, only a very catholic knowledge of Jewish character, tradition, and sociology in order to be understood. They are often understood and appreciated by Jews with widely disparate levels of Jewish education, religious knowledge, and ritual participation. Indeed, many non-Jews are also appreciative auditors and raconteurs of such "Jewish" jokes and anecdotes.

The Jewish humor on the phonograph record was entirely different, however. First, the humor was in the form of songs and comic routines rather than joking narratives. Second, these songs and routines were being disseminated through commercial recordings rather than oral face-to-face communication. Third, and perhaps most striking, these songs and skits, unlike most of the Jewish joke repertoire, presupposed a highly esoteric ethnic and religious knowledge for the comprehension and appreciation of the humor.

This record which generated so much enjoyment and puzzlement turned out to be only one in a series of albums entitled *Rechnitzer Rejects*.[1] The first volume in this series was issued in 1982, and five volumes were issued in subsequent years through 1988. The records are the creation of Perfect Impressions, a "public relations and entertainment management" firm based in New York that specializes in Jewish entertainment.

The six albums consist of ninety-two bands or tracks. Sixty-one of these are songs, while the remaining selections are comic routines, many of which involve music. The great majority of songs are parodies and most of these are based upon standard and contemporary popular tunes including: "Puttin' on the Ritz," "O My Papa," "Shake, Rattle, and Roll," "Thunderball," "Feelings," "Memories," "Saturday Night Fever," "Tie a Yellow Ribbon," the theme from "Flashdance," and "We are the World." A few of the songs are parodies of specifically ethnic material: of Yiddish songs such as "*Mayn shteytele Belz*," "My Zadie," and "Roumania"; of contemporary pop-Hasidic material such as "Just One Shabbos," and "The Time is Now"; and of popular Israeli songs like "*Kahol ve-lavan*," "*Hay, hay, hay,*" and "*Al kol eleh.*"

The comic routines take several forms. A number involve *khazones* or cantorial renditions of liturgy supplemented with appropriate sound effects. Five routines are telephone conversations that a *meshulekh* or Jewish fundraiser has with the English receptionist of a Jewish doctor, the minister of a black church, the proprietor of an Oriental massage parlor, President Ronald Reagan, and a pre-taped sports news recording. Three routines involve the delivery of inappropriate sermons, while two others are mock Yiddish language tutorials. Two routines are commercials and two political announcements. There is one Jewish game show, a presidential debate, a radio talk show interview, and a filler by someone impersonating Henry Kissinger.

As I already indicated, the most striking aspect of these records is the extraordinary range of cultural data that is required to interpret these performances. From a linguistic point of view, listeners are expected, in addition to English, to have a good knowledge of Yiddish and Hebrew as well as a smattering of Aramaic. They should be able to recognize Yiddish and Hebrew dialects and accents as well as the voices of various leaders who have been involved in Middle Eastern affairs (e.g., Menachem Begin, Ariel Sharon, Anwar Sadat, Henry Kissinger, Jimmy Carter, Ronald Reagan). They need to be familiar with typical Jewish foods (cholent, kishka, kneydlakh, ptcha, chopped liver, and bagels) as well as concepts of kosher and glatt kosher. Musically, listeners are expected to be familiar with *khazones* or cantorial style and be able to identify exaggerated examples of that style. Listeners must also be grounded in contemporary trends in Jewish music including the voices and specific performances of Mordechai ben David, Shlomo Carlbach, Avraham Fried, and Jo Amar. Other musical currents from Israel, the klezmer tradition, and Yiddish theater are also drawn upon.

From the perspective of religious observance and ritual, the songs and skits call for some knowledge of: putting on *tefillin* (phylacteries) and customs associated with reciting the *kriyas shema* ("Hear O Israel") prayer; *dukhenen* (bestowing the priestly blessing) and the ritual washing of the hands performed by the Levites; the singing of *zmires* or hymns during the Sabbath eve meal as well as the names of particular hymns; *aliyes* or summonses to recite blessings over the Torah; the *trop* used in cantillating the Torah; the wearing of wigs or *sheytls* by observant Jewish women as an expression of modesty; the Talmud and the language and gestures associated with its study; as well as specific prayers from the Sabbath and high holiday liturgy.

Lastly, these songs and skits rely upon a more general sociological knowledge of Jews and the Jewish community, such as: the propensity of Jews to enjoy the *shvits* or steambath; the continued existence and operation of the figure of *shatkhn* or matchmaker; resort hotels that cater to an observant Jewish clientel during Jewish holidays; concepts of *yikhes* or pedigree and its relationship to the according of ritual honors in the synagogue; the requirement of ten men to form a *minyan* or quorum for communal prayer; the conflicts that traditionally exist between a rabbi and the congregation that employs him; and the names and locations of particular Jewish communities and their character.

In addition to all of this specifically Jewish knowledge, the humor of the *Rechnitzer Rejects* further requires considerable familiarity with American culture, particularly American popular music and singers, but also other media forms and figures such as radio talk shows, commercials, language instruction records, and celebrities.

The musical presentation is a contributing element to both the aesthetic and the comedic properties of the songs and routines. The musical arrangements are full and strong. The opening notes of a song are usually sufficient to identify the song being parodied because the music so faithfully reproduces the original popular recordings. Those tunes that are "Rechnitzer originals" are melodic or otherwise engaging. The *khazones* is equally accomplished and sung by talented *khazonim* [cantors]. In listening to the record one can easily feel that the comedy does not merit such a degree of musical sophistication. But this disparity between the musical and comedic levels only serves to enhance the quality of the latter. The humor is heighted by the extraordinary musical attention that has been dedicated to the production of a broad humorous text.

It is not possible to survey each of the songs and routines that appear on *Rechnitzer Rejects* here. Instead, I will present and comment on three songs, as songs form the majority of selections on these records.

70   Jokes and Their Relations

The first song is entitled "Home on the Blat" and is sung to the tune of "Home on the Range":

[Spoken:] I was in the *beysmedresh* [Yiddish, Hebrew: house of
  study], learning for a change,
When I heard my *khavruse* [Yiddish: study partner]
  singing "Home on the Range."
He sang it with ease, and *neshome* [Yiddish, Hebrew: soul] of
  course,
And when he was finished, he got off his horse.

[Sung:] Oh give me a *daf* [Hebrew: page], where the *sugye's*
  [issue] not taf [= tough],
Where the Rashi and Tosefos [two medieval commentaries] is
  small,
Where seldom is heard, an Aramaic word
And my *rebbe* [rabbi] is always on call.

Oh give me a *blat* [Yiddish: page]
Where I'm able to learn *pashut peshat* [Hebrew: simple
  literalism]
Where *tana'im* [teachers of the Mishnaic period] report, an
  encouraging *vort* [Yiddish: word]
And *rishonim* [post-Talmudic codifiers and commentators of
  the late Middle Ages] don't argue a lot.

Oh give me relief from *kashes* [difficulties] so deep,
That they threaten to fracture my thumb.
And bring someone keener, to the lone *hava amine* [premise]
When it seems the *maskone* [conclusion] won't come.

A *kalvekhoymer's* [an *a fortiori* argument] okay,
But his friend *tsad hashave* [Hebrew: common denominator;
  basis for another hermeneutic principle] "No way!"
But when *im timze lomer* [Hebrew: "And if you should say,"
  indicating the anticipation of counter arguments]
Is like *sefirat ha-omer* [counting the days between
  Passover and Pentecost; i.e., numerous],
I'm tempted to cry out, *"Oy vay!"* [Yiddish: Woe!, My gosh!]

Oh give me a page, where *makhloykes* [Hebrew: controversy] don't
  rage,
And Abbaye and Rava [two Amoraic sages] agree.

> Where the *Mishnah* is *stam* [apparent], and the Rabbenu Tam
> [one of the masters of the Tosefos]
> Doesn't need a *"ve-nireh le-Ri"* ["And it appears to Rabbi
> Isaac"; a reference to another important figure of
> Tosefos activity]
> A *talmid khokhem* [Yiddish, Hebrew: scholar] I'm not,
> I pity the brain that I've got.
> When the *shakle ve-tarye* [Aramaic: balance and throw;
> i.e., debate] is not out to scar ya,
> That's when I feel home on the *blat*.[2]

This song should be completely enigmatic to those unfamiliar with the Talmud. For those who are somewhat familiar with the Talmud, the overall sense of the song probably comes through, although there are still elements that are likely to remain obscure. This song is likely to be completely intelligible only to someone who has actually studied the Talmud. Even the reference to the fractured thumb in the fourth verse which involves no obscure language or terminology depends on familiarity with the traditional gestures associated with Talmudic analysis and argument. Thus, this song provides a good illustration of the depth of Jewish knowledge that is often prerequisite to the appreciation of the humor on *Rechnitzer Rejects*.

Jews are enjoined to study Torah and one of the highest forms of this study is the study of the Talmud. "Home on the Blat" is essentially a complaint about the difficulties of Talmud study. The singer expresses his wish to study an issue that is clear, about which there is no controversy, and upon which the major medieval commentaries of Rashi and the Tosefos (which always appear on the page where the issue is presented and discussed) have little or nothing to say. Indeed, virtually all of the esoteric terminology in this song is dedicated to indicating the desire for a direct and uncomplicated study experience.

The use of the tune "Home on the Range" is not arbitrary or accidental. "Home on the Range" evokes images of pastoral simplicity. A home on the range is a home in the great outdoors, connoting a solitary existence in nature, a life in which "discouraging words" are never heard. The study of the Talmud, however, does not take place on the open plains but in an urban center. It is carried on indoors in crowded houses of study. This study is a loud and intense verbal and gestural interaction within smaller study groups (*khavruses*) where *only* discouraging words are to be heard in the exchange of arguments and counterarguments. A romantic image of the American West stands in direct opposition to the conception of traditional Jewish life as symbolized by the Talmud and its rituals of study. Thus, the parodying of "Home on the Range" involves much more than the utilization of a familiar tune, meter, and an occasional bit of phraseology. As with all successful parody, an awareness of the original song's images and messages is required for a complete appreciation of the comic mutation.

The quest for the simplicity and harmony of the American prairie in the pages of the Talmud is, of course, a ludicrous one. Although the Talmud is the basis of Jewish law, the study of the Talmud is not primarily an exercise in learning and memorizing law. Often an authoritative decision for the case under discussion is never arrived at or stated. Talmudic study is rather a process of examining traditional legal opinions, organizing them, searching for their consistencies, reconciling contradictory opinions, and asking new questions based upon changed circumstances and situations. This process has a life of its own independent of what the actual legal decision may or may not be. This process is of the highest intellectual order. Complexity and controversy are its trademarks. Contrary to the wishes expressed in the second verse of the song, there is no issue devoid of Aramaic words since the greater part of the Talmud involves the Aramaic discussion of earlier Hebrew legal teachings. The desire, in the last stanza, for an issue upon which the sages Abbaye and Rava agree is equally fantastic, because in the Talmud, Abbaye and Rava rarely agree; indeed, their traditional disputations have come to serve as a metaphor for the entire system of Talmudic dialectics.[3]

"Home on the Blat" sends a clear message about the ludicrousness of yearning for American simplifications of Jewish life. The attempt to distill Jewish traditions to a simpler essence can only result in their evaporation altogether. One can never be at home in Jewish life in general, or on a page of the Talmud in particular, if being "at home" signifies being without complexity, conflict, and anxiety. The song clearly communicates the impossibility of a Jewish life that is zealously reconciled with the values of the dominant culture—with the modern, secular values of American society.

The second example that I wish to present is not a parody of a specific song although its music is drawn from a recognizable musical style. The song is entitled "Makhmir":

Shades of black and the Satmar's back,
Gartl [Yiddish: a ritual belt] tight and *peyes* [Yiddish, Hebrew: side
   curls] long;
Socks are white and you know they're right,
Satmar's never wrong.

Shades of blue, he's a special Jew,
Being watched by many eyes;
Shades of green and I know what you mean,
It's a *kheyrem* [Yiddish, Hebrew: ostracism, excommunication] otherwise.

[Chorus:] Half the town they think they're crazy,
But that's nothing new;
To understand the holy plan,
Here's what you must do.
They're off to see,
The *rov* [Hebrew: rabbi] to see,
If strictness is their word.
Makhmir, makhmir [Hebrew: strict, severe]
Makh mir dus and *makh mir* dat [Yiddish pun: Strictness this
   and strictness that; or, make me do this, make me do that];
Makhmir, makhmir,
It's Satmar's secret.

Eenie, meenie, meinie, moe,
Catch a Hasid by the toe;
If he *shokels* [Yiddish: ritual swaying gesture] let him go,
He'll go back to ole Monroe [Monroe, N.Y.]

Shades of pink with a *schnaps* [Yiddish: liquor] to drink,
Simkhes [Yiddish, Hebrew: joyous occasions] make the Satmar sing;
Shades of red like the *rebbe* [leader of Hasidim] said,
He sees everything.

Shades of brown and around the town,
All *misnagdim* [Hebrew, Yiddish: opponents of Hasidism] spurn the
   sect;
Shades of grey well there'll come a day,
That they'll get more respect [repeat chorus].[4]

The Satmar are a group of Hasidim from a town in Northwest Romania (before World War I, a part of Hungary) that settled in Williamsburg after World War II. In 1972 the late Satmar rebbe established a yeshiva and a self-contained community in Monroe, New York. In the eyes of most traditional Jews, the Satmar Hasidim are an extreme manifestation of halakhic or Orthodox Judaism. For example, based upon his interpretation of Jewish law, the leader of the Satmar Hasidim has opposed both Zionism and the State of Israel, claiming that they are sinful and delay the coming of the Messiah. Hasidim in general, and Satmar Hasidim in particular, are opposed to any reconciliation between Jewish tradition and modern society. They are strict (*makhmir*) in their interpretation of the law, leaving no room for the insinuation of alien influences. In every way they attempt to protect Jewish law by removing any potential temptations or occasions for its violation. Thus the traditional dress of the Hasidim, mentioned in the first verse of the song, of black coat, belt, hat, and white socks, insulates them from the wider community and creates an additional barrier against modern institutions and values.

Although the song is ostensibly about Satmar, its real concern is strictness in the interpretation of Jewish law. The Satmar Hasidim are only an extreme representation of this tendency to strictness, for it is a tendency to be found in other segments of the Orthodox community as well. The suggestion in the last verse of the song that a day will come when the Satmar will get "more respect" for their strictness is a ludicrous one. In a certain way, it is as ludicrous as the wish in "Home on the Blat" that the study of the Talmud should be straightforward and uncomplicated. This ludicrousness in "Makhmir" is highlighted by arranging this paean to the Satmar in an exaggerated disco/pop instrumental style.

Both the songs I have presented are similar in that they set lyrics of specifically Jewish content to American popular songs or musical styles. These songs, however, are diametrically opposite expressions. "Home on the Blat" explores the possibility of simplifying Jewish tradition; "Makhmir" explores the possibility that Jewish observance and community will come to resemble that of the contemporary Satmar. From the perspective or stance of the songs, both possibilities are equally ludicrous.

Yet neither perspective is truly ludicrous in its own right. They are only made to seem ludicrous in the songs. Indeed, Reform Judaism, as well as segments of the Conservative movement, is dedicated to the reconciliation of Jewish tradition with modern culture to the extent that modern values determine which elements of traditional Judaism may be rationally maintained. Traditional Orthodoxy, on the other hand, makes no concessions to the modern world if it compromises the observance of the halakhah.[5] The halakhah rules supreme no matter how severe the burden of its observance. It is the halakhah that must extend itself over modern life; not the other way around. As I have said, neither of these positions is inconsistent or ludicrous in its own right. What appears ludicrous, however, is a position that seeks to maintain both perspectives: one that seeks to live in modern society in accordance with modern values *while at the same time* attempting to maintain halakhic Judaism. Yet this is precisely the position of modern Orthodoxy. And it is this dilemma of modern Orthodoxy that is aptly reflected in the tension between the extremes of Satmar severity and feeling at "home on the blat."

While "Home on the Blat" and "Makhmir" stake out the *boundaries* of modern Orthodox identity at the extremes of accommodation and rejection of the mainstream American society and culture, most of the songs in the *Rechnitzer Rejects* albums explore the ludicrousness of the center, the ludicrousness of trying to fuse American culture and values with Orthodox belief and practice. One of the songs that exemplifies this ludicrousness is "Cholent is a-Burnin'." The song concerns the preparation of *cholent*, a traditional Jewish dish, and is sung to the tune of "California Dreamin'."[6]

> All the beans are brown and it's Friday,
> I was so eager to cook for the *Shabes* [Sabbath] day.
> I forgot the water, shouldn't smell this way.
> Cholent was a burnin' on a winter's day.
>
> Stepped into my *shul*, [Yiddish: synagogue] had to walk away.
> I came running home and I began to pray.
> I was so ashamed, having company.
> For cholent was a-burning, and the heat was on me.
>
> Cholent *bren* [Yiddish: "burnt"] is a *nekhtikertog*
>   [Yiddish: literally, "like yesterday's day;
>   colloquially, "of no account"; "a fantasy"] when
> You forget the water and then
> It's the *Shabes* [Sabbath] meal *in drerd* [Yiddish:
>   literally, "in the earth"; colloquially, "gone to
>   hell"].
>
> All the beans are black and it's Saturday.
> Cholent had been burning and it had burnt away.
> I forgot the water shouldn't smell this way.
> My cholent had been burning spoiled my *Shabes* day.
> Oh what can I say,
> Other than, *"Oy vay"* [Yiddish: "Woe!; "Oh my!"].[7]

Cholent is a dish that originated in Europe. It is basically a stew made with beans, meat, potatoes, barley, and spices. The ingredients are covered with boiling water and left at low heat in the oven for a period of fifteen to twenty-four hours. This long period of cooking gives cholent its distinctive smell, color, texture, and flavor.

What is not apparent from the recipe for this dish, however, is the symbolic significance of cholent. Cholent is the quintessential Sabbath dish. It is eaten at luncheon after return from the synagogue.[8] The Jewish Sabbath is traditionally a day of rest on which no "work" is permitted. Halakhic notions of work vary considerably from our modern notions. It is, for example, forbidden for observant Jews to light a fire or to do any cooking on the Sabbath. Lighting a fire or cooking would violate the commandment to observe the Sabbath and keep it holy.

Yet it is also traditional on the Sabbath to eat well, for the Sabbath is a day to be celebrated, not simply observed. According to Jewish Law, it is permitted to keep food that has been cooked before the Sabbath warm; it may be removed from the oven and consumed, although the oven flame may not be extinguished. This makes cholent an ideal Sabbath dish as it can be kept in the oven for long periods of time without danger. Thus what initially appears to be nothing more than a somewhat unusual stew recipe, is really more closely integrated into a ritual context. While cholent is not a ritual dish per se, its particular suitability for the Sabbath endows it with ritual significance. Thus cholent is not merely an example of Jewish ethnic cuisine, but a symbol of the Sabbath and Jewish Law, as well as of Jewish family and community.[9]

But this song about cholent is a ludicrous one. There is clearly something ridiculous in conjoining a song text about ruining a Sabbath meal with the tune of the Mamas and Papas 1960s hit "California Dreamin'." But as with "Home on the Blat," the conjunction of text and tune is not simply arbitrary or fortuitous.

"Cholent is a-Burnin'" inverts several of the key images and themes of the popular original. "California Dreamin'" is about too much *cold* whereas "Cholent is a-Burnin'" concerns the result of too much *heat*. "California Dreamin'" concerns *leaving home* whereas the parody is concerned with company that is *coming to the house*. Also, the *shul* [synagogue] stands in direct opposition to the *church* that figures so prominently in the original song. The Yiddish lexical intrusions further serve to emphasize the differences between the parody and the completely English original.

However, the core contrast between the two songs is thematic. Los Angeles, California, which is the particular object of yearning in "California Dreamin'," occupies a particular niche in American symbology. Los Angeles is thought of as an avant-garde, "laid-back," fun-oriented, sunny paradise. But these attributes conflict rather markedly with the images and values of Orthodox Judaism symbolized by cholent. Orthodox Judaism is conceived of as an Old World, traditional, restrictive, and even anxious way of life. Judaism is associated with a history of persecution and suffering that is not easily reconcilable with the hedonistic philosophy that, in the popular imagination, has come to be associated with the southern California lifestyle.

What "Cholent is a-Burnin'" communicates is the sense of conflict and discordance experienced by members of the modern, American, Orthodox community—that is, by those individuals who are concerned with Jewish law and custom (as in the correct preparation of a Sabbath meal), yet who at the same time are fully competent participants in mainstream American culture. Thus the song makes a statement about the incongruity of the two worlds that modern Orthodox American Jews inhabit.

It should come as no surprise, of course, that the songs of the *Rechnitzer Rejects* reflect the dilemma of modern Orthodoxy. After all, the interpretation and appreciation of *Rechnitzer Rejects* is only open to those who have been immersed in the culture and concerns of halakhic Judaism *and* who have had broad exposure to secular, American, popular culture. But the humor of *Rechnitzer Rejects* is not a modern Orthodox humor only because of the knowledge that is requisite for its understanding; it is a modern Orthodox humor because it iterates the basic incongruities at the core of modern Orthodox identity.

One characteristic of modern Orthodoxy is its orientation toward more liberal interpretations of the halakhah. Modern Orthodox Jews have looked for rabbinic responsa that are *mekel* (lenient), those that make use of legal loopholes that allow for an observance that does not inhibit the pursuit of modernity. They avoid the responsa that are *makhmir* (strict) and that require extreme personal adjustments in living. But the pursuit of this liberal position contributes to a sense of religious ambivalence in many modern Orthodox people. It creates a doubt about the sincerity of their own commitment to the halakhah. It engenders an uneasy feeling that the traditional Orthodox who avoid the honors and rewards bestowed by modern society are more authentic Jews, and that modernist Reform and Conservative Jews are perhaps not so inauthentic. This ambivalence and insecurity about their ritual-status is expressed in endless conversations and evaluations of the status of other members of the community that invariably manifest themselves in pronouncements about being "too *frum*" [Yiddish: pious] or "crazy frum" or "black hats" on the one hand, or "too modern" or "goyim" [Gentiles] on the other.[10] Invariably, it is only others who are characterized in this fashion; one's own degree of observance is usually just right with perhaps only minor deviations from some unstated ideal.

This contradiction in the self-identity of modern Orthodox Jews cannot be easily resolved or summarily dismissed.[11] Elsewhere I have argued that when irresolvable contradictions exist in the definition of self, one method of mastering the conflict engendered by this contradiction is to exaggerate them, externalize them, and celebrate them.[12] And this is precisely what *Rechnitzer Rejects* does. Again and again within individual songs and in the interaction between different songs the contradiction of traditional Jewish and modern life is replayed and broadcast in all its permutations. Proposed solutions, if they are offered, are invariably more ludicrous than accepting and living the contradiction. Ultimately, *Rechnitzer Rejects* communicates that the problems of identity and the conception of self are not so much to be resolved as transcended, and that a major vehicle for this transcendence is to be found in the forms and techniques of humor.

With almost no advertising, the first volume of *Rechnitzer Rejects* sold more than ten thousand copies. The other volumes were also expected to sell this much or more.[13] These kind of sales volumes indicate "hit records" in the Jewish market. What accounts for this kind of popularity? Why should a humor of modern Orthodoxy emerge at this time and prove so popular?

Such questions need to be framed properly. In many respects, the humor of *Rechnitzer Rejects* is not new. For example, the songs of Mickey Katz similarly celebrated the ludicrousness of the encounter between Jewish and American culture.[14] His parodies of American popular songs however, highlighted the encounter between American culture and Jewish ethnic culture; that is, the Yiddish speaking culture of Eastern Europe. Unlike the *Rechnitzer Rejects* albums, his songs contained little Hebrew and no Aramaic and were devoid of references to either Israel or Orthodox religious culture. Nevertheless, Katz's albums clearly demonstrate that a commercial tradition of popular song parodies on Jewish themes is no innovation.

Furthermore, popular song parodies based upon Orthodox Jewish tradition are also not new. Such parodies, however, tended to emerge in the folk culture of modern Orthodoxy rather than in popular and commercial formats. The following is a fragment of a song that was popular among the students of a modern Orthodox elementary school in New York City circa 1955. It was set to the then popular hit song "Black Denim Trousers":

> He wore black denim *tsitses* [fringed ritual garment],
> And *peyes* [sidecurls] two feet long;
> And a black leather *yarmulke* [skull cap],
> With a button on the top;
> He had a hopped-up *gemore* [Talmud],
> That took off like a gun;
> And he was the terror,
> Of *heder* [Hebrew: room] one-o-one.[15]

Although somewhat less sophisticated, this parody is not appreciably different from most of the parodies presented on the *Rechnitzer Rejects* albums. Nor do I believe this example to be idiosyncratic. There is evidence that such traditions of song parody (as well as comic routines) have existed for decades among the youth of modern Orthodox communities, although they have not been documented in any of the folklore or humor collections of which I am aware.

The scope of the questions about the *Rechnitzer Rejects* albums has been somewhat narrowed. A tradition of Jewish parody of American popular song on commercial recordings is not new. Nor does the subject matter of *Rechnitzer Rejects* appear to be entirely new; rather it seems to parallel the folk traditions of modern Orthodox youth of the past several decades. The question that remains is: Why does such material come to be deliberately composed and recorded in the 1980s, and why does it meet with such astounding commercial success? If my interpretation of the basic message of *Rechnitzer Rejects* humor is accepted, the question may be formulated as follows: Why in the 1980s do significant portions of the modern Orthodox community feel the need to project and celebrate this conflict of identity?

I believe the answer to this question lies in the recent compression of the spectrum of Jewish religious practice. That is to say, the range of religious expression that is to be found in Jewish institutional contexts has narrowed considerably in recent years. Furthermore, this compression has been toward the "right"—toward traditional or halakhic forms of expression.

Today, classical Reform Judaism, with its disdain for tradition and ritual, has fewer adherents. No longer is the anecdote about a Christian lawyer who discovered quite accidentally in the midst of a Sunday service that he was in a Reform Synagogue likely to ring true. Today one is more likely to encounter Reform Jews who pray with a *tallis* [prayer shawl] and observe Sabbath and dietary laws.[16] Reform practices, in the return to traditional forms, are becoming indistinguishable from those of the Conservative or even Orthodox congregations. The 1984 call by New York Reform congregation Shaaray Tefila to "join us on Rosh Hashannah for our 'Tashlich' service (casting away of sins)"[17] is merely an extreme example of this movement towards traditionalism.

Similarly there has been movement to the right within Orthodoxy itself. This move to the right is manifested in stricter interpretations of the halakhah with an increasing intolerance for deviation. Modern Orthodox attempts to reconcile the halakhah with modern life have less support and are viewed as mere facades for halakhic deviation.[18] All in all, this compression of Jewish practice along with other developments such as the *havurah* (fellowship) movement,[19] the *baley tshuve* (penitent) phenomenon,[20] and Jewish feminist expression[21] have served to blur traditional denominational boundaries and threaten the identity of a modern Orthodoxy rooted both in the halakhah and the values and attitudes of a liberal democratic society. In this environment, the incongruity between commitments to both secular and religious forms and values is no longer merely a concomitant of modern Orthodox identity, it has become the distinguishing feature of that identity. To know the language of the Talmud and its methods of study, to recognize the lyrics of "Home on the Range" and their expression of naive romanticism, and *to be able to laugh at the conjunction of the two;* that is the measure of modern Orthodoxy. In repeatedly playing upon the incongruity of sacred and secular values, *Rechnitzer Rejects* emerges as an important touchstone of modern Orthodox identity at a time when the elements of that identity are being challenged and no longer seem clearly in focus.

7
Between Jokes and Tales

Humor depends upon the discernment of an appropriate incongruity. This conceptualization holds that humor proceeds upon the apprehension of a structure of ideas rather than from the reaction to particular ideas, motives, or events. However, the necessary and sufficient conditions under which a text qualifies as humorous cannot be used to distinguish the forms of humorous expression. A species cannot be distinguished utilizing the attributes of the class. Consequently, while the notion of appropriate incongruity provides a framework for describing why a particular joke is funny, it provides no basis for assessing why a particular humorous form is a "joke" rather than some other type of humorous expression, or why one joke can be regarded as "funnier" than another.[1]

Here I am interested in exploring such distinctions. What are the differences between humorous narratives that we tend to regard as jokes and those that impress us as some other form of tale? Why do certain representations of jokes seem to be better humor bearing texts than others that exploit the very same appropriate incongruities?

This exploration, to be sure, does not begin in a vacuum, for scholars have identified a rather large number of distinctions between the two forms. The tale is generally longer than the joke which, by comparison, is relatively brief. The world created in the tale emphasizes the normal, the typical, and the rational; the world of the joke invokes the abnormal, the bizarre, and nonsensical. There is a tendency for the tale to be explicitly didactic whereas the joke seems to avoid any explicit moralization. The joke tends to be narrated in the present while the tale is situated in the past. The tale hangs upon deeds and their consequences whereas the joke depends on speech and the peculiarities of language. The tale is frequently multi-episodic and ambles on toward some kind of narrative resolution, whereas the joke is usually restricted to a single scene and culminates abruptly with a punchline.

The above distinctions are derived solely through textual comparison. Other distinctions that have been noted, however, attend the conditions of narration. For example, tales evoke smiles whereas jokes generate laughter. The demands for novelty in joketelling are far greater than in taletelling. Tales and jokes are not usually performed by the same narrators. The taleteller's repertoire endures in memory and remains fairly constant, while the joketeller's changes constantly in response to current joke fashions.[2]

It is, of course, possible to think of counterexamples to many of these distinctions between joke and tale. Jokes are often told in the past tense, and a tale could be narrated in the present tense and still remain essentially a tale. There are numerous jokes whose fictional worlds are normal and realistic, and equally many tales whose contrived scenarios make excessive demands upon the hearer's imagination. Some jokes endure in memory over decades and are continually retold. There are longer jokes and shorter tales, and certainly, there are numerous jokes that are multi-episodic as there are tales that consist of only a single episode. Some jokes elicit only the vaguest of smiles, while certain tales may provoke raucous and sustained laughter. And even a joke can be employed for didactic ends, while a humorous tale may be told without any explicit didacticism whatsoever.

The proliferation of distinctions, in other words, does not clarify the issue. If a joke can be longer than a tale, it does not seem helpful to identify the joke as a shorter form. If a joke can be multi-episodic, it is of little use to characterize it as consisting of a single episode. The only distinction that seems critical in distinguishing the joke from the humorous tale is the presence or absence of what is colloquially referred to as a *punchline*. A joke without a punchline is no joke.[3] Indeed, virtually all the other traits that have been used to distinguish the joke from the tale would seem to be concomitants of the punchline. In other words, it is the punchline that conditions the other conspicuous features of the joke.

That narrative jokes have punchlines seems a rather obvious proposition. It would also seem, however, that this very obviousness has caused the whole issue to be overlooked. Although attention has been given to the techniques of humor,[4] considerably less attention has been devoted to the punchline itself. The notion of the punchline remains largely intuitive.

The punchline is a device that triggers[5] the perception of an appropriate incongruity. It reveals that what is seemingly incongruous is appropriate, or what is seemingly appropriate is incongruous. In any event, the recognition brought about by the punchline must be *sudden*.[6] The punchline must bring about an abrupt cognitive reorganization in the listener. As such, the punchline is not a necessary element of humor but a literary device that characterizes the particular form of humor we label "joke."

> A1. A farmer took himself a real shrew for a wife. After the wedding ceremony, the couple left the church for their new home in a horse-drawn carriage. Along the route, the horse stumbled and the husband said, "That's once!" Further down the road the horse stumbled again and the husband said "That's twice!" When the horse stumbled a third time, the husband got down from the carriage, walked up to the horse, drew a pistol, and shot the horse right between the eyes. His wife immediately started to yell, "What did you do that for? Are you crazy? That was a perfectly good horse. Now we'll have to walk all the way home." The husband looked up at her and said, "That's once!"[7]

Despite having a farmer protagonist, being set in horse and buggy days, and being told in the simple past, this narrative is very much a joke. The final line is a genuine punchline. Its effect is to realign our conceptualization of characters, relations, situations, or events. It triggers the sudden recognition of a serious, though reasonable misapprehension. In the above joke, the farmer's behavior strikes us as totally incongruous. We are appalled at the husband's execution of the horse. It appears an extreme and cruel response to the minor failings of the animal. The warnings the farmer delivers to the horse hardly justify his actions since the poor horse could hardly be expected to understand them. Thus we are moved to silently agree with the shock and indignation of the wife. After all, we are as shocked, indignant, and baffled as she. But in response to his wife's harrangue the farmer offers the seemingly unrelated and inappropriate response, "That's once!" There is a moment of puzzlement. How can this phrase serve as a meaningful and appropriate response to his wife's complaint? An almost simultaneous recognition follows. This is the phrase with which the farmer cautioned the horse of his pique. We therefore reconceptualize the wife's harrangue not as reasonable indignation, but as behavior that irritates the farmer. We are suddenly forced to the recognition that the farmer's behavior toward the horse applies equally to humans, even to his wife, and culminates in the deeper recognition that what seemed an extreme response to the minor failings of his horse was in reality meant to serve as a warning to his wife. What impressed us as impulsive, extreme, and incongruous in the farmer's behavior is recast as controlled, deliberate, and totally appropriate. This transformation is achieved abruptly over the course of, what might be called, a "conceptual instant."[8]

It is not difficult to see how certain features of joke narration would follow naturally from this device of the punchline. A joke is more likely to evoke laughter than the tale because the joke demands a sudden cognitive reorganization. Such reorganizations tend to precipitate laughter. But this reorganization is only possible if the punchline is sudden, and the punchline is sudden only if the joke is novel. If the joke has been heard before, there is nothing to reorganize. The appropriate incongruity is recollected before the punchline is delivered. (Actually this novelty is relative since many hearers know they have heard it before, but as they can't remember how it ends, they are able to listen to it, be surprised by it, and laugh at it again.) The surprise created by the punchline would naturally create a demand for novel materials whose endings had not been heard before and therefore could not be anticipated. Consequently, success would favor narrators who do not rely upon a fixed store of memorized texts but who continually assimilate new material into their repertoires.

The punchline can be characterized in terms of its position in the narrative sequence. A punchline must stand in the final position. This seemingly obvious point is, in actuality, not entirely obvious. And it seems less a matter of joke style than joke grammar. To the extent that this syntagmatic rule is violated, and an appropriate incongruity is revealed in a medial position, this revelation will be muted and the narrative will tend to be conceptualized less as a joke and more as a form of humorous tale.

A2. There was a girl who was unusually domineering, and it was predicted that if she ever got married she would make her husband's life miserable. Finally some farmer asked for her hand, and he was accepted. The wedding took place a short time later, and the groom gave his bride a horse on which she rode home from church. As they were riding along, the horse stumbled. The husband said to the horse, "That's once." When the horse stumbled again a short time later, the husband said, "That's twice." When it stumbled a third time, the husband took out a knife and slit the horse's throat. The wife immediately started berating him for killing the horse. "That's once," he said, and ordered her to pick up and carry the saddle. Well, she was so intimidated that she picked up the saddle and carried that saddle all the way home.

Years passed and the predictions about their marriage were not fulfilled. To the contrary, it was proverbial how obedient the wife was to her husband in all respects.

Once the couple went to a party. After eating, the ladies and gentlemen were in different rooms. The men began to boast about who had the best wife. They agreed to call in their wives from the other room and the wife who obeyed first was the best. The farmers called for their wives. Our woman, who was talking to her sister, quickly stood up. Her sister said, "Don't be in such a hurry," and asked her to stay a while longer. As she hurried to leave the room she said to her sister, "No! You have not carried the saddle like I have."[9]

Despite the fact that our original joke is essentially reduplicated in the first portion of this text, this text is not a joke. The punchline must come at the end of the joke because the abrupt and surprising revelation of an appropriate incongruity marks the end of the joke as a discourse. It is the *point* of the joke—its raison d'etre. A would-be punchline in the medial position is not a punchline. The revelation of an appropriate incongruity in the middle of a narration suggests that this revelation is subordinate to some other narrative program, as it is in the above example. In fact, the importance of the final position is often sufficient to cause the listener to mistake the final line for a punchline, even though it reveals no appropriate incongruity. Thus, "You have not carried the saddle like I have" sounds like a punchline but fulfills none of its cognitive functions. No misapprehension is corrected; nothing new is revealed. We already know why the woman is responding to her husband's summons with such alacrity. We already know she has been intimidated and made to carry the saddle.

It is not unusual to find a narrative concluding with a line that is stylistically, although not structurally, a punchline. Such final lines, however, do not create appropriate incongruities, or if they do, they merely re-present an incongruity that ought to have been perceived earlier in the course of the narrative. These are not true punchlines but "pseudo-punchlines."[10] While they mark the conclusion of the tale, they do not transform the perspective of the listener.

A3. In pioneer days, a man married an ill-tempered young lady. Following the ceremony, they both mounted his horse and started for home. When the old horse stumbled the man glared at it and said, "That's once." Later, when it stumbled again, he said, "That's twice." When they came to a stream and the horse balked at crossing it, he said, "Now that's three times." He told his wife to get down, and he got down and took the saddle off the horse. He stepped back a couple of steps and shot the horse between the eyes. Killed him!

The wife immediately began bawling him out for killing the poor horse. She kept yelling, but he didn't say anything. He merely reloaded his rifle. Finally she quit yelling, and the man said, "Now, that's once." He said, "We'd better get going. Pick up the saddle and let's go." When the wife hesitated to pick up the saddle, he glared at her and said, "That's twice!" Well she picked up the saddle and they headed home. She made him a good wife.[11]

Unlike the preceding tale, the narrative consists of only a single episode, and the revelation of appropriate incongruity occurs significantly closer to the final position. Nevertheless, we are still not quite dealing with a joke. From the point of view of the joke, the husband's "That's twice!" is an unnecessary iteration of his threat. It adds no new information, it alters no perceptions, and reveals no new appropriate incongruities. The concluding description of the woman's acquiescence and the comment that she made a good wife likewise serve to mark this narrative as a form of tale, for it is only the tale that is concerned with the consequence of action within the fictional frame. If "That's once!" is meant by the husband as a threat, then the tale audience may rightfully expect to learn the consequences of that threat. In the joke, however, it is the transformation in the perception of the audience that is the point of the narrative, not the ultimate situation of the characters. Perhaps the most generally inappropriate response that one can make to a joke is to ask, "And then what happened?" This question is not an inappropriate response to a tale, however. The "and they lived happily ever after" employed at the end of "fairytales" in our culture closes narration by denying the possibility of subsequent events. This possibility must be explicitly denied in the tale because further events are, in fact, distinctly possible.[12] As a genre, the tale is naturally "open-ended" and may require formulaic markers of closure that are irrelevant to the joke.

The final position of the punchline also decides the question of whether a joke might have multiple punchlines.

B1. A Russian citizen fills out a request for a telephone. After five years, he receives a notice to come to the ministry. He goes to the ministry and goes to the office in charge of telephone applications. The man behind the desk tells him, "Your application for a telephone has been approved. Your phone will be installed in ten years."

"Morning or afternoon," asks the man.

"It won't be for ten years," the bureaucrat replies. "Why do you care whether it is in the morning or the afternoon."

"Because the plumber is coming in the morning."

This joke could properly end with the line "Morning or afternoon." In fact, versions exist with precisely this ending.[13] But this line, although humorous, is not a punchline of this joke. In this joke the punchline is "Because the plumber is coming in the morning." If this line were removed or replaced, the definition of the narrative as a joke would be severely threatened. For example, were this last line of B1 replaced with: "I am so anxious about getting a phone, and when I get anxious I tend to chatter and ask silly questions," the text would strike us as anomalous. It is the appropriate incongruity created in the final line that defines the punchline, and it is the punchline that defines the joke.[14]

Moralizing or didactic commentaries, which are common in oral and printed repertoires of humorous tales, are invariably absent in jokes. As the joke achieves closure in the punchline, any subsequent commentary—didactic or otherwise—is likely to threaten the conceptualization of the narrative as joke. A joke cannot end with a moral unless the moral *is* the punchline—and then it is not a serious moral and thus not a moral at all.[15] Moralizing commentary embedded within the joke is likely to prematurely reveal information that will destroy the sense of surprise (as frequently happens in the humorous tale). This is not to say that jokes cannot be used for didactic ends. They can be and have been so used.[16] However, any explicit didactic commentary needs to be clearly demarcated from the joke itself. In performance, this may be accomplished by pausing to allow the audience to fully respond to the punchline before commenting on the joke's significance. It may also be accomplished by positioning the didactic commentary as far away from the punchline as possible—that is, in a position *prior* to the telling of the joke.

The inability to conjoin material to a joke after the punchline and the severe limitations upon the use of explicit didactic commentary undoubtedly contributes to what has been described as the characteristic brevity of the joke. However, the joke's brevity probably owes more to the need to control information and prevent overload so that a listener or reader is able to grasp the relationship between the abrupt conclusion and the narrative exposition. If a joke narrative is too rich, too developed, the listener may be unable to recall or select the essential information necessary to effect his cognitive reorganization when the punchline is delivered.

Dan Ben-Amotz, an Israeli writer and humorist, explored the variety of ways a joke can be destroyed in performance. He used a joke about an Israeli trying to smuggle some coffee through the port of Haifa without paying customs duty, which should go something like this:

> C1. A Jew returning through Haifa port tries to smuggle in two sacks of coffee. They ask him, "What have you got in the sacks?" He says, "Bird feed." They open the sacks and see the coffee and ask, "And since when do birds eat coffee?" And he says, "They eat if they want, and if they don't they won't."[17]

One of the joke-destroying techniques that Ben-Amotz explores is what he calls, "The Surplus Details Technique." His formulation is as follows:

> C2. There was this man whose name was, I think, Rabinowitz, who'd been living in France all his life. Well, one day he got a letter from his sister in Tel Aviv, and she wrote to him that she had a headache and she hadn't been feeling at all well recently and things weren't so great with her in general. It doesn't matter. Anyway, she wrote him: It's getting close to Passover, maybe you come to Israel to visit for a while. We'll take a tour to Galilee, there's a lot of beautiful flowers up there now. . . . The man liked the idea and decided to take the trip.
>
> But he must bring his sister some sort of present. Now, what sort of present do you bring to Israel? So he went to the *pletzl* in Paris and asked around what's worthwhile to take to Israel these days. And they told him, "You can bring all sorts of things. You can bring wristwatches in sardine cans; diamonds on your person; radio sets inside a steamroller. It depends what you want. Tell us what you want." So he said, "I don't want to fool around with anything really black market; I'd like something simple, something to eat or drink. . . ."
>
> So they told him, "To eat or drink? Take coffee!" So Rabinowitz asked

them, "What sort of coffee is worthwhile to take?" and they told him, "There's Turkish coffee, and there's Brazilian coffee, and there's this kind of coffee and there's that kind of coffee. . . . It all depends what you want."

So he bought two sacks of fine Argentine coffee and started out on his trip to Israel. Now, he was, what'll I tell you, about forty-five years old at the time and on arriving in Haifa. . . .[18]

Although Ben-Amotz's concern is the creation of humor rather than scientific analysis, he illustrates quite well the danger of an overdeveloped joke narrative. There are simply too many details of potential relevance to the unknown yet anticipated punchline: the protagonist's name, the fact that he is coming from Paris, that he hadn't been to Israel, that it was during the Passover holiday, that the coffee was Argentine, and so on. A listener trying to keep track of so many potential details is in danger of overlooking the single one necessary to the comprehension of the punchline.[19]

Nevertheless, brevity is not the sole means for controlling information. Indeed there are numerous jokes that could be abbreviated without altering their underlying conceptual structures, but whose abbreviation would not necessarily result in better jokes.[20] Yet, there must be some upper limit to the length of a joke narrative. As the joke's raison d'etre is its punchline, a joke can be evaluated only after its punchline is revealed. Too great an emphasis upon narrative development will tip the weight of the joke away from the punchline. Listeners will wonder, in such a case, whether any punchline, no matter how clever, can justify the narrative expenditure.[21] That there are limits to the narrative development in the joke seems clear; what these limits are, however, remains to be ascertained.

If brevity is the tendency in the narrative development of a joke, it is even more characteristic of the punchline. A punchline is rarely more than a "line."[22] Frequently it is much less. Punchlines may be expressed with a noise, an exclamation, a word, a gesture, or even a musical tone. In other words, a punchline is often an unusually compact expression. This compactness is directly related to the function of the punchline as a technical device. The punchline must effect a sudden transformation in apprehension. If the form of the final expression is too protracted, this transformation will not be sufficiently sudden and the surprise element will be lost.

Furthermore, "getting a joke" involves more than being presented with an appropriate incongruity. It requires effort. An appropriate incongruity must, to some extent, be *discovered*.[23] Discovery is an experience, an experience that can only be communicated by engineering a situation in which someone is allowed to repeat that discovery. Being shown the solution to a puzzle is qualitatively different from discovering it oneself.[24] Consequently the joke must establish a balance between revealing too little and revealing too much. If a joke shows too little, the discovery of an appropriate incongruity will not be achieved. If it shows too much, the appropriate incongruity will not be discovered so much as "displayed." While the detail in a joke narrative must be controlled in order to restrict the number of possible ambiguities introduced into the text, the punchline needs to encapsulate a quantum of perplexity to be successful.

> D1. "Is the doctor at home?" the patient asked in his bronchial whisper. "No," the doctor's young and pretty wife whispered in reply. "Come right in."[25]

> D2. "Is the doctor at home?" the patient asked in his bronchial whisper. "No," the doctor's young and pretty wife whispered in reply. "Come right in, handsome."

There is clearly a problem with the punchline in this second text. It is not its absolute length that creates the problem.[26] Certainly, there are effective punchlines that are considerably longer. The joke is inferior because the punchline shows too much. It chooses to explicitly resolve the incongruity involved in the wife's inviting the patient in when the doctor is not at home. It leaves considerably less for listeners to discover on their own.[27]

The task of discovery affects, it would seem, another aspect of joke punchlines. The overwhelming majority of punchlines in narrative jokes are expressed in dialogue—as quoted speech—or in some other kind of performed action: a gesture, a noise, singing.[28] This emphasis of direct discourse in the punchline has little to do with techniques of wordplay. Jokes that make no use of wordplay nevertheless make use of dialogue punchlines. In a book of contemporary jokes containing eighty-one texts,[29] eighty can be categorized as narrative jokes that revolve around characters and situations. Of these, the punchlines of all but four (5 percent) are presented as dialogue. Of those four, two are descriptions of behaviors that likely would be acted out rather than described if the joke were orally performed. Thus only two jokes (2.5 percent) in the collection have punchlines that are not presented as dialogue.

Dialogue, while not the mandatory form of the punchline, is the overwhelmingly favored form of expression. The question is "Why?" Consider the following fifteenth-century joke.

> E1. Francesco Filefio, jealous of his wife, lived in constant fear that she would betray him, so he kept careful watch over her night and day. One night, while sleeping (for we are always occupied in our sleep with that which perturbs the spirit during wakefulness), he beheld a certain demon, who promised security from doubts about his wife if he would do exactly as he was told. In his sleep, he assented, saying he would be grateful, and promised to return the favor. "Take this," said the demon, "and keep it diligently on your finger, for as long as you wear it, your wife will never lay with another man without your knowledge." With great delight he awoke to find that he had his finger in his wife's cunt. This is the best remedy against jealousy, for with it, wives cannot be unfaithful behind their husband's backs.[30]

If we ignore Poggio's ironic coda, this text would seem in almost all respects a joke. In the next-to-last line we are confronted with an incongruity: What has the position of the husband's finger to do with the previous dream? The appropriateness of this incongruity follows almost immediately. A woman's vagina is structurally similar to a ring, and furthermore, a man could indeed insure the fidelity of his wife by wearing such a ring as this. (Poggio's coda would seem ironic as it is not possible for husbands to keep their fingers in their wives' vaginas twenty-four hours a day and thus insure their fidelity; therefore women, in Poggio's view, are fated to be unfaithful.) Thus there is a punchline—an incongruity that is abruptly revealed and resolved in a final, concise statement.

But if "The Vision of Francesco Filefio" is a joke according to structural criteria, it lacks the form of expression common to the majority of current jokes: a contemporary setting, a present-tense narration, and, most important, a dialogic punchline. I believe that Poggio's joke is improved by such changes:

> E2. A guy wakes up his girlfriend in the middle of the night and says, "I know I have always been much too jealous around you. Well I just

dreamt that I went to Heaven where I met an angel who gave me a ring to wear that would guarantee you would always be faithful to me. Somehow, I feel a lot better." "I'm glad you feel better," said the girlfriend, "I'll also feel a lot better when you take your finger out of my cunt."[31]

The joke here is structurally and thematically the same as Poggio's text. The most important transformation is in the way information is communicated. Information that was revealed through exposition and description in the fifteenth-century text is here contained in dialogue. Whether we like the joke or not, I believe this revision is more in keeping with contemporary stylistic preferences.

Dialogue seems a particularly suitable mode for joke punchlines. First, speech in some sense is disruptive. Speech intrudes as a special system of significance into the order of happenings in the world.[32] Events follow from their antecedents (to the extent that they are known) in a chain of cause and effect. Speech seems to elude this chain of causation and is always potentially wild and disruptive. Thus direct speech enhances the punchline that is, after all, designed to disrupt the listener's traditional categories and expectations.

Second, dialogue creates for the listener the illusion of immediacy and presentness. It thrusts the listener up against the here-and-now of the fictional scene. In dialogue, the narrator's voice and whatever guidance it might offer evaporates, leaving the listener to fend for himself utilizing his own interpretive resources.[33] The listener must work to make sense of this fictional world. It is this engagement of the listener that creates the successful joke.

A joke is not a recounting of what happened to certain fictional characters. A joke is something that is *happening* to the hearer at the moment of telling. The tendency of jokes, perhaps more than any other narrative genre, to be told in the present tense (as in, "A guy *goes* into a bar and *orders* a scotch and soda . . ."), to have contemporary settings, and to advance through and culminate in dialogue is probably related to this effort to create an encompassing present in which the listener is, in some sense, the central character.

In the 1950s, Isaac Asimov published a science fiction story about a scientist who programs his computer to analyze jokes in order to discover their origin. His inquiry, and the story, end when the computer ascertains that jokes are extraterrestrial productions introduced by an alien intelligence to assess human psychological functioning.[34] In one respect, the computer was right. Jokes are structures of psychological significance. To date, it has been this psychological dimension that has attracted the bulk of scholarly attention. The joke, however, is also a literary genre, perhaps the most pervasive and popular of modern times. As literature it merits a serious and substantial critique.

8
Freud and Humor
Analytic Reflections

In the interpretation of humor, an encounter with the individual joketeller has been considered superfluous. Either jokes have been regarded as literary texts unrelated to distinct and identifiable personalities, or they have been regarded as vehicles for impulses so common that they hardly could be conceptualized as forms of individual expression.[1] This situation is not entirely surprising. As a joke is rarely a novel creation, there would seem to be a substantial distance between a joke and its teller. Indeed, a joke usually has many tellers. While they may belong to the same social, regional, and cultural groupings, they may also have lived at different times, in disparate cultures, and in diverse environments. Some contemporary jokes were popular a thousand years ago.[2] In other words, a joke is a traditional, public text, and therefore would seem an unlikely vehicle for the expression of personal problems, predilections, or programs.

Psychoanalysis, born in the intimate contact between physician and patient, has been the interpretive paradigm most sensitive to the history, character, and behavior of the individual. Nevertheless, in the psychoanalytic interpretation of jokes, the individual has also been curiously neglected.[3] This neglect began early. In *Jokes and Their Relation to the Unconscious*, written in 1905, Sigmund Freud analyzed only the techniques and thoughts underlying particular joke texts. His discussion of the motives for joking, however, was generic. It was never tied to the investigation of specific cases.

Only once, in fact, did Freud deign to comment on the relationship between a joke and its teller. In *Reisebilder*, in the section entitled "Die Bäder von Lucca," Heinrich Heine introduces the character Hirsch-Hyacinth of Hamburg, lottery agent and extractor of corns, who boasts of his relationship with the Baron Rothschild: "And, as true as God shall grant me all good things, Doctor, I sat beside Salomon Rothschild and he treated me quite as his equal—quite famillionairely."[4]

Freud analyzed this joke at three levels. First he identified the technique of the joke, which he termed *condensation*. "Familiar" and "millionaire" are condensed into the single word "famillionaire," which simultaneously evokes ideas associated with each term.[5] Freud then proceeded to elucidate the underlying *thought* of the joke—that is, the central idea that the joke advances. Hirsch-Hyacinth's characterization of Rothschild's behavior as "famillionaire" posits that Rothschild treated the poor Hyacinth familiarly, but only as familiarly as a millionaire can—which is to say, not familiarly at all.[6]

Freud unraveled the techniques and characterized the underlying thoughts of numerous jokes. Only with this "famillionairely" joke did he move to a third level of analysis; to an exposition of the *relations* between the joke and its teller. In Freud's view, Heine was actually speaking through the mouth of his character. As the character Hirsch had changed his name to Hyacinth (thus maintaining the utility of his signet ring with the letter "H" inscribed on it), Heine with the same economy changed his name from Harry to Heinrich at his baptism. Heine also had a rich uncle named Salomon who played an important part in his life and who treated him as a poor relation, that is, "famillionairely." As Freud stated, "There is not a little evidence to show how much Heine suffered both in his youth and later from this rejection by his rich relations. It was from the soil of this subjective emotion that the 'famillionairely' joke sprang."[7]

While on this occasion, Freud was willing to venture an interpretation of a joke in terms of its teller, he at once cautioned against the facile reduction of jokes to personal factors: "The presence of similar subjective determinants may be suspected in some other of the great scoffer's [Heine's] jokes: but I know of no other one in which this case can be demonstrated so convincingly. For this reason it is not easy to try to make any more definitive statements about the nature of these personal determinants. Indeed, we shall be disinclined in general to claim such complicated determinants for the origin of every individual joke."[8] It would seem that Freud's willingness to explore the personal determinants of the "famillionairely" joke depended, in great measure, upon the fact that Heine was its creator and not merely its raconteur. Undoubtedly Freud would have been reluctant to pursue Heine's personal investment even in this joke had it been drawn from the common stock of traditional humor.

But even traditional texts can be deeply embedded in personal history and invested with personal insignificance. "The Wolfman" was one of Freud's most famous neurotic patients. His appellation derived from a childhood dream in which wolves perched in a tree outside his bedroom window. Freud discovered that this dream was connected to an illustration of a wolf in a book of folktales, and that this folktale had had an enormous influence on the patient as a child.[9] So the fact that an individual is not the author of a text does not mean that it is devoid of personal significance. Indeed, it was Freud who demonstrated that the significance of such traditional texts can be profound.

If a traditional folktale can reflect aspects of individual personality, so can a traditional joke. There is no substantive basis for distinguishing between the two genres in their capacity to reflect private concerns. Of course, one cannot simply assume every joke to be deeply and personally significant for its tellers. Jokes may be told for purely social reasons.[10] A hypothesis of personal significance becomes probable only under certain conditions. I would suggest that the telling of a joke is more likely to be subjectively determined when: (1) the teller claims that the joke is a "favorite" or is "particularly good" or "significant"; (2) the teller tells the same joke in different situations over a long period of time; (3) the teller explicitly identifies with characters or events in the joke; (4) the joke is associated with other personal individualized expressions such as artistic creations or dreams; and (5) a theme is iterated in several jokes rather than restricted to a single example. The more of these conditions that obtain, the greater the justification for hypothesizing a personal relationship of a narrator to his joke.

Below I propose to examine the relationship between Sigmund Freud and the jokes that he told. While this proposal might seem at first sight to be merely clever, there are, in fact, very good reasons to select Freud as the object of such an investigation. Freud has left us with a substantial corpus of jokes to investigate. His *Jokes and Their Relation to the Unconscious* includes nearly two hundred jokes, anecdotes, puns, witticisms, and riddles. His private correspondence is peppered with jokes, sarcastic allusions, and comic metaphors. We also know a great deal about Freud. His psychological writings comprise more than a score of published volumes. He left a good deal of personal correspondence. While only some of this has been published, his biographers have had access to portions of the whole. A good number of friends, disciples, and patients have also recalled their encounters with Freud in their diaries, reminiscences, and memoirs. Furthermore, in choosing Freud, we need not introduce alien or artificial perspectives in the attempt to decipher his joke repertoire. Freud himself proposed the program for the interpretation of jokes. If this program applies to anyone, it should apply to Freud. Finally, Freud is a good subject because there is strong reason to suspect that a portion of his joke repertoire was personally determined. Indeed, in relation to his Jewish jokes, all the conditions that I outlined above are fulfilled.

Virtually every description of Freud by his friends and disciples remarks upon his sense of humor and his penchant for joketelling. Joan Riviere: "The awe inspiring appearance was lightened by the glow of an enchanting humor, always latent and constantly irradiating his whole person as he spoke."[11] Franz Alexander: "He propounded the most significant ideas in a light conversational, casual tone. He liked to illustrate a point with anecdotes and jokes, was an excellent raconteur, and even serious topics were robbed of the artificial austerity with which they are so frequently invested."[12] Ernest Jones: "A Gentile would have said that Freud had few overt Jewish characteristics, a fondness for relating Jewish jokes and anecdotes being perhaps the most prominent one."[13] Thus the telling of jokes was a prominent element of Freud's presentation-of-self; particularly the telling of Jewish jokes.

We also know that Jewish jokes were among Freud's favorites. While Freud felt compelled to include in *Jokes and Their Relation to the Unconscious* many jokes that had been discussed by previous investigators, he also included a number of favorites from his own repertoire. "We must not shirk from the duty of analysing the same instances that have already served the classical authorities on jokes. But it is our intention to turn besides to fresh material so as to obtain a broader foundation for our conclusions. It is natural that we should choose as the subject of our investigation *examples of jokes by which we have been most struck in the course of our lives and which have made us laugh the most*" [my emphasis].[14] The most prominent group of fresh jokes that Freud included in his book were Jewish jokes. These constitute the largest category of jokes that are attributed to no literary or subliterary sources. Undoubtedly, these were from Freud's own oral repertoire. Undoubtedly, these were his favorites—those that struck him and made him laugh the most.

It is clear however that Jewish jokes held a significance for Freud beyond their mere entertainment value. In June 1897, Freud wrote to his friend and confidant Wilhelm Fliess: "Let me confess that I have recently made a collection of deeply significant Jewish jokes."[15] This was written the year after the death of Freud's father and corresponded precisely with the beginning of Freud's self-analysis that gave rise to the fundamental discoveries of psychoanalysis. Certainly to undertake a collection of Jewish jokes at a time of such emotional turmoil and to characterize them as "deeply significant" suggests that these jokes were intimately related to Freud the man. When we add the fact that several of Freud's Jewish jokes served as associations to his dreams[16] and that some of his psychoanalytic insights may have first been suggested to him by Jewish jokes,[17] we must regard the hypothesis that Jewish jokes held a special significance for Freud as virtually incontrovertible.

In the brief space of this essay, it is not possible to examine the full range of Freud's Jewish jokes. Therefore, I will restrict myself to a discussion of only one subset of them—those that concern the figure of the *schnorrer* or beggar. Utilizing these jokes, I hope to illustrate the potential fruitfulness of studying jokes in relation to their individual tellers. But I also hope to contribute something to our understanding of Freud the man—the man who not only broadened our perspectives on humor, but who transformed our conceptions of the world and redefined our sense of place within it.

The character of the schnorrer, or beggar, figures prominently in Jewish folklore and literature. Jokes and anecdotes concerning his behavior are well represented in various anthologies of Jewish humor.[18] These schnorrer anecdotes tend to revolve around a single theme that is clearly discernible in the examples from Freud's own repertoire.

> A *Schnorrer*, who was allowed as a guest into the same house every Sunday, appeared one day in the company of an unknown young man who gave signs of being about to sit down to table. "Who is this?" asked the householder. "He's been my son-in-law," was the reply, "since last week. I've promised him his board for the first year."[19]

The schnorrer presumes upon the largess of his benefactor in order to assume the role of benefactor to his new son-in-law. He does not acknowledge his indebtedness—his dependence—to his charitable host and treats his benefactor's wealth as if it were his own to dispense at will.

In the next example, the protagonist is not a schnorrer proper but a borrower who is in every respect congruent with the schnorrer figure.

> An impoverished individual borrowed 25 florins from a prosperous acquaintance, with many asseverations of his necessitous circum-

stances. The very same day his benefactor met him again in a restaurant with a plate of salmon mayonnaise in front of him. The benefactor reproached him: "What? You borrow money from me and then order yourself salmon mayonnaise? Is *that* what you've used my money for?" "I don't understand you," replied the object of the attack: "if I haven't any money I *can't* eat salmon mayonnaise, and when I have some money I *mustn't* eat salmon mayonnaise. Well, then, when *am* I to eat salmon mayonnaise?"[20]

Again the debtor fails to acknowledge his indebtedness and the consequent responsibility to spend the borrowed funds only on the basic necessities of living. The poor man's justification of his extravagant expenditure is ludicrous because it ignores the implied obligation accompanying the loan of the funds.

The theme of the denial of indebtedness appears even in jokes that are not characterized by Freud as explicitly "Jewish." The following joke Freud cites in connection with his discussion of his dream of "Irma's injection" in *The Interpretation of Dreams*:

A. borrowed a copper kettle from B. and after he had returned it was sued by B. because the kettle now had a big hole in it which made it unusable. His defense was: "First, I never borrowed a kettle from B. at all; secondly, the kettle had a hole in it already when I got it from him; and thirdly, I gave him back the kettle undamaged."[21]

Again we see the denial of what is otherwise an obvious indebtedness. Of course, each denial obviates the preceding one and thus affirms the existence of the debt. In the two preceding examples, a debt is not explicitly denied, but the behavior of the borrower or beggar reveals a total absence of that sense of obligation we might recognize and suppose would exist.

Now what of the relation of these jokes to Freud? It seems appropriate to begin with an assessment of Freud's own financial situation. Freud did not come from a wealthy family. His father was a merchant and, by most accounts, not a very successful one. In his later years, it appears that Freud's father did not produce any income for his family at all.[22] As a student and during his tenure at the General Hospital of Vienna, Freud was always severely strapped for funds. In his early student days, his needs were modest as he lived and ate at home. But in May 1883, he moved from his house to reside at the General Hospital where he had been appointed to the position of *Sekundärarzt* (resident). The previous year Freud had become engaged to Martha Bernays, and he realized he would have to watch his expenses very carefully if he ever hoped to marry. (As it was, their engagement lasted for four and a half years because there were insufficient funds to establish a household.) Freud kept careful accounts of his expenses. He sent any excess funds to Martha to hold for him.[23] His letters to her during their engagement bemoan his impoverished state and are filled with details of earnings and expenditures.[24]

In 1882 Freud was spending one gulden, eleven kreuzer (45 cents) on the two meals that he took daily. Twenty-six kreuzer (ten cents) went for cigars, which Freud considered a "scandalous amount." On one occasion Freud was left with four kreuzer that had to last for three days until he received his miserable salary from the hospital. Freud received thirty gulden a month from the hospital and was also given a small room with a fire. He earned small amounts from his abstracts of medical periodicals as well as small payments from the very occasional private patient. Private students and lecture-demonstrations paid relatively well, but these were difficult to arrange and proved a very unsteady source of income. At the same time, Freud was endeavoring to contribute a minimum of ten gulden a month to support his family.[25]

It does not require a great deal of calculation to conclude that Freud's expenditures exceeded his earnings. Balancing the budget on a day-to-day basis invariably involved borrowing. In Freud's case, we can see a rather strong parallelism with the situation of the schnorrer in the first joke. As Freud wrote to Martha in August 1883: "I am going to tell you a funny little story but you mustn't be sorry for me. When I got home I found a letter from a friend who frequently comes to see me (privately), asking me to lend him *another* gulden till the first of the month, to leave it with the janitor and if I don't have a whole gulden then half a gulden, but at once; on the first everything would be paid up. Well my entire fortune happened to consist of four kreuzer, which I couldn't very well offer him. So I decided that since my ordinary bankers were not at home, to waylay a colleague who owes me some money. . . . But he couldn't be found. . . . Fortunately another colleague appeared from whom I borrowed a gulden in no time. But by then it was too late to send part of it to the other friend. . . . If my debtor pays tomorrow he shall have something. One day he and I will probably be rich, but don't you think this is a funny kind of gypsy life, Marty? Or does this sort of humor not appeal to you and make you weep over my poverty?"[26] Not unlike the schnorrer father-in-law in the joke, Freud must first seek a benefactor in order to be able to provide for others. Furthermore, he saw his situation in a humorous frame, albeit, a somewhat bitter one.

The kind of petty lending and borrowing described in the above letter is common enough among medical students and interns even today. But Freud had also developed a set of economic patrons of some significance, and these patrons loaned or gave Freud substantial amounts of money. These "bankers" of Freud included his old Hebrew teacher, Samuel Hammerschlag; his colleagues at the Brücke Physiological Institute, Josef Paneth and Ernst von Fleischl-Marxow; and most notably, Josef Breuer. In January 1884, Hammerschlag invited Freud to his home and after describing his own situation of poverty in his youth, he offered Freud the sum of fifty florins for his support. Wrote Freud to Martha: "I intend to compensate for it by being charitable myself when I can afford it. It is not the first time the old man has helped me in this way; during my university years he often, unasked, helped me out of a difficult situation. *At first I felt very ashamed*, but later, when I saw that Breuer and he agreed in this respect, *I accepted the idea of being indebted to good men and those of our faith without the feeling of personal obligation.* Thus I was suddenly in the possession of fifty florins and did not conceal from Hammerschlag my intention of spending it on my family. He was very much against this idea, saying that I worked very hard and could not at the moment afford to help other people, but I did make it clear to him that I must spend at least half the money in this way"[27] [my emphasis]. Note that Freud is first "ashamed" of his former teacher's offer, and then resolves to accept indebtedness to those of his faith without feeling a sense of personal obligation. In this sentence we have encapsuled the two trains of thought conjoined in the joke. Freud's shame betrays his sense of indebtedness; on the other hand, he is persuaded to accept charity from his Jewish benefactors without any sense of obligation. In denying this sense of obligation, and against Hammerschlag's advice, Freud again emulates the schnorrer father-in-law of the joke who uses the largess of his benefactor in order to play the benefactor himself to the members of his family.

Ernst von Fleischl-Marxow regularly lent Freud sums of money. Fleischl died in 1891 without being fully repaid by Freud.[28] Josef Paneth also made regular loans to Freud. In 1884, Paneth established a fund for Freud of 1,500 gulden (six hundred dollars) so that Freud might more quickly establish a solid economic base and thus hasten the date of his marriage. The interest from the account could be drawn upon by Freud to finance the expensive visits to Martha, who was residing with her mother in Wandsbek. Freud was also free to draw upon the principal as he saw fit.[29] Freud wrote to Martha of the wonderful economic development: "Isn't it wonderful that a wealthy man should mitigate the injustice of our poor origins and the unfairness of his own favored position?"[30] Again Freud betrayed the attitude of the schnorrers and borrowers in the jokes. He treated the discrepancy between his own economic condition and that of the wealthy Paneth as an "injustice." Freud's use of the funds without a sense of obligation is only "fair." Paneth, like Fleischl-Marxow, died prematurely in 1890. There never was an opportunity for Freud to repay his debt.[31]

We have explicit evidence that Freud viewed himself as something of a schnorrer. In a letter to Fliess, Freud once characterized himself as a schnorrer who had "allotted himself the province of Posen."[32] Freud also used to invent what he himself termed "schnorrer fantasies"; little scenarios in which he imagined himself coming into large sums of money. For example, when Freud was in Paris in 1885-1886, he met the Richettis, an Austrian physician and his wife. They were evidently quite fond of him, and since they were childless, Freud was given to fantasizing about inheriting their considerable wealth. Another such fantasy involved stopping a runaway horse and saving some great personage who rode inside the carriage. Naturally, this person would acknowledge Freud's heroic deed with, "You are my savior—I owe my life to you! What can I do for you?"[33] Such fantasies were truly "schnorrer fantasies" for they implied no sense of indebtedness or obligation on Freud's part.

It is important to recognize, however, that Freud's concern about money never manifested itself in simple accumulation of or glory in the stuff. When Freud came into money, he tended to spend or distribute it. In his later life, he liberally provided his children with money, and he generously contributed to the support of needy friends and acquaintances. He delighted in giving gifts.[34] Freud's concern about money was a concern about the social power it represented.

On the other hand, the gifts and loans that he received from his benefactors generated in Freud feelings of indebtedness, dependence, and resentment. It would seem that these feelings continued throughout his life, despite the subsequent improvements in his economic situation. Thirteen years after Freud married Martha he still complained to Fliess of the helpless poverty he had known and "his constant fear of it."[35] In his final years, Freud undertook a training analysis of an American psychiatrist, Joseph Wortis. Wortis was very much surprised by Freud's "over-emphasis" of money matters. One time, when Wortis paid his monthly bill he requested that Freud receipt it with the conventional German phrase *dankend solviert* (liquidated with thanks). "'Why with thanks . . . ?' Freud said. 'I give you something which is at least as valuable as what you give me.'"[36] Freud was unwilling to abide by the ettiquette of payment if it implied that he was in someone's debt. This exchange took place in 1934. Fifty years earlier, in 1884, Freud had written to Martha: "Oh girl I must become a rich man and then when they want something they will have to come to me."[37]

It may prove worthwhile to review what has been established thus far. First, Freud identified with the figure of the schnorrer. Second, Freud's economic position was for many years a tenuous one in which he, like the schnorrer, was repeatedly forced to accept gifts and loans from his friends. Third, Freud resented the feelings of dependence that resulted from this indebtedness. And fourth, Freud occasionally acted in a manner, like the schnorrer, that tended to deny his indebtedness and dependence.

This conflict can best be seen in Freud's relation to Josef Breuer. Breuer, a respected and successful Jewish physician who made some important contributions in physiology,[38] was fourteen years Freud's senior. By all accounts, he was an intelligent, sensitive, and generous individual who grew very fond of Freud and took a strong interest in his life as well as his career. Freud first met Breuer in the late 1870s. Their relationship grew warm and intimate. Freud admired Breuer and referred to him as "the ever-loyal Breuer"[39] to his fiancée. The Breuers were also friends of the Hammerschlags and lived in the same building.

Like Hammerschlag, Fleischl-Marxow, and Paneth, Breuer was extremely generous in making loans to Freud, and such loans came in almost regular installments. By May 1884, Freud's debt was 1,000 gulden; by July of the following year, 1,500 gulden. Freud's total debt eventually reached some 2,300 gulden, a staggering sum. Although Freud jokingly commented, "It increases my self-respect to see how much I am worth to anyone,"[40] we shall see that there is good reason to suspect otherwise.

It would seem that with Breuer, Freud was capable of playing the classic schnorrer. For example, in 1884 Freud was planning a trip to visit Martha in Wandsbek, and he asked Breuer for an extra fifty gulden for his trip. Breuer refused Freud the amount, claiming that he would only squander it on frivolous extravagances that he could ill afford. Freud asked Breuer not to interfere with his "adventurous style of life," but the plea did not help. Wrote Freud: "It was really dear and intimate of

Breuer not only to refuse me, but to concern himself with my being sensible, but all the same I am annoyed."[41] Freud, like the consumer of salmon mayonnaise, saw nothing wrong in indulging in extravagance with borrowed funds. Breuer, it must be said, was considerably more generous than the lenders in the jokes, for several days later he gave Freud the fifty gulden, explaining that he merely wished to caution Freud about his spending rather than to actually restrict it.[42]

Breuer, of course, was more than an economic benefactor and confidant. In 1882, Breuer introduced Freud to the case of Fräulein Anna O. and the cathartic method, or the "talking cure" as Anna O. herself phrased it.[43] Thus Breuer was not only an economic patron but an intellectual patron as well, providing Freud with the basic capital from which to develop psychoanalysis. Freud eventually persuaded Breuer to collaborate with him on *Studies on Hysteria*, in which Breuer documented the case of Anna O. and Freud presented four cases from his own practice. The book, published in 1895, commenced with an essay they had coauthored in 1893, "On the Psychical Mechanism of Hysterical Phenomena: A Preliminary Communication," followed by the five case studies. Breuer contributed a theoretical chapter, and Freud wrote a chapter on psychotherapy. Even before the work was published a rift between the two men was growing. Freud had had to push Breuer to collaborate on the preliminary communication in 1893, and in 1894, Freud was beginning to dissociate himself from Breuer's theoretical statement even prior to its publication.[44] The scientific difference in opinion seemed to revolve around Freud's claim of a sexual etiology for virtually all neuroses. The ever-cautious Breuer felt that this proposition went way beyond the evidence, although he acknowledged that the essential cause of every hysteria was sexual.[45]

It is not quite clear, in any of the available accounts, how this scientific difference conditioned the severe personal estrangement that developed between the two men. Commentators seem to agree that the primary responsibility for the break was Freud's,[46] and that Breuer would have liked nothing better than to maintain their previous intimate relationship. Already in 1896, Freud was writing his friend Fliess that the mere sight of Breuer "would make him want to emigrate."[47] And there is the rather sad account of Breuer's daughter-in-law, who recalled walking with Breuer when he was already quite old (he died in 1925). Seeing Freud come toward them in the street: "Breuer instinctively opened his arms. Freud passed by pretending not to see him."[48] It is hard to reconcile such hostile behavior with only a difference of scientific opinion.

It would appear that the intensity of Freud's antipathy to Breuer hinged upon Freud's debts, both financial and intellectual. When the differences of scientific opinion developed, Freud wished to emancipate himself totally from Breuer in both spheres, but the fact was that he was bound by his indebtedness.

It was not until January 1898 that Freud was able to send Breuer an installment in payment of his financial debt. Breuer, however, would not accept payment and attempted to write off Freud's debt against medical services Freud was rendering to one of Breuer's relatives. Breuer had always intended the money he gave Freud to be a gift rather than a loan.[49] But for Freud, such a gift implied interminable indebtedness. In 1900 Freud was still complaining to his friend Fliess that he could not break with Breuer completely because of the monetary debt.[50] The payment of this debt in Freud's eyes was prerequisite to his emancipation. Freud's response was complete avoidance.

In a thinly disguised reference to Breuer in *The Psychopathology of Everyday Life*, Freud revealed: "Our intimate friendship later gave place to a total estrangement; after that, I fell into the habit of avoiding the neighborhood and the house. . . . Money played a part [in certain editions: "a great part"] among the reasons for my estrangement from the family living in this building." Freud provided this little history to explain a case of forgetting; forgetting the location of a store that displayed strong boxes in its window. Although he knew that he had passed this store many times, he was unable to locate it despite a thorough search. Eventually he discovered that the store was in Breuer's neighborhood and hence his motivation to forget.[51]

That Freud owed Breuer an intellectual debt he was always scrupulous to acknowledge in his published writings; although even there we may detect a degree of ambivalence in the acknowledgment. For example, in 1909, in delivering a series of lectures at Clark College in Worcester, Massachusetts, Freud attributed the entire discovery of psychoanalysis to Breuer. "If it is a merit to have brought psychoanalysis into being, that merit is not mine. I had no share in its earliest beginnings. . . . Another Viennese physician, Dr. Josef Breuer, first (1880-2) made use of this procedure on a girl who was suffering from hysteria."[52] This generous treatment of Breuer always had something of the character of a reaction formation, especially considering the vigorous "critical opinions" that Freud held about him[53] (opinions that neither Jones nor the editors of Freud's letters saw fit to publish). However, in 1914, Freud was claiming the discovery of psychoanalysis for himself and suggesting that his gratitude to Breuer in his previous lectures might have been expressed "too extravagantly": "As I have long recognized that to stir up contradiction and arouse bitterness is the inevitable fate of psycho-analysis; I have come to the conclusion that I must be the true originator of all that is particularly characteristic in it. I am happy to be able to add that none of the efforts to minimize my part in creating this much-abused analysis have ever come from Breuer himself or could claim any support from him."[54] Freud does go on to credit Breuer with the discovery of the cathartic method, but points out that it was he who had urged Breuer to publish his findings and that this method was only a preliminary stage of psychoanalysis.[55] It would seem that Freud's excessive indebtedness to Breuer is balanced by a desire to minimize his obligation.

Breuer's case of Anna O. was indeed a great discovery. But it was Freud who was the creative inspiration in their collaborative efforts. Even Breuer acknowledged it: "Freud's intellect is soaring at its highest. I gaze after him as a hen at a hawk."[56] To have Breuer follow him in his theories was a way of repaying his debt, of finally having Breuer dependent upon him. Freud actually referred to the period of their collaboration as the time Breuer "submitted to my influence."[57] But Breuer refused to follow. He even attempted to refuse repayment of the loans. In Freud's eyes this could only mean that Breuer could never accept a dependent position and allow Freud to repay his debt.

Jones identifies the main point of reversal in Freud's feelings for Breuer as spring 1896.[58] Freud's first attempt to repay his monetary debt was in January 1898.[59] Somewhere between 1896 and 1898 Freud had undertaken his collection of profound Jewish stories, the schnorrer jokes prominently among them. The message of the jokes probably represented the unconscious wishes of Freud himself: ignore the status of the benefactor and deny the responsibility for the debt.

It is worthwhile to recall the joke about the borrowing of a copper kettle mentioned earlier. In that joke, each denial of obligation contradicted a previous denial and thus affirmed the existence of a debt. The joke was cited by Freud in connection with his discussion of his dream "Irma's injection."[60] The dream is far too complex to review here in its entirety, and the relation of the joke to the dream is somewhat tangential; that is, it is not a direct association to the content of the dream but a joking analogy employed by Freud to demonstrate the incompatibility, indeed the contradictory nature, of the various thoughts underlying his dream. He had this dream in July 1895,[61] two months after the publication of *Studies on Hysteria*.[62] According to Freud, the dream concerned his own feelings of professional competence and expressed the idea that it was not he but his colleagues who were responsible for the persistence of his patient Irma's pains. Dr. M. (Breuer) was one of the figures in the dream, and we learn that Freud was critical of Breuer for refusing to accept a suggestion Freud made to him[63] and also for refusing to concur with Freud's own conclusions concerning the unconscious motivations of Irma's symptoms.[64] In other words, the joke about the denial of indebtedness is clearly associated with Freud's thoughts about Breuer's inability to follow him and be dependent upon him.

It is now possible to see the relationship of another of Freud's Jewish jokes to his personality. The joke is not a schnorrer joke proper, but the underlying thought articulates perfectly with those of the schnorrer series.

> Itzig had been declared fit for military service in the artillery. He was clearly an intelligent lad, but intractable and without any interest in the service. One of his superior officers who was friendlily disposed to him, took him on one side and said to him: "Itzig, you're no use to us. I'll give you a piece of advice: buy yourself a cannon and make yourself independent."[65]

In his discussion of this joke in *Jokes and Their Relation to the Unconscious,* Freud soberly observed that an individual cannot make himself independent in the military where subordination and cooperation are the rule. He noted that the senior officer's advice was patently nonsensical in order to demonstrate that the requirements of military life are not the same as those of the world of business.[66] The joke is nonsensical, however, in the same way that the schnorrer jokes are nonsensical. The schnorrer's behavior ignores the reality of his debt; the officer in this joke urges Itzig to make himself "independent," even though the situation in which he is instructed to do so is manifestly inappropriate. To a great extent, the thought underlying the schnorrer jokes is iterated once again: ignore your obligation! Make yourself independent! This is just the way Freud wished he could behave.

There is another level at which the schnorrer jokes may be understood in relation to Freud's personality apart from considerations of indebtedness. We must first recall that the majority of these jokes are "Jewish jokes" and that this identification is not an irrelevant one. Second, that the "Jewish" aspect of these jokes for Freud was revealed in his own interpretive commentary: "The truth that lies behind is that the

Schnorrer, who in his thoughts treats the rich man's money as his own, has actually, according to the sacred ordinance of the Jews, almost a right to make this confusion. The indignation raised by this joke is of course directed against a Law which is highly oppressive even to pious people."[67]

Freud was correct to point out that the giving of charity is a commandment in Jewish law rather than a spontaneous manifestation of generosity. But Freud was wrong to assume that this was the basic "truth" of the joke, for the joke may be fully understood and appreciated by those who are ignorant of the Jewish legal injunctions to charity. However, it is obvious that Jewish law played an important part in establishing the truth of the joke for Freud, and we shall not be in error if we consider it an association (similar to an association made by a patient to his dream) made by Freud to the joke's contents. With this association, the interpretation of the schnorrer jokes takes on a new dimension. The debt that existed that Freud unconsciously wanted to deny was not a simple monetary and intellectual debt to Josef Breuer, but a much larger debt—the debt to the law, to his Jewish heritage. As with his debt to Breuer, Freud was always scrupulously correct in acknowledging his debt to his people, but this correctness may again belie a deeper emotional conflict about his Jewish identity.

We should recall Heine's "famillionairely" joke discussed earlier. Although it does not involve a schnorrer, it deals with a poor man's relations with a wealthy baron. We have observed that it was the only joke in *Jokes and Their Relation to the Unconscious* that Freud attempts to relate to individual personality determinants. It is also one of the jokes most frequently referred to in the work and merits special attention.

Freud pointed out how the character Hirsch's change of name to Hyacinth paralleled Heine's change of name from Harry to Heinrich. But Freud also changed his name. He was born Sigismund and only later altered his name to Sigmund! There does not seem to be a great deal of consensus as to when this name change took place. In a letter written to his half brother Emmanuel in England in 1863, he signed his name "Sigismund."[68] He was registered in the school roll at the Leopoldstädter Real- und Obergymnasium in 1865 also as "Sigismund."[69] In the annual report for 1871 he was listed as "Sigmund,"[70] yet in 1872 in writing to his friend Emil Flüss he still signed his name "Sigismund."[71] There are several commentators who date his name change to 1878, although they provide no documentary support for this assertion.[72] The commemorative page in the family Bible shows both a Hebrew and German inscription at Freud's birth. In Hebrew, Freud's name is clearly "Schlomo Sigismund"; in the German translation it is "Sigmund."[73] Perhaps the German is a later translation of the Hebrew commemorative page. Or Freud might have had two names assigned to him at birth. The first "Schlomo Sigismund," was his Hebrew name, and "Sigismund" was used by the family. Perhaps the German translation "Sigmund" might have been intended for more public uses. In any event, it would seem that for the first fourteen years of his life Freud was called "Sigismund" and only later adopted for permanent usage the name "Sigmund." The reasons and date for this adoption are not clear, but it would appear to be earlier than the 1878 date subscribed to by most biographers.

It must also be noted that Freud's Hebrew name was "Schlomo," which is the Hebrew equivalent of Salomon, the name of the millionaire baron in Heine's joke. Furthermore, Heine came to grief over his unrequited love for his uncle Salomon's daughter Amalie,[74] and "Amalie" was the name of Freud's mother. There are coincidences here that cannot be ignored. It would seem that the "famillionairely" joke was as personally significant for Freud as he claimed it to have been for Heine.

Heine changed his name on the occasion of his baptism.[75] Might not Freud's own "change of name" have held a similar significance: the desire to escape his Jewish origins and merge with the society of Christian Europe? An observation by Friedrich Heer, *Dramaturg* to the Burgtheater in Vienna, confirms this view. Heer notes that Freud probably changed his name because *Sigismund was a stereotypic Jewish character in Viennese anti-Jewish jokes.*[76] It would seem that Freud was attempting to escape an association with a reviled Jewish caricature to which his name ascribed him.

There is yet other evidence to support the contention that the "famillionairely" joke was personally significant to Freud and implied thoughts of conversion and assimilation.[77] First of all, this joke revolves around the problem of money (or more accurately the absence of money) as do the jokes of the schnorrer series. And it was precisely on the question of money that Heine's own baptism hinged. For many years, his uncle Salomon had been his benefactor.[78] At the point of completing his degree in law at the University of Göttingen, Heine was concerned for his future career and livelihood. He trusted that his conversion would open up possibilities for employment at the university or in government, as Jews were excluded from such positions.[79] As only Heine would put it: "If one could lawfully steal silver spoons I would not have been christened."[80]

Ernest Jones also informs us that when Freud visited Paris in 1885-1886, he made a visit to Père Lachaise cemetery. He looked for only two graves: one was that of Heinrich Heine, the other of Ludwig Börne. Ludwig Börne was a contemporary of Heine's and, like Heine, had been an exile in Paris. Both writers had considerable influence in German letters. Freud had received a collection of Börne's essays as a thirteenth birthday present, and they made a strong impression upon him. In his later years, Freud came to suspect that a number of his psychoanalytic ideas may have been shaped by Börne.[81] More to the point here, however, is that Ludwig Börne was born Löb Baruch in a ghetto of Frankfurt. He changed his name to Ludwig Börne on the occasion of his baptism, and, like Heine and his character Hyacinth, he economized by keeping the same initials.[82]

There are many jokes and witticisms *by* Heine included in *Jokes and Their Relation to the Unconscious*, but there are only three that purport to be *about* Heine. One is the "famillionairely" joke, which, although not explicitly about Heine, Freud personalized with his own unique analysis. Another joke about Heine also revolves around the figure of a wealthy man.

> The story is told of Heine that he was in a Paris *salon* one evening conversing with the dramatist Soulié, when there came into the room one of those financial kings of Paris whom people compare with Midas—and not merely on account of their wealth. He was soon surrounded by a crowd who treated him with the greatest deference. "Look there!" Soulié remarked to Heine, "Look at the way the nineteenth century is worshipping the Golden Calf!" With a glance at the object of so much admiration, Heine replied, as though by way of correction: "Oh, he must be older than that by now."[83]

The prominent image in this joke is the Golden Calf—the worship that was an abomination to the law brought by Moses to the Jews at Sinai.

The last anecdote concerns his death:

> Heine is said to have made a definitely blasphemous joke on his deathbed. When a friendly priest reminded him of God's mercy and gave him hope that God would forgive his sins, he is said to have replied: *"Bien sur qu'il me pardonnera: c'est son metier"* [Of course he'll forgive me, that's his job].[84]

For Freud, Heine was an important author, and along with Goethe, Schiller, and Lessing, was frequently quoted in his works. But the significance of Heine the man to Freud is perhaps best glimpsed through these jokes. Each of Freud's jokes concerning Heine confront or allude to conversion, religious abomination, and blasphemy.

Consciously, Freud was loyal to his Jewish heritage. There are numerous occasions on which he affirmed this loyalty publicly. But there was undoubtedly a strong impulse urging him to renounce this heritage. Yet, Freud sensed that conversion was not the solution to his dilemma. After all, that lesson could be learned from Heine: "I am very sorry I was christened; I do not see that things have gone any better with me since; on the contrary, I have had nothing but ill luck from that time. Is it not foolish? No sooner have I been christened than I am cried down as a Jew."[85] Like Heine, Freud must have felt as though he belonged to two worlds, and there was no way he could successfully renounce either of them. Heine was his mirror image with only the baptismal font separating them.

9
The People of the Joke

There exists a conceptualization of a special relationship between a particular people and a particular form of verbal expression. For some reason, commentators have seen fit to establish a bond between the Jewish people and the joke. Those who for millennia were characterized as "The People of the Book" may now be characterized without excessive exaggeration as "The People of the Joke." This characterization is well-known and confronts us repeatedly in articles, essays, and anthologies of Jewish humor. For example, Ernst Simon: "Hardly anyone will contest the assertion that Jewish wit has a character all its own." Harry Golden: "Humor has been so much a part of Jewish culture that any kind of activity at all is impossible without it." Or Leo Rosten: "In nothing is Jewish psychology so vividly revealed as in the Jewish joke." Or George Mikes: "The Jewish joke is probably the best of all jokes."[1] This list of quotations could be, of course, greatly extended.

What is perhaps more peculiar about this characterization of the Jews as a humorous people is that it seems to be readily endorsed by Jews and non-Jews alike—a pleasant accommodation of insider and outsider perceptions. There is likewise some accord between "scientific" and "folk" perspectives on this matter, for the image is not only perpetuated in scholarly and literary publications but in oral sources as well. Hence the first, oft-cited joke that is recorded in Immanuel Olsvanger's *Röyte Pomerantsen:*

> When you tell a peasant a joke he laughs three times. Once when you tell it, once when you explain it, and once when he understands it.
> When you tell a land-owner a joke he laughs twice; once when you tell it and once when you explain it—he'll never understand it.

The People of the Joke 113

When you tell a military officer a joke he laughs only once—when you tell it. Because he won't let you explain it and of course he doesn't understand it.

But when you tell a Jew a joke, he tells you he's heard it already—and, besides, you're telling it wrong.[2]

This is, of course, one of those curious examples of *metahumor* in which attributes of joking are themselves made the subject matter of a joke.[3]

While most of the claims concerning the humorous predilections of the Jews have been informal and casual, there have been—not unnaturally—some efforts to describe and document this relationship in a more deliberate manner. Thus in his book, *What's the Joke: A Study of Jewish Humor Through the Ages*, Chaim Bermant retraces Jewish history in an effort to delineate the evolution of Jewish humor. He begins his quest, unsurprisingly, with the Bible. According to Bermant, the humorous banter of Sholom Aleichem's Tevye—made so popular in the hit musical and film *Fiddler on the Roof*—is already prefigured in Abraham's tête-à-tête with God over the fate of the cities of Sodom and Gomorrah.[4] Bermant notes further instances of wordplay, irony, and comedy in the Bible and Talmud. Bermant's chapters range from biblical and talmudic humor, to Purim, Heinrich Heine, *shtetl* humor, the Yiddish language, Chelm stories, Sholom Aleichem, Israeli humor, Anglo-Jewish humorists, and American-Jewish humorists, with additional chapters on female humor and graphic humor.

Bermant's book, however, emerges as a compendium of unsubstantiated facts, fanciful speculations, and pseudo-historical theorizing. Did the various expressions and situations strike the ancient Hebrews and talmudic sages with the same comic force as they strike Bermant? Are Gog and Magog truly comic names?[5] Did the casting of Jonah into the sea to be swallowed by a great fish "excite humor"?[6] Did fourth and fifth century rabbis really consider the application of a slaughtered hen to a patient's shaved head only a "tongue-in-cheek" cure for heat stroke?[7]

Certainly the millennium leap from a chapter on the humor of the talmudic sages to one on the humor of Heinrich Heine should alert even the most causal reader that there is no real basis for arguing any sort of evolutionary sequence. Arranging epochs, figures, and themes in chronological order and describing the humor associated with them is a far cry from demonstrating that the humor is developmentally related. There are other curiosities in the book as well: Bermant's chapter on

Israeli humor is devoted to arguing that there isn't any;[8] and there is no discussion of Sephardic humor or the humor of any Oriental Jewish communities whatsoever. Furthermore, Jewish humor is considered in a complete vacuum; as if it were totally self-contained and could have no relations to the humor of the societies of which Jews formed only a part. As an evolutionary account, Bermant's monograph is a failure. It is not even good history. In truth, it is no more likely that Tevye the dairyman's banter with God has evolved from Abraham's style of discourse than the Israeli army has evolved from the militia Abraham organized some four thousand years ago to defeat Chedorlaomer, king of Elam, outside of Damascus.[9]

Bermant's failure, however, is entirely predictable. His is not an inquiry but a demonstration. What Bermant is concerned to demonstrate is that the bond between humor and the Jews is not recent or transitory, but old and imperishable. His book is nothing less than an attempt to establish humor as an integral part of the Jewish psyche that has existed since time immemorial. Indeed, in Bermant's view, "a humourless Jew is, in fact, a dangerous being."[10]

Even for a humorous Jew, not just any humor will do. Bermant clearly is working with a model of Eastern Europe *shtetl* humor as the quintessential Jewish humor. Only humor that can be seen as contributing to or deriving from it does he conceptualize as genuinely Jewish. He is not really interested in the humor of Jews. If he were, he would have paid more attention to Israeli, Sephardic, and Oriental humor. But these do not live up to his standards. Israeli humor is regarded as inferior, and Sephardic and Oriental communities he sees as so far from the Eastern European stream that their humor is not regarded at all.[11]

It should be clear that Bermant is writing something closer to myth than to history. His is an essay of validation, not discovery. But he is not alone. He has merely undertaken to validate what has been taken as self-evident by virtually every commentator on the subject of Jewish humor. He should not be penalized unduly. I single him out only for his thoroughness; not for the singular nature of his vision.

In this essay, I too would like to explore the image of the Jews as a particularly humorous people with a distinctive corpus and style of witticisms, jokes, and anecdotes. What most have failed to recognize, however, is that "Jewish humor" is first and foremost an *idea*. It may be more productive to explore the origin and development of this idea rather than the particular witticisms and jokes to which the term is applied. From this perspective, "Jewish humor" is simply that humor which has been conceptualized as uniquely, distinctly, or characteristically reflective of, evocative of, or conditioned by the Jewish people and their circumstances. I have no particular concern that these conceptualizations of uniqueness can be demonstrated as matters of fact—it is the orientation that defines the subject matter. This perspective affords an escape from the difficulties that have plagued other writers on the subject of Jewish humor, writers who have failed to formulate adequate or generally shared definitions of the subject matter they were studying.[12] On the one hand, this approach is beset with its own inherent limitations, most notably that it is always one step removed from the humor and the jokes themselves and that it is in no position to identify new or old instances of Jewish humorous expression until someone else has identified them as such. For what I claim to discuss is not a literature or a set of expressions and behaviors, but a conceptualization of literature, expression, and behavior. If Jewish humor is a "myth," as was once suggested,[13] it is the myth that is the focus of my inquiry. Ultimately, the value of this approach can only be justified if we are led to new awareness and understanding. That is certainly the goal of this chapter, although I will be satisfied merely to raise the issue to an appropriate level of consciousness so that the inquiry might be broadened and the debate extended to a wider range of scholars and thinkers.

Theoretically this perspective calls for a number of considerations in the analysis of Jewish humor: (1) Who is doing the conceptualizing of the humor? (2) When and where did the conceptualization take place both in chronological and sociological terms? (3) What is the nature of the materials to which the conceptualization applies? (4) What are the characteristics of the conceptualization itself? These considerations would apply whether the conceptualization in question was formally applied in printed publications, or less formally and unreflectively expressed in the normal flow of ordinary, everyday conversation.

Ultimately, if one were to inquire about a great number of oral and printed enterprises in this fashion, one would be in a position to write a history of Jewish humor, with the awareness that because of my definition of Jewish humor as a conceptualization rather than a phenomenon, such a history would necessarily be the history of an idea. In any event, it should be clear that given this perspective, Bermant's book, *What's the Joke*, could offer no solutions to questions of the nature of Jewish humor because it—and all expressions that assume the distinctiveness and genius of a Jewish humor—in fact, constitutes the problem.

I am in no position to undertake such a history here. Constraints of space prove our salvation. What I shall attempt instead is to put forward some hypotheses for consideration and debate concerning the development of the conceptualizations of Jewish humor. Although these hypotheses are stated with some confidence, I have no overpowering commitment to their defense if evidence to the contrary is forthcoming. What I hope to provide is a focus for the discussion of the conceptualization of a Jewish humor and the perception of the Jews as distinctly humorous people.[14]

My first hypothesis may be stated quite straightforwardly: *Jewish humor is a relatively modern invention. The conceptualization of a humor that was in some way characteristic or distinctive of the Jewish people begins only in Europe during the nineteenth century.* In support of this hypothesis, I merely would point out that as late as 1893, Hermann Adler, the Chief Rabbi of London, still found it necessary to defend the Jews against the charge that they were a humorless people.[15] Today, the great collections of Jewish jokes that are instinctively cited to evidence the existence of a Jewish humor are invariably compilations of the twentieth century.

There is no indication that the composers of the Bible or the Talmud or the later commentaries held any awareness of a distinctive Jewish humor. What was conceptualized was a people, a law, a ritual, a language, and a mission in the world that was distinctive—but apparently not a humor. There is evidence that the rabbis were not particularly well disposed toward humor in general;[16] hence they were unlikely to have recorded their impressions of humor in Jewish society other than to condemn its presence. (Exceptions may be noted here with reference to the celebration of Purim in which merrymaking and ritual reversal were positively sanctioned as well as the use of humorous narratives in the disquisitions of itinerant preachers and Hassidic leaders.) This is not to deny that humor was present in biblical, talmudic, and medieval Jewish society, but only to suggest that it held no special place and was not bound up with any national, religious, or ethnic identity.

If the idea of a Jewish humor was the invention of the nineteenth century, the conceptualization was applied to earlier material much as the psychological concept of hysteria might be applied to the conceptualization of witchcraft behaviors reported from earlier centuries. For example, in 1893, Abram S. Isaacs published *Stories from the Rabbis* and *Rabbinical Humor* with the intention of demonstrating that the Jewish sages were not "mere dreamers, always buried in wearisome disputations," but men who were as much impelled by "buoyancy" and "moral cheerfulness" as by intellectual motives.[17] In 1905, J. Chotzner expanded the history of humor in Jewish society by identifying little known Hebrew humorists of the thirteenth, fourteenth, and eighteenth centuries.[18]

At this point I will tender a hypothesis that is little more than a suspicion: *Toward the end of the nineteenth century, the faculty of humor was felt to be one of the signs of a civilized humanity, and Jews felt the necessity to demonstrate that they had participated in this humanity since their emergence as a people.*[19] Consequently, Jewish scholars persued biblical, talmudic, midrashic, and other literary sources to evidence this claim. At present, I lack any weighty evidence to support this contention, but in the enormously successful book *Sex and Character* published in 1903, Otto Weininger, an anti-Semite of Jewish origin, argued that Jews were not readily disposed to humor. According to Weininger, humor recognized the transcendental and was essentially tolerant while wit and satire were essentially intolerant. Thus, "Jews and women are devoid of humour, but addicted to mockery."[20] Granted that the differences between humor, wit, and satire introduce an additional complication here; nevertheless, Weininger's thesis indicates that during this period humor could be and was used as a criterion for bestowing or denying the status of full partnership in civilization.

In their attempts to demonstrate that the prophets and sages were capable of humor, both Isaacs and Adler offered a rudimentary conceptualization of Jewish humor. Each respectively viewed the humor he had culled from earlier sources as a reflection of the "Hebrew spirit that refused to submit to the yoke of any conqueror,"[21] or as "a resilience which enabled . . . [the Jew] to elude effectually all the attempts made at every age, and in every clime, to lay him low."[22] A similar position had been voiced almost twenty years earlier in the *London Athenaeum* in a comment on Heinrich Heine: "In his wit and humor, Heine was a true child of the Hebrew race. However original he may have been, he exhibited the character and peculiarities of Hebrew humor, of the wittiest and most light-hearted people of the world, which in the midst of unparalleled misfortunes and suffering, has preserved an incredible buoyancy and unconquerable spirit of satire."[23]

It is important to note that in the quests for evidence of humor among the Hebrews, the humor was always viewed against the backdrop of Jewish history and experience—a history that was conceptualized as a history of defeat, exile, segregation, and unending persecution. This points to an important clue in our attempt to understand the special relationship that is perceived to exist between the Jews and humor. Since no empirical comparative assessments of the quantity and quality of Jewish humor have been attempted (nor are they likely to be possible), the privileged relationship that is held to obtain between the Jews and humor must derive from elsewhere. Hence, my next hypothesis: *The conception of a Jewish humor derives from a conceptualization of Jewish history as a history of suffering, rejection, and despair. Given this history, the Jews should have nothing to laugh about at all. That they do laugh and jest can only signal the existence of a special relationship between the Jews and humor and suggests that the humor of the Jews must in some way be distinctive from other humors that are not born of despair.*

B. Rohatyn provides a particularly poignant example of how this conceptualization of Jewish experience might effect the notion of Jewish humor. Rohatyn had been interested in all forms of Jewish folklore and collected songs, legends, Märchens, proverbs, folk belief, medical practices, customs, and usages. He knew of the existence of humorous narratives, "but did not consider it necessary to document them."[24] Rohatyn, however, was profoundly moved by the blood libel trials that took place at the turn of the century. The trials made Rohatyn keenly aware of how much his people had suffered. He reflected: "Any means of consolation that otherwise stands open to the Jews seemed to me to fail, and yet how often had our ancestors suffered similar fates and had, as it were, overcome them. Their deep and firm faith had helped them—but also their indestructible and enduring joyfulness, their ability to laugh. Can one better overcome sorrow and gnawing pain than by laughing them away? I began to become aware of the monuments of joy and laughter of our Fathers as they lived in their humorous products, and so I began to collect witticisms and anecdotes of the Jews. What began for me as a consolation and as a pleasure gradually took on the character of an objective scholarly interest."[25] Ultimately, it was only within the context of Jewish despair and suffering that Rohatyn could conceptualize a Jewish humor.

My next hypothesis derives almost directly from the preceding one: *If the background of Jewish suffering did condition the expectation of a distinctive Jewish humor, there was only a limited range of possibilities for articulating this history of suffering with humor. The possibilities were that humor was "transcendent," that the humor was "defensive," or that the humor was* "pathological." In fact, each of these possibilities was explored in the conceptualization of Jewish humor; each possibility suggests a solution to the problem of why the Jew should laugh.

The idea that Jewish humor was in some respects transcendent we have already encountered with Rohatyn's and Isaac's conceptualization of the humor of the ancient rabbis as a triumph of the Hebrew spirit. The major exponent of this conceptualization of Jewish humor, however, was not a scholar, but the dean of Yiddish authors, Sholom Aleichem. Its primary manifestation is in the character of Tevye the dairyman. There is no need to review the literature here because Sholom Aleichem's conceptualization of Jewish humor as transcendent has been clearly recognized.[26] For Sholom Aleichem himself, the conceptualization was quite explicit. In 1911 he wrote: "I tell you it is an ugly and mean world and only to spite it one mustn't weep! If you want to know, that is the real source, the true cause of my constant good spirits, of my, as it is called, 'humor.' Not to cry out of spite! Only to laugh out of spite, *only to laugh.*"[27]

Humor is transcendent when it reflects the unwillingness of the individual to surrender to the impossible conditions of existence and attempts to achieve a measure of liberation from the social, political, economic, and even cosmic forces that remain beyond one's control. Jewish humor is thus conceptualized as transcending the conditions of despair and consequently is distinctive in its reflection of an unperturbable optimism and zest for living. This conceptualization has found its way into numerous popular anthologies of Jewish humor under the slogan of "laughter through tears" or in the characterization of Jewish humor as fundamentally "philosophical."[28]

The characterization of humor as defensive was expressed by Adler, who portrayed it as a "weapon . . . whereby the Jews . . . have been able to survive in the fierce struggle for existence."[29] This conceptualization was greatly amplified in 1905 in Sigmund Freud's *Jokes and Their Relation to the Unconscious*, which, although not ostensibly about Jewish humor, utilized numerous examples of what Freud termed "Jewish jokes." Freud's psychodynamic theory of joking regarded jokes as playful facades that often betrayed serious purposes—particularly hostile or critical purposes.[30] Freud's observations provided a ready-made framework for a conceptualization of Jewish humor as a set of defensive, even retaliatory, measures undertaken in the context of an oppressive environment. Thus according to Alter Druyanow, compiler of the three-volume collection of jokes *Sefer ha-Bediḥah ve-ha-Ḥidud*, there were a host of conditions against which the Jewish joke rebelled: most prominently, the oppression by the non-Jew, the *Goy*. But there were conditions within Jewish society as well which were felt to be oppressive—occupations, the rich, the rabbis, and even God Himself—at which the Jewish joke directed its sharp criticisms.[31]

The conceptualization of the Jewish joke as pathological, an irrational response to the Jewish condition, derives from an aside by Freud on the matter of Jewish jokes in *Jokes and Their Relation to the Unconscious:* "A particularly favorable occasion for tendentious jokes is presented when the intended rebellious criticism is directed against the subject himself, or, to put it more cautiously, against someone in whom the subject has a share—a collective person, that is, (the subject's own nation for instance). The occurrence of self-criticism as a determinant may explain how it is that a number of the most apt jokes . . . have grown up on the soil of Jewish popular life. They are stories created by Jews and directed against Jewish characteristics. . . . Incidentally, I do not know whether there are many other instances of people making fun to such a degree of its own character."[32] Although Freud was not the first to conceptualize self-criticism as distinctive of Jewish humor,[33] set within the framework of his psychology of the unconscious, his observation resonated with new meaning. The observation conditioned analysts Martin Grotjahn's and Theodor Reik's masochistic conceptualizations of Jewish wit.[34] In truth, both Grotjahn and Reik clearly recognized the positive psychological dimensions of Jewish humor, but their fundamental conceptualization of Jewish humor was within the context of psychopathology. Such conceptualizations of the Jewish joke, of course, accorded very well with more general theories of Jewish self-hatred; and the notion that a pathological self-hatred underlies self-critical Jewish jokes is so strongly implied that it often has to be explicitly denied.[35]

As far as I can determine, conceptualizations of Jewish humor rely primarily upon these three characteristics—transcendence, defense, and pathology—the very characteristics that permit the articulation of Jewish suffering and despair with humor. Theoretically, these characteristics are distinct. As they are practically applied to the conceptualization of Jewish humor, however, these distinctions are blurred. Thus Nathan Ausubel, one of the most popular purveyors of Jewish folklore and humor, presents all three possibilities in concert when introducing the concept of Jewish humor to his readers: "By laughing at the absurdities and cruelties of life they [the Jews] draw much of the sting from them. . . . His [the Jew's] satire and irony have one virtue: you never suspect for a moment that his barbs are directed at you. . . . Don't be surprised if you find . . . a large amount of self-criticism disguised as irony, satire, and caricature."[36] The concatenation of these three characteristics by Ausubel is perhaps only to be expected. The three characteristics often seem to be hopelessly intertwined. Thus the transcendent humor of Tevye the dairyman invoked by Sholom Aleichem is belied by Sholom Aleichem's own desperate and spiteful laughter. Indeed, dark and dangerous undercurrents of pathology have been noted in his humorous stories.[37] Even Freud acknowledged that critical and hostile jokes were in some sense liberating and in his later years he came to emphasize the liberating function of humor.[38] And the masochism conceptualized by Grotjahn and Reik was not regarded as a perversion and ultimately could be directed to purposes of defense and liberation.[39]

It would seem that recent conceptualizations of Jewish humor remain firmly rooted in the constructs and categories I have described. Certainly, there have been efforts to identify more precisely the conditions and causes of self-criticism,[40] or the particular character of the dilemmas that the humor was meant to transcend,[41] or the changes in the intensity and targets of hostility and criticism.[42] But it would seem that no new conceptualizations have arisen.

These same conceptualizations even determine predictions concerning the fate of Jewish humor. Some have seen the end of Jewish humor in the rise of the Jewish state, where humor as a weapon has become obsolete.[43] Others foresee a merger between dilemmas of the Jew and "modern man," with the sheer nihilism of the modern age overpowering the transcendental abilities of the Jewish joke.[44] Still others regard the transcendence of Jewish humor as offering an escape from modern forms of despair and imply that Jewish humor and the humor of modernity are merging.[45] As we have seen, it is not really Jewish humor that is at stake. Conceptualizations of the Jewish joke are merely crystallizations of conceptualizations of the Jewish people, their history, and their identity. The notion of Jewish humor will probably persist as long as there remain conceptualizations that fundamentally distinguish Jewish history and experience from the history and experience of a world of nations.

10
Self-Degrading Jokes and Tales

In the seventeenth century, Thomas Hobbes championed what was essentially a megalomaniacal theory of humor. In his view, humor served to exalt the self through contrast with the infirmities of others.[1] In the late nineteenth and early twentieth centuries, however, commentators directed their attentions to the numerous instances in jokes and comic tales in which the *self* seemed to be that infirmed other. Thus Jewish jokes were often characterized as "turned by the speaker against himself,"[2] or marked by a distinctive tendency toward "self-criticism."[3] Such suggestions were part and parcel of broader conceptualizations of self-criticism and self-hatred as characteristically Jewish,[4] conceptualizations later transposed to the assessment of other minority groupings—most notably to blacks in the United States.[5]

The purpose of this chapter is to examine the assumptions that underlie conceptualizations of humor as self-negating. The method is to produce an accumulation of arguments that challenge notions that jokes and tales can be regarded as instruments of self-degradation that betray feelings of self-hatred. Needless to say, some of these arguments are not new and have already been proposed by other commentators.[6] To my knowledge, however, these arguments have not been organized in any systematic critique.

A few terminological considerations are in order. There is a rather large vocabulary of self-negation: "self-hatred," "self-debasement," "self-defeat," "self-deprecation," "self-degradation," "self-abasement," "self-ridicule," "self-criticism," "self-derogation," "self-derision," "self-mockery," "self-denunciation," "self-disparagement," "self-depreciation," "masochism," "self-hatred."[7] Although many of these terms of self-negation seem synonymous and have been used synonymously, they cannot all be so employed. I would suggest the following differentiation of terms.

"Self-mockery," "self-ridicule," and "self-derision" may perhaps be used synonymously as they signify speech or behavior deliberately designed to characterize some aspect of the self as ridiculous. These behaviors are conscious, deliberate, and communicative. They suggest an attempt to provoke some type of laughter from an audience that is directed at the identity of the speaker-actor.

"Self-criticism," although conscious and deliberate, does not necessitate or imply either an audience or a laughter response. It merely suggests the activity of rendering unfavorable self-judgments. It is often accomplished through speech, but it may be an entirely internal process without any external linguistic manifestations.

"Self-degradation," "self-derogation," "self-deprecation," and "self-depreciation" imply the belittling or lowering of the self in value. Degradation is a sociomoral consequence of action. Self-degradation thus necessitates a display before an audience in which communal values are willfully relinquished through action or the marked failure to act. Self-degradation may or may not be marked by laughter.

"Self-defeat" seems to be a term that demands the evaluation of a particular action in terms of its benefit to the individual. It would seem to stress the function of a behavior in some larger program of action.

"Self-hatred" implies a hatred of some part of the self. "Masochism" suggests a disposition towards pain, suffering, and victimization (it may or may not involve accompanying feelings of sexual pleasure).[8] In one sense "masochism" and "self-hatred" are distinct from the other terms. Both refer to psychological conditions that may only be *inferred* from speech and behavior. Self-hatred and masochism endure even in the absence of their symptomatic behaviors and may be and often are entirely unconscious processes.[9]

This perusal of the vocabulary of self-negation reveals (if these formulations are provisionally accepted) a variety—not a unity—of concepts. It would seem that the reason the terms of this lexicon are so often conceptualized and employed synonymously is the following (often unstated) hypothesis: Self-ridicule is an activity that exposes one's negative traits. It is therefore a type of public self-criticism. As the exposure of such unfavorable self-judgements reduce one's value in society, it is therefore a means of self-degradation. Since degradation reduces opportunities for future successful social action, it is therefore self-defeating. The recourse to self-defeating programs can only stem from dynamic internal sources such as self-hatred or masochism.

I have stated the hypothesis in its most elaborate form. The accumulation of terms is not really necessary. Usually the hypothesis is more simply conceptualized: either self-ridicule or self-criticism or self-degradation or self-defeat is caused by—and therefore is a sign of—self-hatred.

Even if one assumes that it is possible to unambiguously assign particular behaviors to the reflexive categories noted above, the overall hypothesis can be questioned at almost every juncture. Instances of self-ridicule may not be self-critical. Instances of self-criticism may not prove degrading. Instances of self-degradation may not prove self-defeating. And self-defeating courses of action may have other than self-hating or masochistic sources. It is easy to imagine situations, for example, in which a *lack* of self-criticism would prove self-defeating; or imagine self-defeating programs that arise from error or lack of insight rather than self-hatred; or imagine self-ridicule raising sociomoral value rather than lowering it; or conceive of self-degradation as contributing to the success of the self and its programs rather than to their defeat. Thus it would seem that a diagnosis of self-hatred might be difficult enough when examining a particular individual's actions in their social and communicative contexts. The difficulty should be compounded when attempting to extract such a diagnosis solely from a perusal of texts.

While there are many joke and tale texts that could serve to illustrate the difficulties attending hypotheses of self-degradation and self-hatred, I have chosen four examples from Daryl Cumber Dance's book *Shuckin' and Jivin': Folklore from Contemporary Black Americans*. The sixth chapter of this volume, entitled "A Nigger Ain't Worth Shit: Self-Degrading Tales," contains forty-nine joke and tale texts. While Dance is by no means the only scholar to recognize jokes and tales as self-degrading,[10] she is one of the few scholars to publish a substantial corpus of texts explicitly characterized as such.

I have selected four texts to illustrate the range of problems that need to be addressed in characterizing a joke as "self-degrading" and attributing it to motives of "self-hatred." There are nine basic problems. Most concern the assumptions upon which textual interpretations are based. Several, however, concern the very notion of self-negation.

Text 1

This fellow say he went out on the battlefield when he was a younger man. Say he was scarry you know. So when they got out to the battlefield, say the battle had started up, and said a fellow shot at 'im. He heard the bullet pass him, and he turned 'round and caught up and passed the bullet.[11]

This tale was collected from a black informant by a black collector. I assume the tale was categorized as a self-degrading tale because it highlights the cowardice of the protagonist. He was *so* afraid as to be driven to extraordinary measures of escape—outrunning a bullet. As cowardice is negatively valued in our society, this tale would serve to reduce the sociomoral value of any teller identified with such a protagonist. However, the following questions must be raised with respect to such an intrepretation.

1. *The social universe of the tale:* Although both the informant and collector of this comic tale text were black, and the purpose of the collecting enterprise was explicitly to document black narrative traditions, it is not clear to what extent this tale can be read as a commentary on black self-image. Even if we assume the protagonist of the tale is likewise black (although this is not explicit in the tale text), we must entertain the very real possibility that this aspect of the protagonist's persona is completely irrelevant. Black people telling tales may create a universe peopled with black characters. The tales, however, are not *about* blacks—they are about cowards, fools, liars, thieves, heroes, or saints. The tales are about humanity, which is viewed as being composed of such variegated characters. Years ago, in Israel, I collected jokes which began, "*Yehudi halakh bareḥov* . . ." which I dutifully translated as "A Jew was walking down the street . . ." since "Yehudi" is the Hebrew word for "Jew."[12] However, in the Israeli context, "Yehudi" is simply a generic person. He might even be a non-Jew.[13] In other words, his ethnic, religious, or national identity is irrelevant. The phrase should be translated, "A guy was walking down the street. . . ." The point is that in order to begin to assess a particular text as speaking to racial, ethnic, or national identity, we must have some inkling of the social universe of the tale. Is the fact that a protagonist is black or Jewish relevant to the teller and his audience? Or for the purpose of a particular text, is the entire universe simply comprised of blacks or Jews? Texts that explicitly identify a protagonist as a black may not necessarily

highlight that identity as a relevant one. In other words, in a fictive universe peopled by blacks we may find all kinds of characters none of whose actions can be read as a commentary on the issue of black character.

2. *Character traits and their relation to established stereotypes:* It seems worthwhile to call attention to the difference between the negative traits highlighted in jokes and tales that do or do not conform to known stereotypes. Thus in the example above, the tale is theoretically self-degrading because it charges blacks with cowardice. However, cowardice is not an element current in the stereotypification of blacks.[14] On the other hand, violence, laziness, and hypersexuality have been and are regularly attributed to blacks. To what extent should we distinguish between narratives that foreground traits that mirror traditional stereotypes from those that do not? For example, should a tale that characterizes a Jew as greedy be considered in the same way as a tale that characterizes a Jew as stupid? In the former case, it would seem that a hypothesis of self-degradation might be more appropriately entertained because the fictive characterization gains strength from its identity with a socially operative stereotype. However, the opposite might also be argued. The charge is more serious and severe when negative traits do not conform to a known stereotype. A stereotype encoded in a humorous narrative is merely a script, a conventional idea, whose truth is easily dismissed or discounted. The novel, unconventional slight may be more damning.

In the case of the tale above, Dance notes that outrunning a bullet is a well-known folk-narrative motif: X1796.2.2: *Lie: man runs as fast or faster than a bullet.*[15] Should a self-derogatory hypothesis be entertained when this tale is encountered in a non-black repertoire as well? This question is not entirely rhetorical. Signs of black self-degradation and self-hatred may be noticed only because they are looked for, whereas similar signs in whites (or other "dominant" groups) are ignored. It may well be that empirical investigation will reveal the levels of self-hatred in the black community to be no greater than those in the white community.[16]

In the tale of the man who outruns the bullet, black identity is not specifically highlighted. Of course, there are numerous tales and jokes in which this identity is highlighted. In such narratives, black character or identity is directly commented upon, or black characters are foregrounded in their opposition to nonblack characters. However, even in these narratives, hypotheses of self-degradation or self-hatred may be difficult to sustain.

Self-Degrading Jokes and Tales   127

Text 2

One time there was a dude in New York, you know. He was standin' on the corner. So then the pohleese come up there to the corner and tol' 'im, say, "Look-a-here," say, "you know I don't allow nobody on my corner." Say, "What's yo' name?"

He says [in a tough voice], "Big Bimbo Bottom, motherfucker, Big Bimbo Bottom."

He say, "What's yo' wife name?"

He say, "Miz Bimbo Bottom, Miz Bimbo Bottom."

He say, "Yeah?" Say, "What kind o' car you got?"

He say, "Cadillac, motherfucker, Cadillac."

He say, "What you smokin' there, buddy?"

He say, "The best o' cigars, motherfucker, the best o' cigars."

He say, "Where you work?"

He say, "Nowhere, NOWHERE!"

So he say, "Well I', gon' take your ass down for vag [vagrancy]."

So he carried him on down the pohleese station, you know. When he got down pohleese station, Judge asked him, he say, "What's yo' name?"

He say, "Big Bimbo Bottom, motherfucker, Big Bimbo Bottom."

He say, "What's yo' wife's name?"

"Miz Bimbo Bottom."

Judge tol' im say, "Well, I'm gon' ask you again, what's yo' name?"

He say, "Big Bimbo Bottom, motherfucker, Big Bimbo Bottom."

Then here come this ole big, *greasy* Black cop. He come in there, say, "Yo' Honor," say, "lemme have that nigger in the back room for a couple of minutes." He say, "I'll find out all the information you want."

So Yo' Honor say, "Yeah, take 'im away."

He carried 'im back in the back room, pull out that blackjack, tol' that nigger, say, "Now what's you name?"

He say, [with slightly less gusto] "Big Bimbo Bottom, motherfucker, Big Bimbo Bottom."

He drawed that blackjack and hit that nigger up side his head: BIP! Say, "What's yo' name?"

[With even less gusto] "Big Bimbo Bottom, you fuckin' motherfucker, Big Bimbo Bottom."

He drawed back and hit that nigger, and let that blackjack stayed on his head and hit him 'bout twenty times: BIP! BRRRRRD! "Nigger, what's yo' name?"

[Whimpering.] "Big Bimbo Bottom, motherfucker, Big Bimbo Bottom."

BIP! BIP! BIP! BIP! "What's yo' name?"

[Crying.] "Hhuh, hhuh. Big Bimbo Bottom, motherfucker, Big Bimbo Bottom."

BIP! BIP! "What's yo' name?"
[Sobbing loudly.] "Thomas Lee."
BIP! "What's yo' wife's name?"
"Hhuh, Luc*ille*."
BIP! "What kinda car you got?"
"Oldsmo*bile*."
BIP! "What you smoking?"
"Chester*fields*."
BIP! "What changed yo' mind?"
"The blue *steel*."
BIP! "If I turn you loose, will you go home?"
[Completely humbled.] "I showly *weel-l-l*."[17]

I imagine that the conceptualization of this tale as self-degrading is based upon the image of the "big *greasy* black cop" who resorts to violence and humiliates a member of his own group. He certainly seems less humane than the (white) policeman who made the arrest or the judge who interviews him at the station. There is also the image of the black hustler who is forced to abandon his boastful street image and humble himself in response to the policeman's intimidation. Nevertheless, the conceptualization of this tale as self-degrading must address the issue of social identities.

3. *The differentiation of social identities:* Do the social identities of the characters in the joke or tale correspond to the social identities of the tellers of that joke or tale? Is the joke about social roles or types with whom the teller identifies? Dan Ben-Amos, in rejecting the thesis of the self-critical, masochistic nature of Jewish humor bases his argument solely upon this point—the status-specific notion of self. He states: "For the thesis of the masochism of Jewish humor to be valid, there should be a direct relationship of social identification between the narrator and the subject of the joke. A matchmaker has to mock matchmakers, a *mohel* [ritual circumciser] has to ridicule *mohels*, and a mother-in-law should laugh at mothers-in-law and not any other figures in the community."[18] Dance also recognizes this factor as do others.[19]

I am perhaps less certain than Ben-Amos that the thesis of the self-critical nature of Jewish humor is overturned on this argument alone. Certainly identities and differences may be perceived on bases other than mere "social status." It would seem quite possible for an ordinary Jew to identify with rabbi or mohel characters as symbols of Jewish community. This would be particularly true in jokes or tales in which these characters act in opposition to non-Jewish figures. The "rabbi trickster" jokes offer one example of the possibility of such identification[20] as Ben-Amos recognizes.[21] And if we admit the possibility of a positive identification with a character of a status other than one's own, we must be prepared to admit the possibility of a negative identification with a social status other than one's own.

Conversely, it is not difficult to imagine a distancing and differentiation from fictional characters with the same social status as the teller of that fiction. After all, there may be good and bad mohels, good and bad rabbis. Certainly, Ben-Amos unnecessarily abandons to the hypothesis of masochism all those instances in which there exists a status identity between tellers and joke characters or in which no specific statuses are delineated at all. (What would Ben-Amos do with the old joke: What is the definition of an anti-Semite? Someone who hates Jews more than he has to.)[22] Nevertheless, I believe that Ben-Amos's critique correctly suggests that the degree of identification between tellers and tale protagonists needs to be ascertained before terms such as self-degradation, self-defeat, or self-hatred can be profitably employed. Rarely, however, can this degree of identification be established solely through the perusal of joke texts.

Let us examine another joke in which black identity is highlighted in a seemingly negative fashion.

Text 3

Say three girls [a white girl and a Chinese and a colored girl] was talking together. And the white girl say, "Lawd, a man feels my legs, it makes me so hot!"

And the Chinese girl [said], "A man feel my tiddies, it makes me hot."

And the old colored girl sittin' over in the corner say, "Hrumph, man feel my legs don't make me hot; feel my tiddies don't make me hot neither. Fuck me and don't pay me, that's what makes me hot."[23]

In this particular joke, a black image is clearly foregrounded against those of white and Chinese. While the white and Chinese girls recall what arouses them sexually, what makes them "hot," the black girl indicates no awareness of or concern about sexual arousal. For her, sex is a purely economic relationship, and she gets angry or "hot" only when a man fails to pay her for it.

One could assume that if this joke were told by a black man it would not be considered "self-degrading" but possibly as degrading to black women. Given such tales told by tellers with the same "social identification" as the tale character (i.e., a black woman),[24] what can we say about these jokes as instruments of self-degradation and signs of self-hatred?

4. *Differential perceptions of value:* What is negatively valued by one individual or group may not be so valued by another. The image of the "ba-ad Nigger" was understood by many blacks, if not by many whites, to be good.[25] Thus the black girl who has reduced "sex" to "business" may be regarded negatively by some, yet positively by others. Witness positive feminist orientations towards women who sell their sexual favors rather than squander them within the institution of marriage.[26] The numerous jokes concerning hypervirility provide even more appropriate examples. Although hypersexuality was part of a negative stereotype of black males, there are clearly positive aspects to the image. Being able to perform sexually is not in itself a negative attribute. In deliberately cultivating a hypersexual image in jokes and tales, black raconteurs may be claiming for themselves the positive aspects of that image.[27] It is not uncommon for a dominant group to regard their virtues as vices when they appear in an outgroup.[28] In the tales of black hypersexuality, we may be witnessing the outgroup transforming those vices back into virtues.

The assumption of a negative stereotype may also not prove to be self-critical or self-degrading for other reasons.

5. *Negative self-description as a form of aggression:* There are numerous instances in which the assumption of a negative stereotype is more likely an outwardly directed attack rather than a masochistic display. For example, the image of black hypervirility mentioned above might serve as a deliberate assault on that traditional foundation of white racism—the purity and inviolability of white womanhood.[29] The jokes and tales compound the insult, moreover, because they imply that the threatened miscegenation is not merely the result of the uncontrolled sexual appetites of black men, but because of the sexual dissatisfactions of white women as well.

Nor is it necessary to assume that only those jokes and tales that promote ideas that directly threaten another group's cherished ideas and institutions serve as a means of attack. Any number of self-ridiculing jokes can serve this function.

Text 4

> Riding through the white areas of Georgia, a Black man slipped unnoticed on the bus. He sat beside a white woman unnoticed also. She finally turned around and said, "Nigger!"
> And he shouted, "Where? Where? Where?"[30]

The black man rejects the term "nigger" as applying to himself. Instead, he becomes anxious about the proximity of this figure. (And in an important sense, he is right. The odious image that the term "nigger" invokes refers to some mythical monster and not to some actual being in the real world.) Rather than assume that the joke is self-denying or self-degrading, however, the seeming self-negation can be comprehended as an attack; as a burlesque of the white woman's fear. The absurd anxiety of the black man underscores the ludicrousness of her behavior. It is her hatred and fear that are in fact irrational and hysterical.

Martin Grotjahn has best described this formulation in reference to the Jewish joke: "The Jewish joke constitutes victory by defeat. . . . One can almost see how a witty Jewish man carefully and cautiously takes a sharp dagger out of his enemies hands, sharpens it so it can split a hair in mid-air, polishes it so it can shine brightly, stabs himself with it, then returns it gallantly to the anti-Semite with the silent reproach: Now see whether you can do half so well. . . . It is as the Jew tells his enemies: You do not need to attack us. We can do that ourselves—even better."[31] In other words, the seemingly self-directed hostility is in reality an assault on the intelligence and competence of the persecutor. Cyrano de Bergerac's rhapsodies about the size of his nose (Act I, Scene IV) are a classic literary illustration of this principle. Only in the case of Cyrano, the outwardly directed aggression is transparent. But then Cyrano is an expert swordsman; he has the ability to back up his words with deeds. However, overt Jewish and black responses to provocation were often severely punished. Grotjahn believes that the Jews who told self-ridiculing jokes deflected their own dangerous hostility away from their persecutors and onto themselves.[32] Perhaps; but it may also be that Jewish and black jokes actually add insult to injury because they presume that their persecutors are not clever enough to realize that it is they rather than the Jew or black who is the genuine object of the attack.

We should also note that seemingly self-degrading jokes and tales may be attacks on the conditions that produce the degrading situation. Dance clearly recognizes this possibility in her discussion of the etiological tales in her collection.[33] She argues that these tales reflect a set of unjust forces that the black is unable to alter. No matter what he does he can't win. It is the underlying hypocrisy of the system by which blacks are degraded and defeated that inspires contempt and not the characters themselves.

A classic transformation of a negative image into an attack on the group that created it occurred during the American Revolutionary War. During the last days of the French and Indian War, a British army surgeon had composed a string of verses satirizing the ragged colonial regiments and set them to a popular tune. In the early days of the Revolution, the British would march out playing this "Yankee Doodle" to show their contempt for the American militia. But the Americans made the song their own. When the British under Burgoyne surrendered at Saratoga, it was humiliating for them to hear the Continental Army playing this anthem.[34] A negative image forged by a dominant group was adopted by a subordinate group, even to the point of making it an emblem of their identity. The image was thus tamed and robbed of its power and was even turned back against the dominant group. In adopting a negative image the ingroup communicates that whatever is negative about the image is so untrue as to be comic and unhurtful and that whatever may be true about the image is really not all that negative. Needless to say, this type of reversal was neither invented nor copyrighted by the Continental Army. It has had numerous analogues in the encounter between persons and groups both before and since.

6. *On the truth of humorous images:* What we have been discussing thus far have been negative images communicated in fictional narratives. Furthermore, these narratives are humorous. Humorous communications tend to have an inverse relationship with truth. On the one hand, statements that are patently untrue are often regarded as humorous.[35] On the other, the potentially serious messages encoded in humorous communications are generally taken as "asides" and discounted in an unfolding social encounter. Humorous communications must be deliberately negotiated into serious, factual discourse, and such negotiation is often accomplished only with great difficulty and social risk.[36] In other words, humorous communications, such as the jokes and comic tales we have been considering, are framed as unserious and untrue. That is why insults can be employed as a type of humorous communication between friends. Knowing the insults are false makes them funny,[37] and because intimates recognize such insults as false, humor-

ous insulting serves as a sign of intimacy and affection, not of repressed hatred.[38] The use of the term "nigger" as a term of self-reference among blacks illustrates this point.[39]

Black tales of self-ridicule are generally restricted to all-black audiences.[40] As these audiences know the images depicted in the narratives to be false, these jokes and tales can likewise serve to signal intimacy. When they are told to outsiders, it is because these outsiders also regard the images as false. In other words, these outsiders are, in some sense, intimates.

Self-ridiculing jokes may also be used to establish the right to humorously ridicule others. One may tell a few jokes about one's own group to allay fears over the jokes that they have told or are going to tell about other groups.[41] In such situations, the implied message would seem to be: as the images depicted in these jokes I tell about my own group can only be considered entertaining fictions, so are the images depicted in the jokes that I have told or may tell about your group.

7. *The transcendent function of humor:* There is yet another reason for not assuming that self-degradation, self-defeat, or self-hatred are necessary consequences of joking self-ridicule. It may be that the negative images are precisely what are being transcended in the humor. Freud has stated this hypothesis succinctly: "The grandeur in it [humor] clearly lies in the triumph of narcissism, the victorious assertion of the ego's invulnerability. The ego refuses to be distressed by the provocations of reality, to let itself be compelled to suffer. It insists that it cannot be affected by the traumas of the external world; it shows, in fact, that such traumas are no more than occasions to gain pleasure. . . . Look! here is the world which seems so dangerous! It is nothing but a game for children—just worth making a jest about!"[42] Thus black and Jewish jokes may serve as a means to transcend the pain and humiliation imposed by others. Perhaps these jokes even betray a willingness to admit that as a group and as individuals they have flaws. But that recognition comes with the insight that all humans are flawed. Flaws make us human, and the ability to recognize those flaws, frame them, display them, and laugh at them makes us more human still.

8. *The signs of self-hatred:* The dominant assumption upon which hypotheses of self-hatred have been founded is that the genuine symptoms of self-hatred are to be found in a victimized group's representations of self. But is this necessarily the case? Who hates himself more—the oppressor or the oppressed? Old Marster or his slave? The Gestapo or their victims? The hypothesis that the cruelty and aggression of an

oppressor betray not secure self-esteem but rather profound self-hatred must also be explored.[43] In relation to the self-hatred manifested in violence, oppression, and prejudice, the self-denying motifs of humorous fictions may ultimately prove benign or insignificant.

9. *On the self and the other:* In conclusion we must note that we have been speaking of terms such as self-degradation and self-hatred in a special sense. The self has been collectively denied rather than individually defined. That is, the jokes and tales purportedly reflect the degradation and hatred, not of the subject himself, but of joke and tale characters in whom "the subject has a share."[44] But this conceptualization of self may lead to curious contradictions. For example, the ridicule of these joke and tale characters may in fact be efforts to deny that one has any share in them whatsoever. Thus the attribution of "self-hatred" really only occurs when A distances himself from some character or group to which B feels A properly belongs. This, of course, suggests that one's identity is not a matter of self-determination but something arbitrated by others. The German Jews who ridiculed the Eastern European Jews were self-hating in the eyes of those who perceived the Eastern and Western Jews as a unity and viewed the Eastern Jews as being deserving of brotherhood and identification.[45] Thus "self-hatred," in our collective sense, is a term that may really mean that one is not identifying as someone else feels they should. Certainly, it would seem that the motives of B, who feels that A should identify, are as open to scrutiny as the motives of A who is seen as failing to identify "properly."

Furthermore, attributions of self-hatred seem in themselves efforts to deny relationships to persons with whom one might otherwise feel some identity. In other words, the very use of the term "self-hatred" is an expression of the type of behavior it supposedly labels: that is, the attribution of negative characteristics to individuals for whom one should experience kinship and feelings of identification.[46] For blacks and Jews to label other blacks and Jews as self-hating is to distance themselves from segments of their own groups. Thus the charge of self-hatred may itself prove to be, paradoxically, a sign of such self-hatred.

11
Dyadic Traditions

The motivations and functions of humor are still being conceptualized in sexual and aggressive terms.[1] Although certain scholars have tried to suggest other potential bases for understanding humor,[2] such perspectives have not had a significant impact on the psychological or sociological interpretation of humorous texts, repertoires, and events, where the emphasis on unmasking primitive impulses has remained the default approach.[3] Consequently, ethnographers and analysts of humor have overlooked some striking situations that suggest a thorough questioning, if not refiguring, of the motives of humorous communication might be in order.

In this chapter I wish to focus upon particular communications I call "dyadic traditions." Dyadic traditions are behavioral and linguistic routines that are generated, endowed with significance, and maintained within a dyadic relationship. A dyadic relationship is more or less an enduring interaction between two individuals who relate to one another more as persons than as occupants of social statuses. Thus dyads are characterized by low degrees of formality and embeddedness; that is to say, there is a lack of dependence upon formal role relations, and the relationship is embedded to a very low degree within a larger social organization.[4] Friendships and conjugal relations are the kinds of relationships we might immediately recognize as conforming to these criteria.

The behaviors and linguistic patterns are "traditional" to the extent that they are to some degree recurring or are directly related to previous patterns of behavior. In other words, traditionality is based on the recognition by the members of the dyad that the patterns in question have a history (if only a brief one) in their relationship. Dyadic traditions are primarily private presentations within the dyad itself. Although these traditions occasionally may be performed in the presence of others, their major field of expression remains the dyadic interaction.[5]

Most of the traditions I have collected can be superficially categorized as names, metaphors, gestures, interactive routines, or rituals. The documentation of such traditions was usually accomplished by interviewing people who knew me well and trusted me to respect their relationship and guard their privacy. Such a situation obtains primarily with friends, and even friends remain in fairly complete control of what they choose to reveal. Therefore, I can make no claim to the representativeness of my sample and would be greatly surprised if I have encountered more than a small percentage of the traditions that exist in the two-person groups that I interviewed. Nevertheless, certain regularities do emerge that permit a preliminary characterization of such communications and their potential significance for the assessment of humorous expressions and interactions.

Dyadic traditions illustrate as no others that sources of traditions are *unpredictable*. That is, it would be impossible to predict exactly what aspects of experience are endowed with significance and elevated to the status of tradition by the dyad.[6] For example, one Los Angeles couple in their early forties are given to exclaiming, "Cuernavaca!" whenever they encounter a dead dog, dog wastes, or heavy bus exhausts. The expression derives from their experience in that Mexican city, which they had visited during one of their vacations, on one particular street filled with dogs, dog wastes, a dead dog, and which opened up onto an avenue filled with buses and their polluting diesel exhausts.

This same couple also developed the habit while brushing their teeth of spitting out the toothpaste with the exclamation, "Ptui! Huey, Dewey, Louie" (a traditional Eastern European expression of spitting followed by the names of Donald Duck's nephews). They customarily referred to body odor as "Chef Boyardee" (a food smell and taste they particularly disliked and deliberately mispronounced by accenting the second rather than the third syllable) and toasted one another with "Skolnik!" after the name of a former landlord. The unpredictability and seeming triviality of such traditions cannot be ascribed to the peculiarity of this dyad alone. Many other cases could be cited. Another dyad, for example, derived a set of pseudonyms, regularly used over the course of several years, from the label on the button of an elevator in which they once happened to ride.[7]

What are we to make of such traditions? What do they accomplish?

In the example of the couple who exclaimed "Cuernavaca!" to express their reactions to certain aspects of urban living (dead dogs, dog wastes, and pollution), we might argue that they simultaneously accomplish several things:

1. They test whether the members of the dyad are sensitive to the same aspects of the immediate experience and whether they share a common orientation toward this experience.

2. They symbolize their intimacy through the use of a highly encrypted code that signals they know one another in ways unknown and unknowable to others.

3. They are made to recall a past experience in which they participated. Consequently, such traditions activate a sense of the past and of the shared history of the relationship.

It is noteworthy that such a seemingly trivial stimulus should carry so much import. But objects and experiences are not in themselves significant or insignificant. Significance is something bestowed, and we may hypothesize that in their effort to symbolize intimacy, the dyad tends deliberately to choose the seemingly trivial and fortuitous as the foundation for their traditions.

If it is characteristic of conjugal and friendship dyads to rename the various aspects of ordinary experience using highly esoteric expressions, they are not content merely to rename. Often the traditions they create comment in direct ways upon the relationship itself by characterizing elements of its structure, function, or ethos. For example, Sigmund Freud was accustomed to write *corragio Casimiro* or merely the abbreviation "C.C." in letters to his friend and disciple Karl Abraham. This expression derived from an experience of Abraham's during a vacation in the Italian Alps. He had climbed a mountain in the company of two Italian guides who had brought some raw meat with them for their lunch. When they reached the summit and set to cooking it, the guides discovered the meat had spoiled, but one encouraged the other to eat it saying, "*corragio Casimiro.*" Freud used the expression to encourage Abraham in the formidable task of organizing the psychoanalytic movement and keeping it pure, while Abraham referred to himself as "Casimiro" in his responses.[8]

Another friendship pair described a tradition that arose quite spontaneously between them. Both were males who had known each other for many years. One had been born in the United States. The other had been born in Israel but, having come to the United States while fairly young, he had forgotten much of his Hebrew, and English had become his native language. Both individuals had for many years been formally educated in the Hebrew language and Jewish tradition at religious schools, and although they could converse in Hebrew, they considered their knowledge of the language and tradition far less than warranted by their long years of study. They reported that their tradition arose while dining at a restaurant. When the drinks came, one toasted the other with the Hebrew toast, "*le-Ḥayyim!*" ("to Life!"). The other promptly responded, "*be-yad ha-lashon*" ("in the power of the tongue"). The response was based upon the Hebrew aphorism, "*Mavet ve-ha-ḥayyim be-yad ha-lashon*" ("Death and life are within the power of the tongue" [Proverbs 18:21]). Of course, there is no substantive connection between the toast and the aphorism, except the sharing of the word "*ḥayyim*." The response was consequently perceived as incongruous. But both members of the dyad agreed that the malapropism came to serve as a concise and appropriate comment on the level of their knowledge of the Hebrew language and Jewish tradition, and thus they maintained the expression in their active repertoire of routines.

One last example of this type of tradition that comments on the nature of the relationship between dyad members derives from Martha Weinman Lear's book *Heartsounds*. The book is about Mrs. Lear's husband, Harold, and their relationship following his heart attack. Harold, it seems, had a more developed sense of responsibility and the work ethnic than his wife, and he had a tendency toward occasional expressions of self-righteousness and sanctimoniousness. As Mrs. Lear reported: "I had joked about it, or tried to. Once, just a year married, he had frozen into the righteous stance about something-or-other, and I had made my face go sour and dour, quite like the faces of American Gothic, and held up a table fork as though it was a farmer's pitchfork and said, "Quick! What painting am I?" He had broken into laughter. . . . And after that, anytime he started getting righteous, I would hold up the fork or three fingers, and yell, 'Pitchfork! Pitchfork!' and he would laugh."9

In this last example, we can see how a particular dyadic tradition depended upon a more pervasive cultural symbolism. Dyads regularly utilize ideas and behaviors common to the larger society, but endow these with unique characteristics or meanings. One couple regularly celebrated their anniversary with a bottle of champagne. This rather ordinary ritual would seem to be a simple enactment of a more widespread tradition of anniversary celebration and, indeed, had begun as such. On their first anniversary, this couple decided to open a bottle of champagne in keeping with a traditional cultural model. As they were not accustomed to drinking much champagne, and as their experience with opening champagne bottles was minimal, the husband took elaborate measures to insure that nothing untoward occurred. He wrapped the bottle with a towel, pointed the cork in a relatively safe direction, and stood near the kitchen sink in case the bottle should overflow. The bottle was opened without incident, but before the champagne could be poured, the bottle slipped out of his hand, rolled across the floor, and emptied its contents under the refrigerator. It took several hours for them to clean it up. For the past twenty years this couple has celebrated their anniversary with champagne. Observation alone would lead one to believe that this couple was observing a cultural tradition. What they have traditionalized, however, is the *difference* between their own first anniversary celebration and the one they imagine to be common and appropriate in the larger society. Theirs was a dyadic tradition. The forms of the two celebrations were identical; their meanings were significantly different.

Another couple actually incorporated an object from popular culture into their interaction. The couple had been married for thirty years and both husband and wife were workaholics. Both worked long hours at demanding jobs and never took vacations. Weekends were rarely spent in leisure activities. One day the wife came across an ad in a newspaper from the Colorado Tourism Board which depicted an adult and small child skiing. The adult was supporting the child between its legs as they skied. The caption read: "Nobody ever looked back and wished they'd spent more time at work." The wife cut out the ad and taped it to her husband's toothbrush in the medicine cabinet. When he found it that night it led to their reminiscing about the times they had had together when their kids were still small. Several days later the wife found the ad in the potato bin. The ad continued to be placed in surprising locations over the next several years, but usually in some context that communicated more time should be taken for the things that each of them enjoyed. When their twenty-five-year-old son married, they passed on a copy of the advertisement to him.[10]

Many dyadic traditions are *ephemeral*. They can spring into existence and disappear in relatively short periods of time. Many names, metaphors, and linguistic routines are not only dropped but forgotten as well. Several informants indicated they had a host of expressions and routines but could remember only a few. Undoubtedly, some are only seemingly forgotten and constitute a passive repertoire that may be reactivated at any moment, but the informants are also correct that many of their traditions are irretrievably lost.

Dyadic traditions seem capable of extraordinary and rapid *evolution*, as can be demonstrated in the instance of a pet name. The woman's name was "Judith" but because the couple was Jewish, a development took place from Judith to its Hebrew equivalent "Yehudit" and to its Yiddish diminutive "Hudl." From "Hudl" it was transformed to "Hud" and "Huds." From "Hud" it became "Huk" and "Hukus" (through affixture of the deliberately mispronounced last syllable of the Yiddish word *tukhus* meaning "buttocks"), finally stabilizing for a brief period of time between "Hud," "Hukus," and "Tukhus."

Another conjugal pair reported that the male on occasion referred to the female as "penis breath," a phrase borrowed from one of the characters in the movie *E.T.* This sobriquet eventually evolved to "*tepuli* breath" after the male finished Gary Jenning's novel *Aztec* in which this Nahuatl word for penis repeatedly appears.[11]

While the transformation and extinction of traditions are by no means unusual, the excessive rate of such change for dyadic traditions is startling. Yet, as a numerically minimal social unit, the dyad is particularly prone to such change because the decision of only a single member is required for a tradition to disappear. If one ceases to participate, the tradition cannot be maintained within the unit. In larger organizations, the decision of a single member or even a few members rarely has such impact on the culture of the organization as a whole. Furthermore, in larger organizations, there is the moral and political force of the majority. Dissenters are often asked or made to conform. In dyads, there is no majority. The traditions established result from implicit and explicit negotiations between two persons and consequently are subject to changes initiated by either one.[12]

But there may be other reasons why dyadic traditions change so rapidly. The dyad, by definition, is an organization that cannot grow by adding or replacing members or expanding structurally. Instead dyads may grow culturally with the sense of exclusive knowledge each member feels he or she has about the other; that is, in the growth of intimacy.[13] The deliberate creation, transformation, and extinction of traditions may come to reflect and participate in this growing sense of intimacy.

Some dyadic traditions are thematically traditional rather than comprised of traditional content. Thus one couple traded greetings according to predetermined linguistic rules:

He: Hi toots!
She: Hi boots!
He: Hi shmoots!
She: Hi doots!

The exchange by no means needed to utilize the same phrases each time. It could begin with an entirely different opening yet progress along similar lines by altering the first consonants and maintaining the end rhyme:

He: Hi babes!
She: Hi shmabes!
He: Hi grabes! etc.

I have already noted that dyadic traditions may serve to test whether members of the dyad share a common orientation toward present experience. In the example just cited, we may hypothesize that such exchanges serve to communicate about the mood-states of the dyad members and ascertain whether a unity or harmony in mood exists. Such communications are especially important in dyads where moods have a disproportionate effect on the process of interaction.[14] Formal role relations involve culturally defined and relatively predictable expectations of behavior. Mechanisms that serve to evaluate mood-states of members of the dyad may increase the predictability of behavior and reduce the potential for conflict in the interaction.

The members of another friendship pair were accustomed to trade insults that assailed the intellectual capacities of the other. No particular utterances were repeated, but each understood that when the opportunity arose, one could attack his compatriot along traditional thematic lines. Here are some particular examples:

A: I think I'll blow my brains out.

B: I suggest you use a small caliber weapon.

A: I have been getting these severe headaches. I'll bet I have a brain tumor.

B: I'm sure it's not a *brain* tumor.

A: I've been doing some hard thinking.

B: Any thinking you do is hard.

Intellectual capacity was not the only traditional theme for such exchanges. Sexual capacity, physical appearance, and the quality of the relationship itself were also noted as themes for creative exchange in this and other dyads.

Dyadic communication often seems to involve *insult,* and this tendency toward insulting communication deserves comment. We have already encountered it to some extent in connection with the pet names "Hukus" and "Tukhus" as well as "tepuli breath." Some would dismiss this phenomenon as an instance of "ambivalence" or the result of temporary resentments and regard it as sufficiently explained.[15] Rarely, however, is this ambivalence or resentment demonstrated, let alone correlated, with the language or frequency of insult, so the hypotheses remain more truisms than clarifying concepts. Others would suggest that certain relationships provide the *license* to insult. To the extent that this interpretation is true, it also tends to mask the processes underlying the exchange of insults among intimates and tends to dismiss such behavior as merely another instance of ritual license or permitted disrespect.[16]

The examination of insult in dyadic relations is instructive. Traditionally exchanged insults are not perceived as insults. Rather, they are regarded as their opposites: expressions of intimacy and affection. The principle seems to be that the better two people know one another as persons, the less they depend upon the literal meaning of messages to communicate. The knowledge of the relationship they bring to their interaction frames all messages, particularly those dealing with the relationship itself. This frame transforms—inverts—their messages so that literal insults emerge as signs of affection.[17]

A particularly illuminating example of the operation of this transforming principle derives from my own experience. I have a close friend, a physician by occupation, with whom I frequently exchange traditional insults not unlike those already described. I am also in the habit of asking his medical opinion of occasional physical symptoms I experience. One time, after he questioned me closely about a symptom I had brought to his attention, I asked him what it all meant. He assured me quite soberly that it really didn't mean anything, and there was absolutely nothing to worry about. He must have seen the look of consternation that crossed my face because he immediately started laughing. What he realized was that if he truly wanted to reassure me, he should have said, "You'll be dead by morning." For a moment he had forgotten the transforming frame of our relationship and had employed a mode of reassurance appropriate only outside the dyad. I, on the other hand, had employed the frame in interpreting his message: if he were literally reassuring me, something must be desperately wrong.

In this case, the *failure* to threaten or insult caused the communicative problem. The situation cannot be adequately explained in terms of emotional ambivalence or notions of license. The principle called to our attention is precisely the one that explains the preponderance of traditional insult and threat in dyadic units: the more intimate the people communicating, the more their relationship transforms the literal meaning of a message than does the literal meaning of a message transform their relationship.

The preceding discussion leads to a more general principle concerning the nature of dyadic traditions. The intimacy and sincerity of a dyadic relationship is established and maintained through the regular violation of normal proprieties. That is, it depends to a great extent upon the violation of the rules that regulate the encounters between strangers.[18] Traditionalizing the response to dog wastes or body odors, ritualizing spitting into the bathroom sink, reveling in the exchange of insulting epithets or childish rhyming names are all to some degree violations of the behaviors thought to constitute social propriety. In dyads, improprieties are created, traditionalized, and celebrated in the effort to both engender and symbolize the intimacy of the relationship.

Finally we must recognize that dyadic traditions are basically *humorous* traditions. The names, metaphors, gestures, routines, and rituals were not merely encrypted or idiosyncratic; they were regarded by the individuals who used or engaged in them as funny. While it is possible that humorous traditions were the only ones that my informants cared to reveal, it is also clear that humor is a predominant mode of dyadic expression.[19]

Georg Simmel has argued that the dyad is an endangered and irreplaceable social unit. The death or secession of either member destroys the whole. Consequently, dyadic relations engender ever-present feelings of melancholy and tendencies toward the sentimentalization of the relationship.[20] While Simmel's assessment is logical enough, melancholy and sentiment do not seem to directly express themselves through the dyad's traditions. But then Simmel was a nineteenth-century man. In the late nineteenth century, direct, crafted expressions of sentiment were acceptable, indeed compulsory.[21] In the late twentieth, such expressions have, by and large, been repudiated, often in favor of more indirect—indeed humorous—formulations. For example, the humorous card has to a great extent superseded the sentimental card in the communication of birthday, anniversary, friendship, and holiday greetings.[22] The reasons for such shifts in interpersonal communicative style, though interesting and important, are not at issue here. What is at issue is the fact that modern sentiments have come to be situated within humorous communications. Dyadic traditions reveal humor to be one of the basic languages of intimacy and affection. Those who would reduce humor to disguised expressions of hostility and aggression might well ponder whether humor might not serve to mask expressions of love and tenderness as well.[23]

Notes

1. Appropriate Incongruity

1. Sigmund Freud, *The Standard Edition of the Complete Psychological Works of Sigmund Freud*, 24 vols., trans. under the general editorship of James Strachey in collaboration with Anna Freud (London: Hogarth Press and the Institute of Psycho-Analysis, 1953-74), 8:9-238 (henceforth cited as *S.E.*).

2. Freud outlines this idea quite clearly in his description of the evolution of smut into the sexual joke. *S.E.* 8:99-100.

3. This has been the predominant notion from Plato and Aristotle through the seventeenth century. See the outline of humor theory in Ralph Piddington, *The Psychology of Laughter: A Study in Social Adaptation* (London: Figurehead, 1933), pp. 152-221, passim.

4. Thomas Hobbes, *Leviathan: Or the Matter, Form, and Power of a Commonwealth, Ecclesiastical and Civil* (London: Routledge, 1907 [1651]), p. 33.

5. Henri Bergson, *Laughter*, trans. Cloudesley Brereton (New York: Macmillan, 1928 [1911]), p. 135.

6. James Beattie, *Essays: On Poetry and Music, as They Effect the Mind; On Laughter and Ludicrous Composition; On the Utility of Classical Learning* (Edinburgh for W. Creech and for E. Dilly in London, 1778), p. 347.

7. I derive the phrase from D.H. Monro, *Argument of Laughter* (Carlton: Melbourne Univ. Press, 1951) although Monro prefers to talk about "appropriateness in the inappropriate"; p. 255. I find my usage somewhat more felicitous.

8. Incongruity theory has been reformulated several times in recent years, most notably by Arthur Koestler for whom humor is the result of "perceiving of a situation or idea . . . in two self-consistent but habitually incompatible frames of reference." Victor Raskin also sees humor engendered by "two overlapping scripts perceived as opposite in a certain sense." See Arthur Koestler, *The Act of Creation* (New York: Macmillan, 1964), p. 35; and Victor Raskin, *Semantic Mechanisms of Humor* (Dordrecht, Holland: Reidel, 1985), p. 100.

9. Generally those riddles that do rely on soundplay are characterized as "conundrums" rather than true riddles. See Jan Harold Brunvand, *The Study of American Folklore*, 3d ed. (New York: Norton, 1986), p. 96.

10. See Robert A. Georges and Alan Dundes, "Toward a Structural Definition of the Riddle," *Journal of American Folklore* 76 (1963): 111-18.

11. There are answers, however, that do not depend upon formal analogy. For example, a "ship" might satisfy the demands of the riddle question because the toilet on a ship is referred to as "the head." To my knowledge traditional children's riddling in the United States has not utilized this answer, probably because by the time "ship's head" becomes part of one's vocabulary, one is no longer a child and the riddle has been abandoned as a form of humorous entertainment. There are other possible answers to this riddle question depending upon the status of the riddler and riddlee. A professor, for example, might answer the question with "an undergraduate" or a southerner might answer the question with "a Yankee." Such answers, however, are parodies of the traditional riddle because they depend upon knowledge of the traditional solutions for these solutions to be accepted and perceived as humorous. Joke parodies of the riddle are discussed in chapter 2.

12. Raskin holds that humorous communication is predicated upon the expectation that a joke will include only as much information as is necessary for the joke. Therefore, information that might at first sight seem extraneous is usually crucial for discerning the appropriate incongruity; Raskin, pp. 103-5.

13. There are some people who cannot tell jokes and whose attempt to tell the joke about the doctor and the husband might produce such a horrific result. The performance might still be hysterically funny but only to those who already knew the joke and what it was supposed to sound like. The performance becomes a parody of proper performance with its own independent appropriate incongruities. There are a number of jokes that deal with someone's inability to tell jokes properly; see, for example, Alan Dundes, *Cracking Jokes: Studies of Sick Humor Cycles and Stereotypes*, (Berkeley: Ten Speed, 1987), pp. 152-55.

14. This is the case for oppositional riddles; see Georges and Dundes, pp. 114-15.

15. Some of these conventions are discussed in chapter 2.

16. The distinction Yigal Zan makes between image base and verbal report is a useful one. See "The Scientific Motivation for the Structural Analysis of Folktales," *Fabula* 30 (1989): 210.

17. After Mildred Meiers and Jack Knapp, *5600 Jokes for All Occasions* (New York: Avenel, 1980), p. 225.

18. William J. Pepicello and Robert W. Weisberg, "Linguistics and Humor," in *Handbook of Humor Research*, 2 vols., ed. Paul E. McGhee and Jeffrey H. Goldstein (New York: Springer-Verlag, 1983), 1:61.

The solubility potential of riddles extends to nonoppositional riddles as well. Nonoppositional riddles do not present an explicit incongruity but provide an extended metaphorical description for which a referent must be found. The stated or implied problem is, "What is X?" with X limited to objects or activities whose structure articulates with that of the metaphor. I do not mean to suggest that riddle answers are necessarily or even usually guessed—only that they are guessable. The "neck riddle" is a special problem because it is virtually unguessable, but it usually functions as a narrative motif rather than as an interactive routine. See Brunvand, pp. 93-94.

19. Paul Schiller, "A Configurational Theory of Jokes and Puzzles," *Journal of General Psychology* 18 (1938): 217-34.

20. I will focus my remarks on verbal humor but virtually all would apply to nonverbal forms as well.

21. When I first analyzed this joke, the price of the drink was only a dollar seventy-five. I have had to raise the price in this version in order to retain the sense of the joke. Inflation would seem to affect the joke world as much as the real one. See Elliott Oring, *Israeli Humor: The Content and Structure of the Chizbat of the Palmah* (Albany: State Univ. of New York Press, 1981), pp. 40-41.

22. Raskin, pp. 195-96.

23. This joke would be better if the American's knowledge of sexual positions were based solely upon his reading of the *Kama Sutra*, while the Frenchman's knowledge, though inferior in the number of positions, were rooted solely in experience. This would heighten the distinction between their claims—one theoretical, one practical—and consequently underscore the superiority of the Frenchman despite his seemingly inferior knowledge.

24. Raskin, p. 81.

25. Gordon W. Allport, *The Nature of Prejudice*, abr. ed. (Garden City, N.Y.: Doubleday Anchor, 1958), p. 187.

26. For Raskin, the notion of script is not merely employed to differentiate it from stereotype. He is trying to formalize incongruity theory within semantic theory; Raskin, pp. 59-147.

27. Quoted by Freud in *S.E.* 8:92.

28. *S.E.* 8:17-89.

29. Ibid., p. 42.

30. G.B. Milner, "Homo Ridens: Towards a Semiotic Theory of Humor and Laughter," *Semiotica* 5 (1972): 17.

31. For some other discussions of humorous technique see John Allen Paulos, *Mathematics and Humor* (Chicago: Univ. of Chicago Press, 1980); and Charles F. Hockett, "Jokes," in *Studies in Linguistics in Honor of George L. Trager*, ed. M. Estellie Smith (The Hague: Mouton, 1972), pp. 153-78.

32. I am using this term in a more restricted sense than "vacuous recombination." See Robert Hetzron, "On the Structure of Punchlines," *Humor: International Journal of Humor Research* 4 (1991): 73.

33. Brunvand, p. 100.

34. Evan Esar, *The Humor of Humor* (New York: Bramhall, 1952), p. 93.

35. For a discussion of jokes on vaginal size see G. Legman, *Rationale of the Dirty Joke: An Analysis of Sexual Humor, First Series* (New York: Grove, 1968), pp. 377-82.

36. After *S.E.* 8:33.

37. For a discussion of the developmental aspects of humor production and appreciation see Paul E. McGhee, *Humor: Its Origin and Development* (San Francisco: Freeman, 1979).

38. Joel Sherzer, "Puns and Jokes," in *Handbook of Discourse Analysis*, vol. 3, ed. Teun A. Van Dijk (London: Academic, 1985), p. 219.

39. *S.E.* 8:16-17, 23. By serious, Freud meant only that these thoughts were expressible as nonhumorous formulations. Freud chose to elucidate the thoughts of only *some* of the jokes he analyzed. He fell short of demonstrating that every joke could be unequivocally reduced to a nonhumorous proposition.

40. Charles R. Gruner has reviewed the experimentation on the influence of

humor and satire on persuasion and found that it has little or no effect. See *Understanding Laughter: The Workings of Wit and Humor* (Chicago: Nelson-Hall, 1978), p. 148ff.

41. See Joan P. Emerson, "Negotiating the Serious Import of Humor," *Sociometry* 32 (1969): 169-81.

42. Henny Youngman, *Take This Book, Please*, 3 vols. in one (New York: Grammercy, 1987), 2:11.

43. I am using the term "opposition" somewhat loosely here. I am not suggesting that incongruities are invariably genuine oppositions of the "door and not-a-door" variety. Raskin, however, is happier with the term "opposition" than "incongruity"; Raskin, pp. 99, 107-14.

2. To Skin an Elephant: On the Presumption of Aggression in Humor

1. Sigmund Freud, *Jokes and Their Relation to the Unconscious*, in *The Standard Edition of the Complete Psychological Works of Sigmund Freud*, 24 vols., trans. under the general editorship of James Strachey in collaboration with Anna Freud (London: Hogarth Press and the Institute of Psycho-Analysis, 1953-74), 8:97 (henceforth cited as *S.E.*). Although this perspective was meant to apply only to the class of jokes Freud characterized as "tendentious," it is not clear that any jokes are completely innocent or nontendentious; ibid., p. 143; Richard Wollheim, *Sigmund Freud* (New York: Viking, 1971), pp. 101-2.

2. G. Legman, *Rationale of the Dirty Joke: An Analysis of Sexual Humor, First Series* (New York: Grove, 1968), p. 9. See also *Rationale of the Dirty Joke: An Analysis of Sexual Humor, Second Series [No Laughing Matter]*, (New York: Breaking Point, 1975). For my review of these works see *Western Folklore* 36 (1977): 365-71.

3. Martha Wolfenstein has suggested that jokes, unlike dreams or fairytales, transform the feelings toward their self-contained wishes by depicting them as ridiculous or harmless; *Children's Humor: A Psychological Analysis* (Glencoe, Ill.: Free Press, 1954), pp. 29, 31, 51-52. This perspective, however, is not adhered to throughout her analysis, nor does she make clear why wishes so carefully hidden from consciousness should require such devaluation. Legman also alludes to a similar perspective (*First Series*, p. 21; *Second Series*, p. 619), but likewise ignores it in his analysis.

4. Alan Dundes realized this problem and could suspend his aggression theory to deal with it: "Despite the clearcut pejorative cast of most of the ethnic slurs, it is important to realize that most of the slurs are told and enjoyed by members of the group concerned. . . . Part of the reason for this may be that ethnic slurs are part of ethnic identity"; "A Study of Ethnic Slurs: The Jew and the Polack in the United States," *Journal of American Folklore* 86 (1971): 202. For a discussion of the difficulties associated with self-aggressive hypotheses, see chapter 10 in this volume.

5. See Paulette Cross, "Jokes and Black Consciousness: A Collection with Interviews," in *Mother Wit from the Laughing Barrel*, ed. Alan Dundes (Englewood Cliffs, N.J.: Prentice-Hall, 1973), pp. 649-69.

6. Roger D. Abrahams and Alan Dundes, "On Elephantasy and Elephanticide," *The Psychoanalytic Review* 56 (1969): 228. The essay has been reprinted in

Alan Dundes, *Cracking Jokes: Studies of Sick Humor Cycles and Stereotypes* (Berkeley, Calif.: Ten Speed, 1987), pp. 41-54.

7. Abrahams and Dundes, pp. 229-37.

8. Ibid., pp. 237-38.

9. The joke examples that follow are drawn from my own collection as well as from Mac E. Barrick, "The Shaggy Elephant Riddle," *Southern Folklore Quarterly* 28 (1964): 266-90; and Ed Cray and Marilyn Eisenberg Herzog, "The Absurd Elephant: A Recent Riddle Fad," *Western Folklore* 26 (1967): 27-36.

10. See Archer Taylor, "The Riddle," *California Folklore Quarterly* 2 (1943): 129-47, and Robert A. Georges and Alan Dundes, "Toward a Structural Definition of the Riddle," *Journal of American Folklore* 76 (1963): 111-18.

11. Unfortunately, there are no reports of joke sessions that describe the actual sets or sequences in which elephant jokes were performed. I would expect, however, to see in such sequences creative alterations in the expectations being violated. No session should be composed of jokes violating only one kind of rule.

12. James Manns, "Two Faces of the Absurd," *Humor: International Journal of Humor Research* 1 (1988): 259-68.

13. Barrick, p. 266.

14. Barrick sees the illogic of the jokes as reflecting a revolt against an overly scientific-minded society; ibid., p. 268. I would contend that is but one aspect of a larger phenomenon.

Furthermore, I suspect that the jokes were not popular among the minority who were at the centers of the counterculture movement. They would have been popular among the majority who were caught up and affected by it. Through their absurd violation of rules, the rules are actually confirmed (Manns, p. 266), for the rules are the consensual base from which the joking violations are recognized and appreciated. The violations produce laughter and are not taken seriously. They are not accepted as legitimate intellectual transactions. Thus the jokes would seem to reflect a distancing from rather than an embracing of disestablishment tendencies.

15. There are features of the elephant, other than the phallic, that have been emphasized in interpretation. Joseph Boskin focuses upon the elephant's size and relates it to the theme of gigantism in America. See *Humor and Social Change in the Twentieth Century* (Boston: Trustees of the Public Library of the City of Boston, 1979), pp. 79-84.

16. *S.E.* 8:173-80.

17. Ibid., pp. 110, 115.

18. "Humour" in *S.E.* 21:162-63.

19. For example, see Jonathan Gutman and Robert F. Priest, "When is Aggression Funny?" *Journal of Personality and Social Psychology* 12 (1969): 60-65; Jay M. Davis and Amerigo Farina, "Humor Appreciation as Social Communication," *Journal of Personality and Social Psychology* 15 (1970): 175-78.

20. Gregory Bateson, "A Theory of Play and Fantasy," in *Steps to an Ecology of Mind* by Gregory Bateson (New York: Ballentine, 1972), p. 180.

3. Jokes and the Discourse on Disaster

1. Matthew 25:14-30; Luke 19:11-26.

2. Quoted in Sigmund Freud, *Jokes and Their Relation to the Unconscious* in

The Standard Edition of the Complete Psychological Works of Sigmund Freud, 24 vols., trans. under the general editorship of James Strachey with the collaboration of Anna Freud (London: Hogarth Press and the Institute of Psycho-Analysis, 1953-74), 8:92 (henceforth cited as *S.E.*). The witticism is discussed in chapter 1, p. 9.

3. Barbara Kirshenblatt-Gimblett, "Toward a Theory of Proverb Meaning," *Proverbium* 22 (1973): 821-27.

4. The jokes in this essay are mainly from my own collection, but several were communicated to me by Charles G. Kelley of the University of Georgia.

5. Roger Simon, "The Jokes That Speak the Unspeakable," *Los Angeles Times*, 23 Feb. 1986, Pt IV, p. 11.

6. All of these opinions are quoted in Steve Emmons, "'Sick' Jokes: Coping with Disaster," *Los Angeles Times*, 30 May 1986.

7. Willie Smyth, "Challenger Jokes and the Humor of Disaster," *Western Folklore* 45 (1986): 243-60.

8. Susan Crittendon, "Space disaster was 'inevitable' former Hoosier astronaut says," *Indianapolis Star*, 29 Jan. 1986.

9. We should note that these jokes were being told before the empowering of the commission that investigated the accident and before its revelations of NASA's negligence in overseeing the safety of the mission.

Since the explosion of the Challenger, a number of NASA delays, mistakes, and failures have prompted humorous comment in the media, if not in oral tradition. See "Cartoon Gallery," *Discover* 12 (Jan. 1991), pp. 54-55.

10. Actually, only CNN covered the launch live. But within minutes, the other networks were running monitored film of the flight. Don Kowet, "Tasteful TV coverage pays homage to crew without being morbid," *Washington Times*, 29 Jan. 1986.

11. Rosalind Jackler, "Let students talk about deaths, experts urge," *Houston Post*, 29 Jan. 1986; "Death of a School Teacher," *New York Times*, 29 Jan. 1986, p. A22.

12. Viewers called into local television stations to complain about this endless repetition of explosion footage. See R.C. Morgan-Wilde, "Shuttle-disaster coverage costly and controversial," *Tallahassee Democrat*, 31 Jan. 1986; David Jones, "Kudos, knocks on shuttle coverage," *Columbus Dispatch*, 31 Jan. 1986.

13. Although not known until some months after the accident, it seems that the members of the shuttle crew survived the booster explosion and were killed only when their cabin struck the ocean. They were dismembered on impact. After months of submersion, the soft body tissues of the crew members had become gelatinous and there was damage from shrimp and crabs. NASA prevented the release of pictures of the cabin and apparently conspired to keep all non-NASA personnel from seeing the bodies—even authorized county medical examiners. It would seem that the gruesome images conjured up in the jokes proved remarkably accurate. See Dennis E. Powell, "Challenger 'horror stories' hidden by NASA," *San Jose Mercury News*, 13 Nov. 1988.

14. The battle over last words erupted with the Challenger mission as well. Although they had released a transcript in 1986, NASA refused to make public the tape recording itself claiming that it would violate the privacy of the victims' families and subject them to the media's "morbid fascination" with grief. The *New York*

Times had to sue for release of the tape. See "Challenger tape ordered released," *Santa Rosa Press Democrat*, 4 June 1987; Lee Hockstader, "Release of Challenger Tape Ordered," *Washington Post*, 30 July 1988.

15. ABC reported that 80 percent of 1,200 calls received by their network offices in New York on the day of the crash complained about the preempting of soap operas by Challenger coverage; Morgan-Wilde, "Shuttle-disaster coverage."

16. There were complaints about the excessive attention paid to Christa McAuliffe in relation to the other astronauts; ibid.; Jones, "Kudos, knocks."

17. Elizabeth Radin Simons, "The NASA Joke Cycle: The Astronauts and the Teacher," *Western Folklore* 45 (1986): 261-77.

18. "'On Tuesday night, Rather and Brokaw both recited poetry in a feeble effort to put the tragedy into perspective. I found it melodramatic and offensive. Poetry is best left to the preachers. Let the newsmen report the news.'" Quoted in Jones, "Kudos, knocks."

19. Smyth, p. 259.

20. Nicholas von Hoffman, "Shuttle Jokes," *The New Republic*, 24 Mar. 1986, p. 14.

21. S.E. 8:173-80.

22. Alan Dundes and Thomas Hauschild, "Auschwitz Jokes," *Western Folklore* 42 (1983): 243-60; Alan Dundes, "A Study of Ethnic Slurs: The Jew and Polack in the United States," *Journal of American Folklore* 84 (1971): 186-203; "The Dead Baby Joke Cycle," *Western Folklore* 38 (1979): 145-57; "At Ease, Disease—AIDS Jokes as Sick Humor," *American Behavioral Scientist* 30 (1987): 72-81.

23. Simon Bronner, "What's Grosser than Gross?" *Midwestern Journal of Language and Lore* 11 (1985): 39-49.

24. Mary Kasdan, "The joke's on you—or is it?" *L.A. Life, Daily News*, 29 June 1986, pp. 4-5.

4. On the Structure of a Humorous Repertoire

1. James Beattie, *Essays on Poetry and Music, as They Effect the Mind; On Laughter and Ludicrous Composition; On the Utility of Classical Learning* (Edinburgh: for W. Creech and for E. Dilly in London, 1778), p. 347.

2. Arthur Koestler, *The Act of Creation* (New York: Macmillan, 1964), p. 35.

3. "There is an element of appropriateness in the inappropriate" is the way D.H. Monro phrased it in *The Argument of Laughter* (Melbourne: Melbourne Univ. Press, 1951), p. 255. I believe the actual term is my own.

4. Victor Raskin, *Semantic Mechanisms of Humor* (Dordrecht, Holland: Reidel, 1985), p. 99.

5. "The purpose of the proposed semantic theory of humor is to formulate a set of conditions which are both necessary and sufficient conditions for the text to be funny. . . . If a text is funny, all the conditions in the set obtain; and conversely, if all the conditions in the set obtain for a text, the text is funny." Ibid., p. 57.

6. Yigal Allon, *The Shield of David: The Story of Israel's Armed Forces* (New York: Random, 1970), and Yigal Allon, *The Making of Israel's Army* (New York: Bantam, 1971).

7. Hayyim Guri, *Dapim Yerushalmi'im* [Jerusalemite Leaves] (Israel: Hakibutz Hameuchad, 1968), p. 147.

8. Dahn Ben-Amotz, personal communication, 4 Feb. 1970.

9. Elliott Oring, *Israeli Humor: The Content and Structure of the Chizbat of the Palmah* (Albany: State Univ. of New York Press, 1981), pp. 47-48, 150-51. All chizbat texts cited in this essay are drawn from translations appearing in my book. References to the original Hebrew sources as well as additional discussion may be found there.

10. Ibid., pp. 90, 232.

11. Ibid., p. 246.

12. Ibid., pp. 98, 197.

13. Ibid., pp. 64-65, 178-79.

14. J.E. Hanauer, *Folk-Lore of the Holy Land*, New and enlarged ed. (London: Sheldon, 1935), p. 202.

15. Oring, pp. 103, 183.

16. Ibid., pp. 104, 199.

17. Ferdynand Zweig, *Israel: The Sword and the Harp* (London: Heinemann, 1969), pp. 3-12.

18. D. Shhori, *Al Hamishmar*, 30 Mar. 1981; cited in Tamar Katriel *Talking Straight: Dugri Speech in Israeli Sabra Culture* (Cambridge: Cambridge Univ. Press, 1986), p. 85.

19. Eli Yassif in his review of *Israeli Humor* categorized my analysis of the chizbat as based on "the binary opposition theory of Levi-Strauss"; *Kirjat Sefer* 57 (1982): 142.

20. Claude Levi-Strauss, "The Structural Study of Myth," *Journal of American Folklore* 67 (1955): 428-44.

5. Redundancy in Repertoire

1. See J.R. Pierce, *Symbols, Signals, and Noise: The Nature and Process of Communication* (New York: Harper Torchbook, 1961), pp. 149-50.

2. The kumzits still remains a powerful signifier in the presentation of images of Israeli song and story. It is used as the setting for *Sing Along with Israel* (Tel Aviv: Vinona, 1988), billed as "the first Israeli 'Sing-Along' video ever."

3. Elliott Oring, *Israeli Humor: The Content and Structure of the Chizbat of the Palmah* (Albany: State Univ. of New York Press, 1981), p. 201. All chizbat texts cited in this essay are drawn from translations appearing in my book. References to the original Hebrew sources as well as additional discussion may be found there.

4. Ibid., pp. 246-47.

5. Ibid., p. 245.

6. To know that the chizbat is set in the Galilean village of Yavne'el, one has to know who the narrator of the chizbat was.

7. The iteration of themes is the only kind of redundancy that concerns the analysts of myth; see Claude Levi-Strauss, "The Structural Study of Myth," *Journal of American Folklore* 67 (1953): 428-44; and Edmund R. Leach, "Genesis as Myth," *Discovery* (May 1982), pp. 30-35.

8. Oring, pp. 138-39, 141-42, 158-60, 172-73, 180, 184-86.

9. Ibid., p. 166.
10. Ibid., p. 191.
11. Ibid., 151-52.
12. This chizbat is not pure fantasy. There were early settlers in the Galilee who never mastered Hebrew, and there were Arabs who could converse in both Hebrew and Yiddish.
13. Oring, p. 264.
14. Ibid., pp. 220-22.
15. For a discussion of Israeli jokes concerning the figure of Trumpeldor see Yael Zerubavel, "The Last Stand: On the Transformation of Symbols in Modern Israeli Culture" (Ph.D. diss., Univ. of Pennsylvania, 1980).
16. Although this chizbat is perfectly aesthetic and communicative, it is enhanced by familiarity with Melnikov's actual sculpture. For, in a sense, this chizbat is saying that as Melnikov's stylized sculpture only obliquely resembles a real lion, the image of a lion only obliquely resembles the spirit of pioneering and sacrifice. The Palmach on occasion referred to themselves as "lions"; ibid., pp. 159, 210.
17. Ibid., p. 158.
18. This seems to have been what happened during the War of Independence when the chizbat became a conscious token in the game of identity; see ibid., p. 134.
19. I do not want to leave the reader with a mystical feeling about redundancy in repertoire. I believe that it is important in the analysis of the repertoire to look at the assemblages of chizbat texts told in individual sessions, and to evaluate whether they manage to articulate a balanced and coherent message within the performance event. An assessment of how often synoptic texts are performed and whether there is some distribution of thematic, motif, and plot codings within each session is also desirable. It is no longer possible to do this with the chizbat, but it should be possible for other joke repertoires.

6. *Rechnitzer Rejects:* An Unorthodox Humor of Modern Orthodoxy

1. *Rechnitzer Rejects*, vol. 1 (HP29561), vol. 2 (HP29565), vol. 3 (HP29568), vol. 4 (HP29572), vol. 5 (HP29574), vol. 6 (HP29576). The records are produced and written by Martin Davidson with Seymour Rockoff as a contributing writer. Copies of the records may be obtained from Perfect Impressions, 1697 Broadway, New York, N.Y. 10019.

The name *Rechnitzer Rejects* seems to imply that these are songs or tunes rejected by some Hasidic leader (rebbe) from the town of Rechnitz. A town of Rechnitz did exist in the Austrian Burgenland along the Hungarian border, but the "Rechnitzer" here seems to evoke the word "recht" meaning "right" or "proper," implying that this is a rebbe who sees his own way of doing things as the "right" way for everybody. The producer of the records recalled that as an adolescent he would tell people in synagogue he followed the custom of the Rechnitzer Rebbe when they tried to tell him the "correct" ritual observance (Martin Davidson, personal communication, Nov. 1985).

2. *Rechnitzer Rejects*, vol. 2 (HP29565), Side 2, Band 3.
3. "*Havayot de-Abbaye ve-Rava*," Reuben Alcalay, *The Complete Hebrew-English Dictionary* (Tel Aviv and Jerusalem: Massadah, 1965), s.v. "*havayah.*"

4. *Rechnitzer Rejects*, vol. 2, Side 2, Band 1.

5. "Halakhah" is regularly listed in English dictionaries although it is spelled "halakah" or "halacha." Generally the term refers to the legal portion of Jewish literary tradition. Specifically it refers to the numerous legal injunctions and prohibitions that govern daily Jewish life.

6. *If You Can Believe Your Eyes and Ears: The Mamas and the Papas* (Dunhill DS-50006), Side 2, Band 1.

7. *Rechnitzer Rejects*, vol. 3 (HP 29568), Side 2, Band 5.

8. The association between the end of the synagogue service and eating cholent is so strong there is even an etymology that derives the word "cholent" (or variously "shulent") from "*shul ende*"—"synagogue is over." *Encyclopedia Judaica* (Jerusalem: Keter, 1972), 16 vols.; s.v. "cholent."

9. A cookbook published by the Lubavitch Women's Organization quotes a tale from the Talmud in which "cholent" is substituted for the generic "Sabbath dishes" of the original. See *The Spice and Spirit of Kosher-Jewish Cooking* (n.p.: Lubavitch Women's Organization—Junior Division, 1972), p. 121.

10. Samuel C. Heilman, *Synagogue Life: A Study in Symbolic Interaction* (Chicago: Univ. of Chicago Press, 1973), pp. 12-19; Edward S. Shapiro, "Orthodoxy in Pleasantdale," *Judaism* 34 (1985): 167.

11. Charles S. Liebman has noted: "Orthodoxy has responded by compartmentalizing Judaism. . . . Orthodox Jews, by and large, do not search for consistency between their Jewish and non-Jewish life. On the contrary, *they make a virtue of their inconsistency*" [my emphasis]; "Orthodox Judaism Today," *Midstream* 25 (1979): 34. "Cosmopolitan parochialism" is how Heilman describes this same characteristic; pp. 7-8.

12. Elliott Oring, *Israeli Humor: The Content and Structure of the Chizbat of the Palmah* (Albany: State Univ. of New York Press, 1981), p. 129.

13. Martin Davidson, personal communication, 29 Sept. 1986.

14. Herbert J. Gans, "The 'Yinglish' Music of Mickey Katz," *American Quarterly* 5 (1953): 213-18.

15. Personal communication, 15 Sept. 1986; oral witticisms also reflect this conjunction of sacred and secular, see Heilman, pp. 203-4.

16. Jonathan D. Sarna, "The Great American Jewish Awakening," *Midstream* 28 (1982): 30.

17. Charles E. Silberman, *A Certain People: American Jews and Their Lives Today* (New York: Summit, 1985), p. 257.

18. Liebman, pp. 21-22.

19. Silberman, pp. 256-57.

20. Ibid., pp. 244-54; Sarna, pp. 31-32.

21. Silberman, pp. 262-67.

7. Between Jokes and Tales

1. Victor Raskin, "Telling Good Humor from Bad: Limitations of the Linguistics of Humor," in *The Fifth International Conference on Humor*, ed. Desmonde MacHale (Dun Laoghaire, Ireland: Boole, 1985), p. 87.

2. The above traits are gathered from Hermann Bausinger, "Schwank und

Witz," *Studium Generale* 11 (1958): 699-710; Siegfried Neumann, "Volkprosa mit komischen Inhalt: Zur Problematik ihres Gehalts und ihrer Differenzierung," *Fabula* 9 (1967): 137-48; Francis Lee Utley, "The Urban and the Rural Jest (With an Excursus on the Shaggy Dog)," *Journal of Popular Culture* 2 (1969): 563-77; Lutz Röhrich, *Der Witz: Figuren, Formen, Funktionen* (Stuttgart: Carl Ernst Poeschel Verlag, 1977), pp. 6-11.

3. "The punchline is the obvious keystone of the joke. . . . The punchline determines whether the text qualifies as a joke"; Hannjost Lixfeld, "Jokes and Aggression: Toward a Determination of the Concept and the Function of a Text Type," in *German Volkskunde: A Decade of Theoretical Confrontation, Debate, and Reorientation, (1967-1977)*, ed., trans. James R. Dow and Hannjost Lixfeld, (Bloomington: Indiana Univ. Press, 1986), p. 235. The centrality of the punchline, however, is not recognized by everyone: "The term 'joke' refers to any episode or story that is laughable, obviously fictional, based on one event, and which ends abruptly, usually with a 'punchline' "; Jan Harold Brunvand, "The Study of Contemporary Folklore: Jokes," *Fabula* 13 (1972): 10.

4. See, for example, Sigmund Freud, *Jokes and Their Relation to the Unconscious*, in *The Standard Edition of the Complete Psychological Works of Sigmund Freud*, 24 vols., trans. under the general editorship of James Strachey in collaboration with Anna Freud (London: Hogarth Press and the Institute of Psycho-Analysis, 1953-74), 8:16-89 (henceforth cited as *S.E.*); also see Evan Esar, *The Humor of Humor* (New York: Bramhall, 1952), passim; and Charles F. Hockett, "Jokes" in *Studies in Linguistics in Honor of George L. Trager*, ed. M. Estellie Smith (The Hague: Mouton, 1972), pp. 153-78.

5. The "semantic script-switch trigger" is what introduces the second script in Victor Raskin's formulation. See Victor Raskin. *Semantic Mechanisms of Humor* (Dordrecht, Holland: Reidel, 1985), pp. 114-17.

6. Ibid., pp. 33, 42, 146.

7. A1, A2, and A3 are constructed from texts included in Jan Harold Brunvand, "The Taming of the Shrew Tale in the United States," in *The Study of American Folklore*, by Jan Harold Brunvand, 2nd ed. (New York: Norton, 1978), pp. 360-71.

8. What Röhrich calls "die Momentaufnahme"; p. 9.

9. Based on Brunvand, *The Study of American Folklore*, pp. 360-61.

10. The terminology "true" and "pseudo" is merely used to distinguish concluding lines structurally and functionally. It is not meant to serve as a basis for aesthetic evaluation. The "true" punchline defines the joke, whereas the pseudo-punchline characterizes the tale. For a discussion of an example of a pseudo-punchline, see Elliott Oring, *Israeli Humor: The Content and Structure of the Chizbat of the Palmah* (Albany: State Univ. of New York Press, 1981), pp. 51-52. The distinction between true and pseudo-punchlines is not entirely unequivocal. If a listener fails to apprehend an unfolding incongruity in the course of a tale and only grasps it when the pseudo-punchline is uttered, we must acknowledge that what was only a pseudo-punchline for others is, in actuality, a true punchline for that listener. There are yet other equivocalities to be reckoned with, but they are beyond the scope of this chapter.

11. Based on Brunvand, *The Study of American Folklore*, pp. 363-64.

12. In fact, independent tales can be and often are chained together in performance; Stith Thompson, *The Folktale* (Berkeley: Univ. of California Press, 1977 [1946]), p. 415. See, for example, Type 516B: "The Abducted Princess" in Antti Aarne and Stith Thompson, *The Types of the Folktale*, FF Communications No. 184 (Helsinki: Suomalainen Tiedakatemia, 1964), p. 185.

13. William Novak and Moshe Waldoks, eds., *The Big Book of Jewish Humor* (New York: Harper & Row, 1981), p. 61.

14. Charles F. Hockett holds that a joke may have more than one punchline, and he distinguishes simple from compound and complex jokes on the basis of the number of punchlines they contain. Since Hockett regards the punchline merely as a concise humor-producing mechanism, a joke text may contain more than one punchline. However, Hockett is interested in distinguishing between types of jokes. As I am more interested in distinguishing the joke from the comic tale, I emphasize the final position of the punchline. In my view, only a humor-producing trigger in the final position is a punchline. Any material that follows this trigger threatens the perception of the narrative as a joke. While Hockett also acknowledges that joke grammar requires a punchline follow the joke "build-up," he does not insist upon the final position of the punchline. Material may be conjoined after the punchline, in his view, without generic consequence. See Hockett, pp. 155-56.

15. See for example, Larry Wilde, *The Official Religious/Not So Religious Jokebook* (New York: Pinnacle, 1976), p. 73.

16. Sigmund Freud regularly told jokes for didactic purposes. See Elliott Oring, *The Jokes of Sigmund Freud: A Study in Humor and Jewish Identity* (Philadelphia: Univ. of Pennsylvania Press, 1984), pp. 2-3.

17. Dan Ben-Amotz, "There's More Ways Than One to Kill a Joke," in *The Big Book of Jewish Humor*, ed. William Novak and Moshe Waldoks (New York: Harper & Row, 1981), pp. 133.

18. Ibid., p. 134. It should be noted that this piece, although humorous, has no punchline and is not a joke.

19. Hockett also explores the ways in which jokes can be "blown" in telling, although he does not consider the overdevelopment of the joke narrative or build-up as one possibility.

20. The principles for non-bona-fide-communication would seem to suggest otherwise; Raskin, *Semantic Mechanisms of Humor*, p. 103. But expansion is possible so long as it remains within limits and does not interfere with processing the punchline. Indeed, in many instances, expansion enhances a joke. If this were not the case, "one liners" would probably supplant narrative joketelling almost entirely.

21. This is precisely the point of the "Shaggy Dog Story," which develops a protracted multi-episodic narrative concluded by a non sequitur or atrocious pun. The Shaggy Dog Story (and it seems significant that it is labeled as a type of "story") is a parody of the narrative joke. See Utley, pp. 568-69.

22. Two jokes immediately come to mind in which the punchline consists of three lines. In each case, however, the first two lines condition the third. They summarize relevant aspects of the situation in a specific linguistic or conceptual format. Based on this format, the third line triggers an appropriate incongruity. See *S.E.* 8: 49-50, 115.

23. Neumann, p. 141.

24. A joke is just a special case of puzzle solving. See Paul Schiller, "A Configurational Theory of Jokes and Puzzles," *The Journal of General Psychology* 18 (1938): 217-34.

25. This is the model text for Raskin's analysis; *Semantic Mechanisms*, pp. 117-27.

26. The addition of "handsome" does not move this joke into bona fide communication. Raskin takes an extreme position in creating a "botched" version of this joke. What he manages to do is create something analogous to a humorous tale, albeit without dialogue or concluding episode; ibid., p. 145.

27. Hockett sees this issue solely in terms of the length and diffusiveness of the punchline. The word "handsome" in joke D2, however, adds appreciably to neither. Yet the addition of that word is sufficient to impair the effectiveness of the joke. See Hockett, pp. 168-69.

28. Esar, p. 29.

29. Mr. "J," *The World's Best Dirty Jokes* (New York: Ballantine, 1976).

30. Tale CXXXII in *The Facetiae of Giovanni Poggio Bracciolini*, trans. Bernhardt J. Hurwood (New York: Award, 1986), p. 118.

31. This text, which is my own adaptation of Poggio's joke, is not without parallels in the literature. See Larry Wilde, *The Last Official Sex Maniac's Joke Book* (Toronto: Bantam, 1982), p. 38.

32. Paul Goodman, *Speaking and Language: Defence of Poetry* (New York: Random, 1971), pp. 19, 22, 29, 72, 76.

33. A.A. Mendilow, "The Position of the Present in Fiction," in *The Theory of the Novel*, ed. Philip Stevick (New York: Free Press, 1967), pp. 275-77.

34. Isaac Asimov, "The Jokester," in *Earth is Room Enough* by Isaac Asimov (Garden City, N.Y.: Doubleday, 1957), pp. 149-61.

8. Freud and Humor: Analytic Reflections

1. These two views find their expression in the works of literary theorists, on the one hand, whose analyses generally cease when they have uncovered the structures or techniques of humor; and psychologists, on the other, who evaluate their subjects' responses to preselected experimental materials. For an example of the former view see Victor Raskin, *The Semantic Mechanisms of Humor* (Dordrecht: Reidel, 1985); for the latter see J. Levine, ed., *Motivation in Humor* (New York: Atherton, 1969).

2. See *The Philogelos or Laughter Lover*, trans. Barry Baldwin (Amsterdam: Gieben, 1983).

3. While there are several papers that relate the jokes of patients to their particular situations and conditions, the basic psychoanalytic works on humor ignore this approach entirely. Examples of the exceptional papers include Israel Zwerling, "The Favorite Joke Technique in Diagnostic and Therapeutic Interviewing," *Psychoanalytic Quarterly* 24 (1955): 104-15; Saul A. Grossman, "The Use of Jokes in Psychotherapy," in *It's a Funny Thing, Humor*, ed. Anthony J. Chapman and Hugh C. Foot (Oxford: Pergamon, 1977), pp. 149-52; and Atalay Yorukoglu,

"Favorite Jokes of Children and Their Dynamic Relation to Intra-Familial Conflicts," ibid., pp. 407-12.

4. Sigmund Freud, *Jokes and Their Relation to the Unconscious* in *The Standard Edition of the Complete Psychological Works of Sigmund Freud*, 24 vols., trans. under the general editorship of James Strachey in collaboration with Anna Freud (London: Hogarth Press and the Institute of Psycho-Analysis, 1953-74), 8:16 (henceforth cited as *S.E.*).

5. Ibid., pp. 19-20.

6. Ibid., p. 17.

7. Ibid., pp. 141-42.

8. Ibid., p. 142.

9. Sigmund Freud, "From the History of an Infantile Nerosis," *S.E.* 17:29-32.

10. This purely social aspect of joking is addressed in Thomas A. Burns with Inger H. Burns, *Doing the Wash: An Expressive Culture and Personality Study of a Joke and Its Tellers* (Norwood, Penn.: Norwood, 1975), pp. 14-18.

11. Joan Riviere, "An Intimate Impression," in *Freud as We Knew Him*, ed. Hendrik M. Ruitenbeek (Detroit: Wayne State Univ. Press, 1973), p. 129.

12. Franz Alexander, "Recollections of Bergasse 19," in *Freud as We Knew Him*, pp. 133-34.

13. Ernest Jones, *The Life and Work of Sigmund Freud*, 3 vols. (New York: Basic, 1953-57), 1:22.

14. *S.E.* 8:15.

15. *The Origins of Psycho-Analysis: Letters to Wilhelm Fliess, Drafts and Notes, 1887-1902*, ed. Marie Bonaparte, Anna Freud, and Ernst Kris, trans. Eric Mosbacher and James Strachey (New York: Basic, 1954), p. 211 (henceforth cited as *Origins*).

16. Sigmund Freud, *The Interpretation of Dreams*, *S.E.* 4:119-20, 194-95, 204-5.

17. Hanns Sachs, *Freud: Master and Friend* (Cambridge: Harvard Univ. Press, 1946), p. 100; Theodor Reik, "Freud and Jewish Wit," *Psychoanalysis* 2 (1954): 18.

18. For example see Nathan Ausubel, ed., *A Treasury of Jewish Folklore* (New York: Crown, 1948), pp. 267-86; Henry D. Spaulding, comp. and ed., *Encyclopedia of Jewish Humor* (New York: Jonathan David, 1969), pp. 27-39.

19. *S.E.* 8:112. For other schnorrer jokes see pp. 112-13.

20. Ibid., pp. 49-50.

21. Ibid., p. 62; 4:119-20.

22. Jones 1:60, 157.

23. Ibid., pp. 61, 64, 154-55.

24. For example see *The Letters of Sigmund Freud*, ed. Ernst L. Freud, trans. Tania and James Stern (New York: Basic, 1960), pp. 27-28, 44, 53, 127, 148-49, 168-69 (henceforth cited as *Letters*).

25. Jones 1:155-59.

26. *Letters*, p. 49.

27. Ibid., p. 87.

28. Jones 1:161.

29. Ibid.

30. *Letters*, p. 104.
31. Jones 1:166.
32. *Origins*, p. 211.
33. Jones 1:188.
34. Ibid., p. 154; 2:92, 195, 388-91. Also see Bruno Grinker, "Some Memories of Sigmund Freud," in *Freud as We Knew Him*, pp. 266-68.
35. *Origins*, p. 298.
36. Joseph Wortis, *Fragments of an Analysis with Freud* (New York: Simon and Schuster, 1954), pp. 22, 62.
37. *Letters*, p. 116.
38. Most notably the discovery of the self-regulative function of the vagus nerve in respiration known as the Hering-Breuer reflex and the elucidation of the functions of the semicircular canals in regulating posture, equilibrium and movement. See Frank J. Sulloway, *Freud: Biologist of the Mind* (New York: Basic, 1979), pp. 51-52.
39. Jones 1:166-67, 223.
40. Ibid., p. 160.
41. Ibid., p. 167.
42. Ibid., p. 168.
43. Ibid., pp. 224, 226.
44. *Origins*, pp. 64, 95.
45. Sulloway, p. 85.
46. Jones 1:255.
47. Ibid.
48. Paul Roazen, *Freud and His Followers* (New York: New American Library, Meridian, 1971), p. 80.
49. Jones 1:255-56.
50. Ibid.
51. *S.E.* 6:137-38.
52. Sigmund Freud, *Five Lectures on Psycho-Analysis*, *S.E.* 11:9.
53. Jones 1:289.
54. Sigmund Freud, "On the History of the Psycho-Analytic Movement," *S.E.* 14:8.
55. Ibid., pp. 8-9.
56. Jones 1:242.
57. Sigmund Freud, "Joseph Breuer," *S.E.* 19:280.
58. Jones 1:255.
59. *Letters*, pp. 234-35.
60. *S.E.* 4:107-20.
61. Ibid., p. 107.
62. Ibid. 2:xv.
63. Ibid. 4:112.
64. Ibid., pp. 115, 119.
65. Ibid. 8:56.
66. Ibid., p. 58.
67. Ibid., p. 113.
68. Ernst Freud, Lucie Freud, and Ilse Gubrich-Simitis, eds., *Sigmund*

Freud: His Life in Pictures and Words (New York: Harcourt Brace Jovanovich, 1976), pp. 56-57.

69. Ibid., p. 61.
70. Ibid., p. 64.
71. Ernst Freud, "Some Early Unpublished Letters of Freud," *International Journal of Psycho-Analysis* 50 (1969): 421.
72. Maryse Choisy, *Sigmund Freud: A New Appraisal* (New York: Citadel, 1963), p. 25; William M. Johnston, *The Austrian Mind: An Intellectual and Social History, 1848-1939* (Berkeley: Univ. of California Press, 1972), p. 222; Friedrich Heer, "Freud, the Viennese Jew," trans. W.A. Littlewood, in *Freud: The Man, His World, His Influence*, ed. Jonathan Miller (Boston: Little Brown, 1972), p. 6.
73. Ernst Freud et al., *Sigmund Freud*, p. 46.
74. Jeffrey L. Sammons, *Heinrich Heine: A Modern Biography* (Princeton: Princeton Univ. Press, 1979), pp. 42-46.
75. He was baptized Christian Johann Heinrich Heine. Ibid., p. 107.
76. Heer, p. 6.
77. In the chapter immediately following the "famillionairely" joke in "Die Bäder von Lucca," the character Hirsch-Hyacinth is questioned as to his religious preferences. He points out that Catholicism is good for a wealthy man of leisure but not for a practical man like himself who must earn a living. Protestantism he finds devoid of spirituality. And the old Jewish religion, says Hyacinth, "I don't wish it to my worst enemy. It brings nothing but abuse and disgrace. I tell you it ain't a religion, but a misfortune." See Heinrich Heine, *Pictures of Travel*, trans. Charles Godfrey Leland (Philadelphia: Schaefer and Koradi, 1882), p. 331.
78. Sammons, p. 51.
79. Ibid., p. 108.
80. Heinrich Heine, *Heinrich Heine's Life Told in His Own Words*, ed. Gustav Karpeles, trans. Arthur Dexter (New York: Henry Holt, 1893), p. 130.
81. The idea of free association may have been suggested by Börne's essay, "The Art of Becoming an Original Writer in Three Days." See Jones 1:246.
82. Ibid.
83. S.E. 8:47-48.
84. Ibid., p. 114.
85. Heine, p. 145.

9. The People of the Joke

1. Ernst Simon, "Notes on Jewish Wit," *Jewish Frontier* 15 (1948): 42; Harry Golden, *The Golden Book of Jewish Humor* (New York: G.P. Putnam's Sons, 1972), p. 12; Leo Rosten, *The Joys of Yiddish* (New York: McGraw Hill, 1968), p. xxix; George Mikes, *Laughing Matter* (New York: Library Press, 1971), p. 111.
2. Immanuel Olsvanger, *Röyte Pomerantsen* (New York: Schocken, 1965), p. 3; trans. in Naomi Katz and Eli Katz, "Tradition and Adaptation in American Jewish Humor," *Journal of American Folklore* 84 (1971): 216.
3. Alan Dundes, "Metafolklore and Oral Literary Criticism," in *Analytic Essays in Folklore*, by Alan Dundes (The Hague: Mouton, 1975), pp. 52-53.
4. Chaim Bermant, *What's the Joke: A Study of Jewish Humor Through the Ages* (London: Weidenfeld and Nicolson, 1986), pp. 9-10.

5. Ibid., p. 8.
6. Ibid., p. 18.
7. Ibid., p. 27.
8. "The early settlers were thus either humourless to start with, or the heat of the Holy Land steamed the humour out of them, and no one today would recommend their memoires—which form a not inconsiderable library—for light reading. If their lack of humour was an acquired characteristic, they nevertheless managed to transmit it to their sons and grandsons;" ibid., p. 152.
9. Gen. 14:1-16.
10. Bermant, p. 249.
11. See Isaac Jack Levy, "Sephardic Humor: One Has to Laugh to Live," *Southern Folklore* 47 (1990): 147-61.
12. See the critique of Heda Jason, "The Jewish Joke: The Problem of Definition," *Southern Folklore Quarterly* 31 (1967): 48-54.
13. Dan Ben-Amos, "The 'Myth' of Jewish Humor," *Western Folklore* 32 (1973): 112-31. Ben-Amos does not really suggest that Jewish humor is a myth. He uses the term merely to characterize the assessments of Jewish humor as self-critical as incorrect.
14. It should be noted that in Yemen, Jews—particularly women—are recognized by their Muslim neighbors for their singing and not for their humor. Shalom Staub, personal communication, 1982.
15. Hermann Adler, "Jewish Wit and Humor," *The Nineteenth Century* 33 (1893): 457-69.
16. Alter Druyanow, *Sefer ha-Bediḥah ve-ha Ḥidud*, 3 vols. (Tel. Aviv: Dvir, 1963), 1:ix.
17. Abram S. Isaacs, *Stories from the Rabbis* (New York: Bloch, 1911), pp. 7, 114.
18. J. Chotzner, *Hebrew Humor and Other Essays* (London: Luzac, 1905).
19. Nathan Ausubel seems to agree: "Wit and irony can be regarded as the likely attributes of a civilized mentality." Nathan Ausubel, ed., *A Treasury of Jewish Folklore* (New York: Crown, 1948), p. xx.
20. Otto Weininger, *Sex and Character* (London: Heinemann, 1906), pp. 318-19.
21. Isaacs, p. 7.
22. Adler, p. 458.
23. *London Athenaeum*, 15 Jan. 1876; quoted in Sig Altman, *The Comic Image of the Jew: Explorations of a Pop Culture Phenomenon* (Rutherford, N.J.: Fairleigh Dickinson Univ. Press, 1971), pp. 144-45.
24. B. Rohatyn, "Die Gestalten des Juedischen Volkshumor," *Ost und West* 11 (1911): 122.
25. Ibid., p. 123.
26. Shmuel Niger, "The Humor of Sholem Aleichem," in *Voices from the Yiddish*, ed. Irving Howe and Eliezer Greenberg (Ann Arbor: Univ. of Michigan Press, 1972), pp. 41-50.
27. Quoted in Charles A. Madison, *Yiddish Literature: Its Scope and Major Writers* (New York: Fredrich Ungar, 1968), p. 96.
28. For example, Ausubel, *A Treasury of Jewish Folklore*, p. xx; Nathan Ausubel, ed., *A Treasury of Jewish Humor* (Garden City, N.Y.: Doubleday, 1951),

p. xvi; Rosten, p. xxiv; William Novak and Moshe Waldoks, eds., *The Big Book of Jewish Humor* (New York: Harper and Row, 1981), p. xiv.

29. Adler, p. 458.

30. Sigmund Freud, *Jokes and Their Relation to the Unconscious* in *The Standard Edition of the Complete Psychological Works of Sigmund Freud*, 24 vols., trans. under the general editorship of James Strachey in collaboration with Anna Freud (London: The Hogarth Press and the Institute of Psycho-Analysis, 1953-74), 8:102-116 (henceforth cited as *S.E.*).

31. Druyanow, pp. ix-xix. Also see Donald C. Simmons, "Protest Humor: Folkloristic Reaction to Prejudice," *American Journal of Psychiatry* 120 (1963): 567-69.

32. *S.E.* 8:111-12.

33. Adler, p. 468.

34. Martin Grotjahn, *Beyond Laughter: Humor and the Subconscious* (New York: McGraw-Hill, 1966), pp. 21-25; Theodor Reik, *Jewish Wit* (New York: Gamut, 1962), pp. 217-42.

35. Novak and Waldoks, p. xvi.

36. Ausubel, *A Treasury of Jewish Humor*, pp. xvi, xvii.

37. Irving Howe and Ruth Wisse, eds., *The Best of Sholom Aleichem* (New York: Washington Square, 1979), pp. ix-xxi.

38. *S.E.* 8:105; "Humour," *S.E.* 21:161-72.

39. Grotjahn, p. 22; Reik, p. 202.

40. Bernard Rosenberg and Gilbert Shapiro, "Marginality and Jewish Humor," *Midstream* 4 (1958): 70-80.

41. Irving Kristol, "Is Jewish Humor Dead?: The Rise and Fall of the Jewish Joke," *Commentary* 12 (1951): 431-36.

42. Ed Cray, "The Rabbi Trickster," *Journal of American Folklore* 77 (1964): 331-45.

43. Salcia Landmann, "On Jewish Humor," *Jewish Journal of Sociology* 4 (1962): 198.

44. Kristol, p. 436.

45. Ruth R. Wisse, *The Schlemiel as Modern Hero* (Chicago: Univ. of Chicago Press, 1971).

10. Self-Degrading Jokes and Tales

1. Thomas Hobbes, *Leviathan: Or the Matter, Form, and Power of a Commonwealth, Ecclesiastical and Civil* (New York and London: Routledge and Sons, 1907 [1651]), p. 33.

2. Hermann Adler, "Jewish Wit and Humor," *The Nineteenth Century* 33 (1893): 468.

3. Sigmund Freud, *Jokes and Their Relation to the Unconscious*, in *The Standard Edition of the Complete Psychological Works of Sigmund Freud*, 24 vols., trans. under the general editorship of James Strachey in collaboration with Anna Freud (London: Hogarth Press and the Institute of Psycho-Analysis, 1953-74), 8:111-12 (henceforth cited as *S.E.*).

4. Sander L. Gilman, *Jewish Self-Hatred: Anti-Semitism and the Hidden Language of the Jews* (Baltimore: Johns Hopkins Univ. Press, 1986), pp. 286-308.

5. Roger D. Abrahams, *Deep Down in the Jungle: Negro Narrative Folklore from the Streets of Philadelphia* (Hatboro, Penn.: Folklore Associates, 1964), p. 31; Eldridge Cleaver, "As Crinkly as Yours," in Alan Dundes, ed., *Mother Wit from the Laughing Barrel: Readings in the Interpretation of Afro-American Folklore* (Englewood Cliffs, N.J.: Prentice-Hall, 1973), pp. 9-21; Abram Kardiner and Lionel Oversey, *The Mark of Oppression: Explorations in the Personality of the American Negro* (Cleveland: Meridian, 1962 [1951]), pp. 302-5; Charles E. Silberman, *Crisis in White and Black* (New York: Vintage, 1964), pp. 68-122; Kurt Lewin, *Resolving Social Conflicts* (New York: Harper Brothers, 1948), p. 189; Thomas F. Pettigrew, *A Profile of the Negro American* (Princeton: Van Nostrand, 1964), pp. 7-11; Roderick W. Pugh, *Psychology and the Black Experience* (Monterey, Calif.: Brooks/Cole, 1972), p. 5.

6. Mahadev L. Apte, *Humor and Laughter: An Anthropological Approach* (Ithaca N.Y.: Cornell Univ. Press, 1985), pp. 108-48; Dan Ben-Amos, "The Myth of Jewish Humor," *Western Folklore* 32 (1973): 112-31; Lawrence W. Levine, *Black Culture and Black Consciousness: Afro-American Folk Thought from Slavery to Freedom* (New York: Oxford Univ. Press, 1977), pp. 298-366; and most recently by Christie Davies, "Exploring the Thesis of the Self-deprecating Jewish Sense of Humor," *Humor: International Journal of Humor Research* 4 (1991): 189-209.

7. Daryl Cumber Dance, *Shuckin' and Jivin': Folklore From Contemporary Black Americans* (Bloomington: Indiana Univ. Press, 1978), pp. 3-4, 77-78; Theodor Reik, *Jewish Wit* (New York: Gamut, 1962), p. 219; Theodor Isaac Rubin, *Compassion and Self-Hatred: An Alternative to Despair* (New York: David McKay, 1975), p. 34; Irving Howe, "The Nature of Jewish Laughter," *The New American Mercury* 72 (1951): 211-12; Bernard Rosenberg and Gilbert Shapiro, "Marginality and Jewish Humor," *Midstream* 4 (1958): 74.

8. Sigmund Freud, "The Economic Problem of Masochism," in *S.E.* 19:165.

9. Rubin, pp. 29-33.

10. For examples, Edmund Bergler, *Laughter and the Sense of Humor* (New York: Intercontinental Medical, 1956), p. 111; Martin Grotjahn, "Jewish Jokes and Their Relation to Masochism," in *A Celebration of Laughter*, ed. Werner M. Mendel (Los Angeles: Mara, 1970), pp. 135-43; Arthur J. Prange and M.M. Vitols, "Jokes Among Southern Negroes: The Revelation of Conflict," in Dundes, p. 633; Russell Middleton and John Moland, "Humor in Negro and White Subcultures: A Study of Jokes Among University Students," *American Sociological Review* 24 (1959): 66; Chaim Bermant, *What's the Joke: A Study of Jewish Humor Through the Ages* (London: Weidenfeld and Nicolson, 1986), p. 242; Rosenberg and Shapiro, p. 74.

11. Dance, p. 83.

12. Elliott Oring, *Israeli Humor: The Content and Structure of the Chizbat of the Palmah* (Albany: State Univ. of New York Press, 1981), p. 31.

13. Dahn Ben-Amotz and Netiva Ben-Yehudah, *Milon olami le-ivrit meduberet* [*The World Dictionary of Hebrew Slang*], 2 vols. (Tel Aviv: Zmora, Bitan, 1982); s.v. "yehudi."

14. Cowardice was attached to black soldiers in World War I and that script was

attached to black soldiers after that war. See Christie Davies, *Ethnic Humor Around the World: A Comparative Analysis* (Bloomington: Indiana Univ. Press, 1990), pp. 225-33.

15. Ernest W. Baughman, *Type and Motif-Index of the Folktales of England and North America* (The Hague: Mouton, 1966).

16. E. Earl Baughman, *Black Americans: A Psychological Analysis* (New York: Academic, 1971), pp. 41-42.

17. Dance, pp. 80-81.

18. Ben-Amos, p. 122.

19. Dance, p. 78; Harry Oster, "Negro Humor: John and Ole Marster," *Journal of the Folklore Institute* 5 (1968): 42-57; Levine, p. 339.

20. Ed Cray, "The Rabbi Trickster," *Journal of American Folklore* 77 (1964): 331-45.

21. Ben Amos, p. 128.

22. Rosenberg and Shapiro, p. 75.

23. Dance, p. 99.

24. The sex of the informant is not noted by Dance. She notes the tale was recorded 20 Nov. 1974 in Richmond, Virginia. Dance's Richmond informants seem about equally divided between males and females. But of the texts collected in Richmond on that date, two of them (no. 45 and no. 269) are clearly from female informants while none are clearly from male informants, so it is quite possible that this text was also related by a female. That women frequently tell such stories is indicated by the large number of female informants who contributed to chapter 8, "I Could Eat Her Up: Tales about Women." Beyond this, we can assume a female teller, if only for the sake of argument.

25. H.C. Brearley, "Ba-ad Nigger," in Dundes, pp. 578-85.

26. Robbie Davis Johnson, "Folklore and Women: A Social Interactional Analysis of Folklore of a Texas Madam," *Journal of American Folklore* 86 (1973): 211-24.

27. Levine, p. 338.

28. Robert K. Merton, *Social Theory and Social Structure* (Glencoe, Ill.: Free Press, 1957), pp. 426-30.

29. Neil A. Eddington, "Genital Superiority in Oakland Negro Folklore: A Theme," in Dundes, pp. 642-48.

30. Dance, p. 99. A similar joke is cited by Anton C. Zijderveld who is also opposed to reading such jokes as unambiguous signs of self-hatred. The version Zijderveld cites has the black elegantly and the white only shabbily dressed, so the black man's "success and the white man's failure are equal parts of the punchline"; "The Sociology of Humor and Laughter," *Current Sociology: La Sociologie Contemporaine* 31 (1983): 54-55. I do not believe that such distinctions of dress or class are necessary for the joke to be regarded positively.

31. Martin Grotjahn, *Beyond Laughter: Humor and the Subconscious* (New York: McGraw-Hill, 1966), pp. 22-23. Zijderveld similarly cites Grotjahn, p. 51.

32. Ibid.

33. Dance, pp. 5-6.

34. Tristram Potter Coffin, *Uncertain Glory: Folklore and the American Revolution* (Detroit: Folklore Associates, 1971), pp. 94-101.

35. William Labov, "Rules for Ritual Insults," in *Rappin' and Stylin' Out:*

Communication in Urban Black America, ed. Thomas Kochman (Urbana, Ill.: Univ. of Illinois Press, 1972), pp. 296-98.

36. Joan Emerson, "Negotiating the Serious Import of Humor," *Sociometry* 32 (1969): 169-81.

37. Labov, p. 297.

38. See chapter 11, pp. 142-43.

39. Levine, pp. 335-36. The term "nigger" also illustrates the previous point about how a negative image can be tamed and used as a means of counterattack.

40. Dance, p. 77; Langston Hughes, "Jokes Negroes Tell on Themselves," in Dundes, p. 641.

41. Seth Kravitz, "London Jokes and Ethnic Stereotypes," *Western Folklore* 36 (1977): 275-301.

42. Sigmund Freud, "Humour" in *S.E.* 21:162, 166.

43. Jean-Paul Sartre, *Anti-Semite and Jew*, trans. George J. Becker (New York: Schocken, 1948), pp. 26-28; T.W. Adorno, Else Frenkel-Brunswik, Daniel J. Levinson, R. Nevitt Sanford, *The Authoritarian Personality*, abr. ed. (New York: Norton, 1982), pp. 279-80. Or as Rubin states, "Murder is the ultimate form of displaced and projected self-hate," p. 70.

44. *S.E.* 8:111.

45. Gilman, p. 286.

46. Ibid., p. 307.

11. Dyadic Traditions

1. "American humor is violent—and often sexist, racist, brutal, and disgusting as well," is just another in a long line of similar formulations. See William Keough, *Punchlines: The Violence of American Humor* (New York: Paragon, 1990), p. xi.

2. R.L. Coser, "Some Social Functions of Laughter," *Human Relations* 12 (1959): 171-82; Joan Emerson, "Negotiating the Serious Import of Humor," *Sociometry* 32 (1969): 169-81; and most recently, Christie Davies, *Ethnic Humor Around the World: A Comparative Analysis* (Bloomington: Indiana Univ. Press, 1990) and "An Explanation of Jewish Jokes about Jewish Women," *Humor* 3 (1990): 363-78.

3. This has been true despite a realization of the limits of aggression or disparagement theories. See Dolf Zillman, "Disparagement Humor," in *Handbook of Humor Research*, ed. Paul E. McGhee and Jeffrey H. Goldstein, 2 vols. (New York: Springer-Verlag, 1983), 1:85-107.

4. George J. McCall, Michal M. McCall, Norman K. Denzin, Gerald D. Suttles, Suzanne B. Kurth, "A Collaborative Overview of Social Relationships," in *Social Relationships*, ed. George J. McCall et al. (Chicago: Aldine, 1970), p. 172.

5. Dyadic traditions fall within the concept of "idioculture"; Gary Alan Fine, "Small Groups and Cultural Creation: The Idioculture of Little League Baseball Teams," *American Sociological Review* 44 (1979): 733-45. However, dyadic traditions are not coextensive with idioculture. Dyadic traditions are conceptualized by the dyad as unique properties of the unit or unique enactments of more widely shared properties. My notion of tradition also does not accord entirely with that of

Edward Shils who requires "two transmissions" over three "generations" for a pattern or a belief to be considered a tradition; Edward Shils, *Tradition* (Chicago: Univ. of Chicago Press, 1981), p. 15. Dyadic traditions require a minimum of two transmissions, but only within two generations. Dyadic traditions are oscillating rather than linear transmissions. Dyadic traditions are created and maintained, but they are rarely passed on.

6. Fine has described the "triggering events" for the creation of the idioculture as potentially infinite and hence unpredictable; Fine, pp. 742-43.

7. While specific traditions for specific dyads are unpredictable, it might be possible to anticipate the kinds of materials that might be utilized by any number of dyads. For example, in the movie "Fiddler on the Roof," a husband sings to his wife of twenty-five years a song in which he questions whether she loves him. I have interviewed a dyad that utilizes elements of this song in their relationship, and its use has been reported by others as well. See Paola Tavarelli, "Dyadic Traditions in Mixed Couples," *Folklore and Mythology Studies* 11-12 (1987-88): 73-74.

8. Sigmund Freud and Karl Abraham, *A Psycho-Analytic Dialogue: The Letters of Sigmund Freud and Karl Abraham, 1907-1926*, ed. Hilda C. Abraham and Ernst L. Freud (New York: Basic, 1965), pp. 146, 157-58.

9. Martha Weinman Lear, *Heartsounds* (New York: Simon and Schuster, 1980), p. 91.

10. Kathy Fletcher, "'Where My Navel String is Buried': Folklore Memories of Home from Employees of ETI," unpublished manuscript, Feb. 1990, pp. 61-69.

11. Gary Jennings, *Aztec* (New York: Avon, 1980), p. 80, passim.

12. Simmel, p. 137.

13. Ibid., pp. 126-28.

14. Ibid., pp. 135-36.

15. Love and hate are acute, transitional states so that "there is no contradiction in expecting the best of friends to be temporarily annoyed with one another, a circumstance that should motivate mirth from witnessed disparagement." Zillman 1:91.

16. See Max Gluckman, *Order and Rebellion in Tribal Africa* (New York: Free Press of Glencoe, 1963), pp. 118, 168-69; C. Masheter and L.M. Harris, "From Divorce to Friendship: A Study of Dialectic Relationship Development," *Journal of Social and Personal Relationships* 3 (1986): 179.

17. Gregory Bateson, "A Theory of Play and Fantasy," in *Steps to an Ecology of Mind* (New York: Ballantine, 1972), pp. 177-93.

18. Gerald D. Suttles, "Friendship as a Social Institution," in McCall et al., *Social Relationships*, pp. 101-10.

19. See Regina Bendix, "Marmot, Memet, and Marmoset: Further Research on the Folklore of Dyads," *Western Folklore* 46 (1987): 171-91; Paola Tavarelli, "Dyadic Traditions in Mixed Couples"; Robert A. Bell, Nancy L. Buerkel-Rothfuss, Kevin E. Gore, "'Did You Bring the Yarmulke for the Cabbage Patch Kid?': The Idiomatic Communication of Young Lovers," *Human Communication Research* 14 (1987): 47-67.

20. Simmel, p. 124.

21. See Carl Bode, *The Anatomy of American Popular Culture, 1840-1861* (Berkeley: Univ. of California Press, 1959), pp. 188-200.

22. Men are often characterized as unable to talk about their feelings and to express intimacy other than through sex; Francesca M. Cancian, *Love in America: Gender and Self-Development* (Cambridge: Cambridge Univ. Press, 1987), pp. 4, 7, 70-71, 91-97. I would suggest that humor is one such means of intimate communication.

23. While I would be prepared to allow that some particular traditions are the result of repressed or suppressed aggression, I do not believe that such hostilities account for all, or even most, of these dyadic traditions.

Index

Abraham, 113, 114
Abraham, Karl, 137
Abrahams, Roger D. and Alan Dundes, 17-19, 27
absurdity, 19-26. *See also* drama, absurd
Adler, Hermann, 116, 117, 119
Aleichem, Sholom, 113, 114, 119, 121
aggression theory. *See* humor: as aggression
appropriate incongruity, ix-x, 2-15, 19-22, 30, 41-42, 44-49, 51-52, 57-58, 81, 83, 84, 85, 145 n 7, 148 n 43, 151 n 3; in jokes, 3-9; in riddles, 2-3, 20
Ausubel, Nathan, 120-21, 161 n 19

Beattie, James, 1-2, 41
Ben-Amos, Dan, 128-29, 161 n 13
Ben-Amotz, Dahn, 88-89
Bergson, Henri, 1
Bermant, Chaim, 113-14
Bible, the, 113, 116
binary opposition. *See* myth, structural analysis of
bisociation, 41. *See also* incongruity theory
Börne, Ludwig, 110, 160 n 81
Breuer, Josef, 101, 103-7, 159 n 38

"California Dreamin'," 75-77
chizbat, 42, 43-52, 53, 54-66, 152 nn 9, 19, 3, 6; 153 nn 12, 16, 18, 19; dissimilarity of, to joke, 43-44, 49-51; stance of, 49-51; underlying message of, 53, 55, 56, 59, 61-62, 64, 66, 68, 153 n 19
cholent, 75-76, 154 nn 8, 9
"Cholent is a-Burnin'," text of, 75
Chotzner, J., 117

conundrum, 146 n 9
countercultural revolution, 26, 27, 149 n 14
Cyrano de Bergerac, 131

Dance, Daryl Cumber, 124, 126, 131-32, 164 n 24
Davidson, Martin, 153 n 1
didacticism, 87, 156 n 16
drama, absurd, 26
dreams, dissimilarities of, to jokes, 39
Druyanow, Alter, 119-20
Dundes, Alan, 34, 148 n 4. *See also* Abrahams, Roger D., and Alan Dundes
dyad, 135, 140, 143
dyadic tradition: definition of, 135-36, 165-66 n 5; ephemeral nature of, 139-40; evolution of, 140; function of, 136-37, 140-41, 142-43; predictability of, 136, 166 nn 6, 7

Fiddler on the Roof, 113, 166 n 7. *See also* Aleichem, Sholom
Fine, Gary Alan, 166 n 6
Fleischl-Marxow, Ernst von, 101-2
French and Indian War, 132
Freud, Sigmund, 1, 10, 13, 16, 27-28, 39, 94-111, 119-20, 137, 145 n 2, 147 n 39, 148 n 1, 156 n 16; identification with schnorrer, 99-108; Jewish identity of, 107-11, 160 n 77

galut image, 49-51, 53, 62, 65. *See also* identity
Grotjahn, Martin, 120, 121, 131

halakhah, 74-78, 79-80, 154 n 5
Hammerschlag, Samuel, 101
Hasidim. *See* Satmar
Heine, Heinrich, 94-95, 108-11, 117, 160 nn 75, 77
Hobbes, Thomas, 1, 122
Hockett, Charles F., 156 nn 14, 19
"Home on the Blat," text of, 70-71
"Home on the Range," 70-72
humor: appreciation of, 12-13, 147 n 37; as aggression, ix, 1, 16-19, 27-28, 33, 39, 122, 130-32, 135, 142, 144, 148 nn 1, 4; 165 nn 1, 3; 166 n 15; 167 n 23; as defense, 119-21; as masochism (*see* self-hatred); as manifestation of Oedipal complex, 17; as pathology, 120-21; as persuasion, 13, 147-48 n 40; as play, 16, 28; as self-aggression, 17, 122, 148 n 4 (*see also* self hatred); as sexual expression, 1, 16, 28, 135, 145 n 2, 165 n 1; as superiority, expression of, 145 n 3; as therapy, 34, 39, 150 n 6; as transcendence, 118-19, 120-21; context of, x, 15; cultural knowledge in, 7-9, 68-69, 147 nn 21, 23; function of, ix; Israeli, 42-51, 53-66, 113-14, 152 nn 2, 3, 6, 9, 19; 153 nn 15, 16, 18, 19; 161 n 8; psychoanalytic theory of, 1, 16, 39, 94, 157 n 3; shtetl, 114; social aspects of, 96, 158 n 10; truth of, 132-33; underlying message of, 13-15; use of language in, 2-4, 6-8. *See also* chizbat

identity, 50-51, 53, 56-66, 75, 77-80, 153 n 18; black, 126-28, 129-30; differences in social, 128-30, 164 n 24; Israeli, 42; Jewish, 128-29, 134; Palmach, dirty/clean, 48-49; Palmach, Levantine/European, 45-46; opposition of, 45-51; Palmach, primitive/civilized, 46-48, 57-58. *See also* Freud, Sigmund, identification with schnorrer; galut image; sabra image
idioculture, 165-66 n 5, 166 n 6
incongruity theory, ix-x, 1-2, 41-42, 51-52, 145 n 8, 147 n 26, 151 n 3. *See also* appropriate incongruity
incongruous assemblages, 41. *See also* appropriate incongruity
insult, 141-43
inversion. *See* myth, structural theory of
Isaacs, Abram S., 116, 117

iteration: of motif, 58-59, 65; of plot, 59-62, 65; of texts, 56, 65; of theme, 56-58, 65, 152 n 7

Jewish humor, conceptions of, 114-15
Jewish verbal culture, classifications of, 42
joke: absurd, 26; as argument, 13, 147-48 n 40; base meaning of, 30, 31; brevity of, 88-89, 156 nn 20, 21; complex, 87, 156 n 14; compound, 87, 156 n 14; conventions of, 5-6; conventions of, narration, 82; conventions of, texts, 81-82; distinctions of, from tale, 81-93, 154 n 2; 155 nn 3, 10; 156 nn 12, 14, 18, 21; 157 n 26; information in, 146 n 12; intelligibility of, 39; performance meaning of, 31; propositional meaning of, 13-14, 30-31; relation of, to the individual, 94-97, 157 n 3; seriousness of, 13-15, 147 n 39, 149 n 14; simple, 87, 156 n 14; underlying message of, 95
joke cycle. *See* jokes: elephant; jokes: Challenger
joke-destroying technique, 88-89, 156 n 19, 157 n 26
joke grammar, 84, 156 n 14
joke repertoire, 20
joke sequence, 23-24, 149 n 11
joke session, 18, 149 n 11
joke texts: Arab beats his wife, 46; asking for fruit, 44; asking for water in Galilee, 60-61; bank door without crack, 56; beadle sleeps on Sundays, 5; Big Bimbo Bottom, 127-28; biggest vagina, 11; black man sits next to white woman on bus, 131; brushing teeth with soda, 49; businessman and secretaries, 29-30; buying a cannon, 107; capitalism-communism, 10; carrying an immigrant, 59; Challenger jokes, 32-33; concerts give headaches, 45; copper kettle returned, 99; definition of anti-Semite, 129; doctor and husband, 3, 4, 5; elephant jokes, 17-26; "famillionairely," 94-95; fork forgotten, 57; ghosts disbelieved, 9, 30; golden calf, 110; Heine's deathbed remark, 110; hyenas as psychological warfare, 47-48; kangaroo in bar, 6-7; lamp thrown in lake, 65; lion sought, 62-64; mare examined, 61; martinis-breasts, 13; outrunning a bullet, 125; patient invited by doctor's wife, 90;

poetry addressed to girl, 60; rarely beautiful girl, 11; rifle is not an ear, 48; ring that keeps woman faithful, 91-92; Russian requests telephone, 87; salmon mayonnaise, 98-99; schnorrer's son-in-law, 98; sexual positions, 8; smuggling coffee, 88-89; telling a joke to Jews, 112-13; "That's once!", 83, 84-85, 86; veterinarian's instruments, 46; violin of Palmach, 57; woman lays back a bit, 11; women discuss what makes them "hot," 129

jokes: black, 124, 129-30, 131; Challenger, 31-39, 150 nn 4, 9; elephant, 17-28, 149 nn 9, 11, 15; ethnic, 16-17, 18, 148 n 4. *See also* Jewish, 97-98, 107-8, 122, 128-29, 131; rabbi trickster, 129; riddles, color; schnorrer, 98-99; sexual, 29-30, 40; sick, 40

Jokes and Their Relation to the Unconscious, 1, 16, 94, 96, 97, 107, 108, 110, 119, 120, 148 n 1

Katz, Mickey, 78

last words, 36-37, 150 n 14
Legman, G., 149 n 3
Levi-Strauss, Claude. *See* myth, structural analysis of
Liebman, Charles S., 154 n 11

McAuliffe, Christa, 32-34, 36, 37, 151 n 16
makhmir, 72-74, 77-78, 80
"Makhmir," text of, 73
masochism. *See* self-hatred
media: commercial messages, 38; news, 35-39, 150 nn 10, 12, 14, 15, 16, 18
mekel, 77-78
metahumor, 113
Monro, D.H., 145 n 7
moralization. *See* didacticism
mutilation, 36, 150 n 13
myth, structural analysis of, 51-52, 152 nn 17, 5.7; relation to incongruity theory, 51-52, 152 n 19

narrative, multi-episodic, 84-85, 156 n 21
NASA, 34-35, 150 nn 9, 13, 14

Oedipus myth. *See* myth, structural analysis of
orthodoxy, 74-75, 77-80, 154 n 11

palindrome. *See* techniques of humor, vacuous reversal
Palmach, 42-43, 50-51; ethos of, 43; history of 42-43; identity (*see* identity, Palmach)
Paneth, Josef, 101-2
"Parable of the Talents," 30
parody: performance, 146 n 13; riddle, 146 n 11; song, 68, 71-72, 74, 76-77, 78-79
performance setting, 55, 152 n 2
Poggio Bracciolini, Giovanni, 91-92
psychoanalysis, history of, 104, 105-6
psychoanalytic theory of humor. *See* humor: psychoanalytic theory of
pun, 12, 156 n 21
punchline, 82-85, 86-87, 89-92, 155 nn 3, 10; 156 nn 14, 20; 157 nn 26, 27; brevity of, 89, 156 n 22, 157 n 27; as dialogue, 90-92; diffusiveness of, 89-90, 157 nn 26, 27; position of, 84-87, 156 n 14; pseudo-, 84-85, 153 n 10; as trigger mechanism, 83-84, 155 n 5, 156 n 14

Raskin, Victor, 145 n 8, 146 n 12, 147 n 26, 148 n 43. *See also* semantic theory of humor
Rechnitzer Rejects, 67-80, 153 n 1
redundancy in communication, 53-54, 152 n 7, 153 n 19
Reform Judaism, 74, 80
Reik, Theodor, 120, 121
Reisebilder (Pictures of Travels), 94-95, 160 n 77
repertoire: humorous, 53, 55-56, 153 n 19; joke, 20
riddle, 2-3, 5-6, 146 nn 11, 18; conventions of, 5-6, 20-24 (*see also* conundrum); nonoppositional, 146 n 18; oppositional, 146 n 14; parodies of, 146 n 11; violations of conventions of, 20-27, 149 n 11
riddles, color, 18-19
Rohatyn, B., 118

sabra image, 49-51, 53, 62, 65. *See also* identity
Satmar, 73-75
script, 9, 52, 126, 145 n 8, 147 n 26, 163 n 14; compatibly opposed, 41. *See also* incongruity theory
self-degradation, 123-28, 129-33; as outward aggression, 130-32, 164 n 30, 165 n 39

self-hatred, 123-24, 128-30, 133-34; paradox of, 133-34
semantic theory of humor, 147 n 26, 151 n 5
sentimentalization, 143-44
shaggy dog stories, 156 n 21
Shils, Edward, 165-66 n 5
Shuckin' and Jivin': Folklore from Contemporary Black Americans, 124
Simmel, Georg, 143-44
Simon, Roger, 33-34, 35, 37, 39
speakability, 36-40
stereotype, 9, 126-28, 147 n 26
"Surplus Details Technique," 88-89
synoptic text, 62-65, 153 n 19

tale: conventions of, narration, 82; conventions of, texts, 81-82; social universe of, 125-26
Talmud, 71-72, 113, 116
techniques of humor, ix, 10-12; condensation, 10, 95; contrastive iteration, 11; double meaning, 10, 35; reversal, 10, 11-12; transparency of, 12, 35; vacuous reversal, 10-11, 147 n 32
Tevye, the dairyman. *See* Aleichem, Sholom
texts: discreteness of, 23-24, 27; linked, 55, 56, 153 n 19
tradition, 135, 165-66 n 5
transcendence, 133

value, perception of, 130
viewability. *See* speakability

Weininger, Otto, 117
What's the Joke: A Study of Jewish Humor Through the Ages, 113-14
Wortis, Joseph, 102-3

"Yankee Doodle," 132

Zijderveld, Anton C., 164 n 30